*To Pat
from John*

THE PENGUIN SPORTS LIBRARY

THE SUMMER GAME

In 1962, six years after joining the *The New Yorker* as a fiction editor, Roger Angell was asked by the editor of *The New Yorker*, William Shawn, if he could try writing about spring baseball training. Angell hasn't missed a spring in Florida or Arizona since. *The Summer Game*, his first book on the sport, was originally published in 1972. Then came *Five Seasons* (1977), *Late Innings* (1982), and *Season Ticket* (1988). All have received widespread critical praise. A typical reaction came from Jonathan Yardley in *The Washington Post*, who wrote, "No other sport has been so well served by any other writer."

Roger Angell is New Yorker born and bred. His mother, Katherine White, was fiction editor of the magazine in 1925, the year *The New Yorker* was founded. Angell's stepfather was E. B. White. In addition to writing about baseball and other sports, Angell over the years has written short stories for *The New Yorker*, casuals and comment pieces in addition to "Talk of the Town" articles, parodies, and humor pieces. Today, as *The New Yorker*'s senior fiction editor, Angell is responsible for the work of John Updike, Ann Beattie, Garrison Keillor, Bobbie Ann Mason, and V. S. Pritchett among others. He lives in Manhattan with his wife, Carol. He has three children, Caroline, Alice, and John Henry.

THE
SUMMER
GAME

Roger Angell

PENGUIN BOOKS

PENGUIN BOOKS
Published by the Penguin Group
Viking Penguin, a division of Penguin Books USA Inc.,
40 West 23rd Street, New York, New York 10010, U.S.A.
Penguin Books Ltd, 27 Wrights Lane,
London W8 5TZ, England
Penguin Books Australia Ltd, Ringwood,
Victoria, Australia
Penguin Books Canada Ltd, 2801 John Street,
Markham, Ontario, Canada L3R 1B4
Penguin Books (N.Z.) Ltd, 182–190 Wairau Road,
Auckland 10, New Zealand

Penguin Books Ltd, Registered Offices:
Harmondsworth, Middlesex, England

First published in the United States of America by
Viking Penguin, a division of Penguin Books USA Inc., 1972
This edition with a new introduction by the author
published in Penguin Books 1990

10 9 8 7 6 5 4 3 2 1

The material in this book, with exception of the introduction,
first appeared in *The New Yorker*, some of it in different form.

LIBRARY OF CONGRESS CATALOGING IN PUBLICATION DATA
Angell, Roger.
The summer game/Roger Angell.
p.   cm.
Reprint. Originally published: New York: Viking Press. 1972.
ISBN 0 14 01.3121 3
1. Baseball—United States.   I. Title.
GV863.A1A54 1990
796.357'0973—dc20   89-26548

Printed in the United States of America

FOR MY FATHER

Introduction

Eighteen seasons have gone by since this first baseball book of mine was published, and my pleasure at finding myself still in the game feels like a natural extension of the expressions of appreciation and hope with which its foreword concludes. For me, that time has passed both swiftly and slowly, just as ballgames often seem to droop and drag and also rush along almost simultaneously. But everything about baseball's time is mysterious, which must be why expert fans can weigh and taste its events almost at the instant they are happening. Baseball, Bill Veeck liked to say, is meant to be savored. The players described in these pages have all left the field, but the look of them— young Reggie Jackson in his first flower, Bob Gibson glaring down the next batter, Tom Seaver firing the fastball through the afternoon din at Shea—is clearer to this fan than my knowledge of who and where they are today. Old Timer's Days are not for me.

One of the first great shocks to me when I started covering the sport was the realization that many of the players were not fans of the game (later, I noticed that some of them *became* fans as they got older and began to sense that the quicksilver skills of their youth would have to be replaced by craft and cogitation if they were to remain in the show), and it has become apparent to me more recently that not all baseball writers are baseball fans, either, although they all must have begun that way. Beat writers, the true professionals of my calling, must sustain at least a superficial appearance of neutrality in their work, and this stricture, along with the rigors of their weary, March-to-November season; their need to generate awesome flows of copy; their ceaseless travels; their necessary but profoundly unappreciated presence in the daily lives and doings of the players; and the incessant demands for freshness and a sense of youthful energy in their writing, does wear down a few of the scribes to cynicism and bitterness. It's painful to grow older in a world of play and unaltered youth, and the only escape available may be to hold on to one's credentials as a fan. I've been exempted from some of these strains, because I've been permitted to express my own partisan hopes in my *New Yorker* "Sporting Scene" pieces (which were later translated into four baseball books), and because I've noticed that watching almost any team over a span of a bare four or five games still seems to win my attachment to its players and fortunes for weeks or seasons to come. One can't belong to baseball in the abstract, as Mike Barnicle noted in *The Boston Globe*, many seasons ago. "Baseball isn't a life-and-death matter," he wrote, "but the Red Sox are."

Rereading these chapters, I can see that I was not particularly knowing about the game back in the Sixties, even though I tried to sound that way. I seemed to catch on a little as I went along. My real innocence about baseball shows itself in an ongoing indignation with the owners, who were then engaged, year by year, in dismantling the sport I had known all my life and turning it into something quite different—adding franchises, uprooting old teams, taking up the grass, building domes and shopping-mall stadiums, and inviting in the television networks as the ruling partner of baseball. (Free agency, salary arbitration, player agents, and three-million-dollar player salaries were still ahead.) But this book seems to show something else happening to its author as the decade slid along, which was my deepening pleasure in the game itself, the stuff out on the field, as I watched more and more innings and seasons. I kept running into amazing baseball luck, it seemed—the brilliant World Series played out in succession in 1967, '68, and '69, for instance: each better than the last, and each still vividly held in memory—and only slowly did I begin to see that surprise and good luck (sudden feats, complex confrontations, the constant exceeding or dashing of deeply held expectations) is an inextricable and self-renewing part of the sport.

I know baseball better today than I did back in 1962, but so do we all. Fans today are not only more numerous than they used to be (twenty-one million fans watched the twenty teams engaged in the 1962 season, as against fifty-five million plus at twenty-six ballparks in 1989), but far more expert about how the game is played and won. Television, to give it its due, created this vast audience and has coached it in the subtleties and hidden stratagems of the action. Along the way, we have lost some of our self-deceiving ignorance of the business side of baseball, and some of our innocence about the players, as well—not all of it, I trust. Baseball may not be held as close to our hearts as it used to be, but it is far better appreciated. It is exciting for me, an old fan now, to go back to this book and pick up the first gleams, out on the diamond, as that sentimental education began.

—Roger Angell, 1989

Foreword

These pieces cover a span of ten years, but this book is certainly not offered as a comprehensive baseball history of the period. Most of the great winning teams and a good many of the horrendous losers of the decade are here, while the middle ground is often sketchy. I have written about some celebrated players—Sandy Koufax, Bob Gibson, Brooks Robinson and Frank Robinson, Willie Mays—again and again, while slighting equally admirable figures such as Hank Aaron and Mickey Mantle. It is unfair, but this book is the work of a part-time, nonprofessional baseball watcher. In most of these ten seasons, I was rarely able to attend as many as twenty-five games before the beginning of the World Series; I watched, or half-watched, a good many more on television. Enthusiasm and interest took me out to the ballpark; I never went out of a sense of duty or history. I was, in short, a fan. Unafflicted by daily deadlines or the weight of objectivity, I have been free to write about whatever I found in the game that excited or absorbed or dismayed me—and free, it will become evident, to draw large and sometimes quite mistaken conclusions from an emaciated body of evidence. I have added some updating and footnotes in an attempt to cover up the worst mistakes.

When I began writing sports pieces for *The New Yorker*, it was clear to me that the doings of big-league baseball—the daily happenings on the field, the managerial strategies, the celebration of heroes, the medical and financial bulletins, the clubhouse gossip—were so enormously reported in the newspapers that I would have to find some other aspect of the game to study. I decided to sit in the stands—for a while, at least—and watch the baseball from there. I wanted to concentrate not just on the events down on the field but on their reception and results; I wanted to pick up the feel of the game as it happened to the people around me. Right from the start, I was terribly lucky, because my first year or two in the seats behind first or third coincided with the birth and grotesque early sufferings of the Mets, which turned out to be the greatest fan story of all.

Then I was lucky in another way. In time, I made my way to the press box and found friends there, and summoned up the nerve to talk to some ballplayers face-to-face, but even with a full set of World Series credentials flapping from my lapel, I was still faking it as a news reporter. Writing at length for a leisurely and most generous weekly magazine, I could sum things up, to be sure, and fill in a few gaps that the newspapermen were too hurried or too cramped for space to explore, but my main job, as I conceived it, was to continue to try to give the feel of things—to explain the baseball as it happened to me, at a distance and in retrospect. And this was the real luck, for how could I have guessed then that baseball, of all team sports anywhere, should turn out to be so complex, so rich and various in structure and aesthetics and emotion, as to convince me, after ten years as a writer and forty years as a fan, that I have not yet come close to its heart?

R.A.

Contents

PART **I**

Rustle of Spring

Box Scores

Today the *Times* reported the arrival of the first pitchers and catchers at the spring training camps, and the morning was abruptly brightened, as if by the delivery of a seed catalogue. The view from my city window still yields only frozen tundras of trash, but now spring is guaranteed and one of my favorite urban flowers, the baseball box score, will burgeon and flourish through the warm, languid, information-packed weeks and months just ahead. I can remember a spring, not too many years ago, when a prolonged New York newspaper strike threatened to extend itself into the baseball season, and my obsessively fannish mind tried to contemplate the desert prospect of a summer without daily box scores. The thought was impossible; it was like trying to think about infinity. Had I been deprived of those tiny lists of sporting personae and accompanying columns of runs batted in, strikeouts, double plays, assists, earned runs, and the like, all served up in neat three-inch packages from Pittsburgh, Milwaukee, Baltimore, Houston, and points east and west, only the most aggressive kind of blind faith would have convinced me that the season had begun at all or that its distant, invisible events had any more reality than the silent collision of molecules. This year, thank heaven, no such crisis of belief impends; summer will be admitted to our breakfast table as usual, and in the space of half a cup of coffee I will be able to discover, say, that Ferguson Jenkins went eight innings in Montreal and won his fourth game of the season while giving up five hits, that Al Kaline was horse-collared by Fritz Peterson at the Stadium, that Tony Oliva hit a double and a single off Mickey Lolich in Detroit, that Juan Marichal was bombed by the Reds in the top of the sixth at Candlestick Park, and that similar disasters and triumphs befell a couple of dozen-odd of the other ballplayers—favorites and knaves—whose fortunes I follow from April to October.

The box score, being modestly arcane, is a matter of intense indifference, if not irritation, to the non-fan. To the baseball-bitten, it is not only informative, pictorial, and gossipy but lovely in aesthetic structure. It represents happenstance and physical flight exactly translated into figures and history. Its totals—batters' credit vs. pitchers' debit—balance as exactly as those in an accountant's ledger. And a box score is more than a capsule archive. It is a precisely etched miniature of the sport itself, for baseball, in spite of its grassy spaciousness and apparent unpredictability, is the most intensely and satisfyingly mathematical of all our outdoor sports. Every player in every game is subjected to a cold and ceaseless accounting; no ball is thrown and no base is gained without an instant responding judgment—ball or strike, hit or error, yea or nay—and an ensuing statistic. This encompassing neatness permits the baseball fan, aided by experience and memory, to extract from a box score the same joy, the same hallucinatory reality, that prickles the scalp of a musician when he glances at a page of his score of *Don Giovanni* and actually hears bassos and sopranos, woodwinds and violins.

The small magic of the box score is cognominal as well as mathematical. Down the years, the rosters of the big-league teams have echoed and twangled with evocative, hilarious, ominous, impossible, and exactly appropriate names. The daily, breathing reality of the ballplayers' names in box scores accounts in part, it seems to me, for the rarity of convincing baseball fiction. No novelist has yet been able to concoct a baseball hero with as tonic a name as Willie Mays or Duke Snider or Vida Blue. No contemporary novelist would dare a supporting cast of characters with Dickensian names like those that have stuck with me ever since I deciphered my first box scores and began peopling the lively landscape of baseball in my mind—Ossee Schreckengost, Smead Jolley, Slim Sallee, Elon Hogsett, Urban Shocker, Burleigh Grimes, Hazen Shirley Cuyler, Heinie Manush, Cletus Elwood Poffenberger, Virgil Trucks, Enos Slaughter, Luscious Easter, and Eli Grba. And not even a latter-day O. Henry would risk a conte like the true, electrifying history of a pitcher named Pete Jablonowski, who disappeared from the Yankees in 1933 after several seasons of inept relief work with various clubs. Presumably disheartened by seeing the losing pitcher listed as "J'bl'n's'i" in the box scores of his day, he changed his name to Pete Appleton in the semi-privacy of the minors, and came back to win fourteen games for the Senators in 1936 and to continue in the majors for another decade.

The Old Folks behind Home

Sarasota, March 20

This winter, a local mortician named Willie Robarts sent Sarasota residents and visitors a mailing of cards printed with his name and with the schedule of baseball games to be played here by the Chicago White Sox, who conduct their spring training in Payne Park, right in the middle of town. This must be interpreted as a pure public service, rather than as an attempt to accelerate business by the exposure of senior citizens (or "senior Americans," as they are sometimes called here) to unbearable excitement; only last night I was informed that a Sarasota heart specialist has ordered one of his patients to attend every Sox game as a therapeutic measure. Big-league ball on the west coast of Florida is a spring sport played by the young for the divertissement of the elderly—a sun-warmed, sleepy exhibition celebrating the juvenescence of the year and the senescence of the fans. Although Florida newspapers print the standings of the clubs in the Grapefruit League every day, none of the teams tries especially hard to win; managers are looking hopefully at their rookies and anxiously at their veteran stars, and by the seventh or eighth inning, no matter what the score, most of the regulars are back in the hotel or driving out to join their families on the beach, their places taken by youngsters up from the minors. The spectators accept this without complaint. Their loyalty to the home club is gentle and unquestioning, and their afternoon pleasure appears scarcely affected by victory or defeat. If this attachment were deeper or more emotional, there would have been widespread distress here three years ago when the Boston Red Sox, who had trained in Sarasota for many years, transferred their spring camp to Scottsdale, Arizona, and the White Sox moved down from Tampa, but the adjustment to the new stocking color, by all accounts, was without trauma. The Beach Club Bar, out on Siesta Key, still displays photographs of Bobby Doerr and Dom DiMaggio and other members of the fine Red Sox teams of the forties, and at the ballpark I spotted a boy of ten or twelve wearing a faded junior-size Red Sox uniform (almost surely a hand-me-down from an older brother), but these are the only evidences of disaffection and memory, and the old gentlemen filing into the park before the game now wear baseball caps with the White Sox insigne above the bill.

Caps are the preferred millinery for both male and female fans in Payne Park—baseball caps, long-billed fishing caps, perforated summer-weights, yachting caps with crossed anchors, old-fashioned John D. Rockefeller linen jobs. Beneath them are country faces—of retired farmers and small-town storekeepers, perhaps, and dignified ladies now doing their cooking in trailers —wearing rimless spectacles and snap-on dark glasses. This afternoon, Payne Park's little sixteen-row grandstand behind home plate had filled up well before game time (the Dodgers, always a good draw, were here today), and fans on their way in paused to visit with those already in their seats. The ushers greeted the regulars by name, and I saw one of them offering his arm to a very old lady in a blue hairnet and chatting with her as he escorted her slowly to her seat. Just after the national anthem, the loudspeaker announced that a lost wallet had been turned in, and invited the owner to come and claim it—an announcement that I very much doubt has ever been heard in a big-city ballpark.

There were elders on the field, too. Early Wynn, who has spent half of his forty-two years in the major leagues and has won 292 games, started for the Sox. He pitched carefully, slowly wheeling his heavy body on the windup and glowering down on the batters between pitches, his big Indian-like face almost hidden under his cap. He has a successful construction business in Venice, Florida, south of here, but he wants that three-hundredth game this year; as for the Sox, if they are to be contenders they must have ten or fifteen wins from him. Duke Snider led off the Dodger second. He is as handsome and cheerful-looking as ever —he has the classic ballplayer's face—but he is a bit portly now, and beneath his helmet the sideburns were white. As he stepped up, a man somewhere behind me shouted, "C'mon, Duke! C'mon, Grandpa—belt one!" and a lady just in front of me murmured to her companion, "Now, really, I think that's *very* offensive." (Clapping and small, encouraging cries are heard in Florida parks, but boos and personal epithets are bad form.) Duke's feelings didn't seem hurt; he swung viciously and grounded out to second, running it out fast all the way.

Wynn pitched three innings, shutting out the Dodgers and giving up only two hits, and was succeeded by Herb Score. The crowd was pulling for Score with every pitch; they knew his story, which is the saddest in modern baseball. Although he has entirely recovered from the terrible injury he suffered when he was struck in the face by a line drive hit by Gil MacDougald in 1957, Score's confidence, his control, and, finally, his form have vanished, and he has never again approached the brilliance of 1956, when he won twenty games for the Indians, struck out 263 batters, and finished with an earned-run average of 2.53. Now he is up from the minor leagues, battling for a job. Today, at least, he was getting batters out, but watching him work was a nervous, unhappy business. Most of his pitches were high, and it was difficult to see why the Dodgers weren't hitting him harder. He kept running into bouts of wildness, and his delivery was a painful parody of what it used to be, for his arm would come to a full, hitching halt at the end of his windup, and he appeared to be pushing the ball. He escaped his four innings with only a lone, unearned run scored against him. Meantime, the White Sox were bleeding for runs, too, as they will be all season. They have traded away their power, Minoso and Sievers, for pitching and defense, hoping for a repetition of their 1959 surprise, and the run they scored in the seventh came on two singles and a stolen base —the kind of rally their supporters will have to expect this year.

The tension of a tied, low-scoring game appeared to distract rather than engross the crowd. The sun slid behind the grand-stand roof, and there was a great stirring and rustling around me as sweaters were produced and windbreakers zipped up; seats began to be vacated by deserters, and the fans in the upper rows, who had been in the shade all afternoon, came down looking for a warmer perch. Brief bursts of clapping died away, and the only sound was the shrill two-note whistle of infielders encouraging their pitcher. The old people all around me hunched forward, their necks bent, peering out at the field from under their cap bills, and I had the curious impression that I was in a giant aviary. Out in right-field foul ground, members of the Sox' big pitching squad began wind sprints. They stood together in clus-ters, their uniforms a vivid white in the blaze of late sun, and four or five at a time would break away from the group and make a sudden sandpiper dash along the foot of the distant sea-green wall, all the way into deep center field, where they stopped just as quickly and stood and stared at the game. At last, in the bot-tom of the twelfth, the White Sox loaded the bases on some sloppy Dodger fielding, and Nellie Fox, his wad of tobacco bulg-ing, delivered the single that broke the bird spell and sent every-one home to supper. "*There*, now," said the woman in front of me, standing up and brushing her skirt. "Wasn't that nice?"

Sarasota, March 21

Watching the White Sox work out this morning at Payne Park reassured me that baseball is, after all, still a young man's sport and a cheerful one. Coach Don Gutteridge broke up the early

pepper games with a cry of "Ever'body 'round!" and after the
squad had circled the field once, the ritual—the same one that
is practiced on every high-school, college, and professional ballfield in the country—began. Batters in the cage bunted one, hit
five or six, and made room for the next man. Pitchers hit fungoes
to the outfielders, coaches on the first and third baselines knocked
out grounders to the infield, pepper games went on behind the
cage, and the bright air was full of baseballs, shouts, whistles, and
easy laughter. There was a raucous hoot from the players around
second when a grounder hopped over Esposito's glove and hit
him in the belly. Two young boys with fielders' gloves had
joined the squad in the outfield, and I saw Floyd Robinson
gravely shake hands with them both. Anyone can come to watch
practice here, and fans from nearby hotels and cottages wandered
in after their breakfasts, in twos and threes, and slowly clambered
up into the empty bleachers, where they assumed the easy, cere-
monial attitude—feet up on the row in front, elbows on knees,
chin in hands. There were perhaps two dozen of us in the stands,
and what kept us there, what nailed us to our seats for a sweet,
boring hour or more, was not just the *whop!* of bats, the climbing white arcs of outfield flies, and the swift flight of the ball
whipped around the infield, but something more painful and just
as obvious—the knowledge that we had never made it. We
would never know the rich joke that doubled over three young
pitchers in front of the dugout; we would never be part of that
golden company on the field, which each of us, certainly for one
moment of his life, had wanted more than anything else in the
world to join.

The Cardinals, who have been having a fine spring, were the
visitors this afternoon, and their high spirits infected everyone.
Minnie Minoso, grinning extravagantly, exchanged insults with
his former White Sox teammates, and Larry Jackson, the big, fast
Cardinal right-hander, laughed out loud on the mound when he
got Joe Cunningham, who was *his* teammate last year, to miss
badly on a big curve in the first inning. Stan Musial had the day

off, and Al Lopez, the Sox' manager, had filled his lineup with rookies. My eye was caught by the Chicago shortstop, a kid named Al Weis, who is not on the team's regular roster but who was having a nifty day in the field. He started double plays in the first and second innings, and in the third he made a fine throw from deep short to get Jackson, and then robbed Gotay with a diving spear of a low, hot liner. At the plate, though, he was nervous and uncertain, anxious to succeed in this one short and, to him, terribly important afternoon. He struck out in the first inning and again in the second, stranding two base-runners.

At about this time, I began to pick up a dialogue from the seats directly behind me—a flat, murmurous, continuous exchange in Middle Western accents between two elderly men.

"Look at the skin on my hands, how dry it is," said one.

"You do anything for it?" asked the other.

"Yes, I got some stuff the doctor gave me—just a little tube of something. It don't help much."

I stole a look at them. They were both in their seventies, at least. Both were sitting back comfortably, their arms folded across their stomachs.

"Watch that ball," said the first. "Is that fair?"

"No, it's foul. You know, I haven't seen a homer this year."

"Me neither."

"Maybe Musial will hit one here tomorrow."

The White Sox, down one run after the first inning, could do nothing with Jackson. Weis struck out again in the fifth, made a wild throw to first in the sixth, and then immediately redeemed himself with another fast double play. The voices went on.

"This wind melts your ice cream fast, don't it?"

"Yes, it does. It feels nice, though. Warm wind."

In the top of the eighth, with the bases loaded, Weis grabbed another line drive and doubled up the runner at second base. There were chirps from the stands.

"It don't seem any time at all since spring training last year."

"That's because we're older now. You take my grandson, he's

always looking forward to something. Christmas and his birthday and things like that. That makes the time go slow for him. You and me, we just watch each day by itself."

"Yes. You know, I didn't hardly think about life at all until I was sixty-five or seventy."

"I know."

Weis led off the bottom of the eighth, and popped up to left. He started still another double play in the ninth, but his afternoon was ruined. The Cardinals won the game, 2–0.

This evening, I looked up Al Weis's record. He is twenty-two years old and was an All-Scholastic player at Farmingdale High, on Long Island. In his three years in organized baseball, he has played with Holdrege, in the Nebraska State League; with Lincoln, in the Three-I League; and with Charleston, in the Sally League. His batting averages in those years—.275, .231, .261 —tell the story: good field, no hit. Time has run out for him this spring, and it must seem to him that it went too quickly. Next week, he will report to the White Sox farm camp in Hollywood, Florida, for another year in the minors.

St. Petersburg, March 22

This is Gerontium, the elders' capital—city of shuffleboard courts, city of sidewalk benches, city of curious signs reading "Youtharama," "Smorgarama," and "Biblegraph." Today it was also the baseball capital of the world, for the game at Al Lang Field was the first encounter between the Yankees and the New York Mets, the new National League team that sprang—not simply full-grown but middle-aged—out of the forehead of George Weiss last winter. Some of the spectators' curiosity and expectancy about this game resembled the unbecoming relish with which party guests watch a newly divorced couple encountering each other in public for the first time, for they could watch General Manager Weiss, in his box behind the home dugout, and Casey Stengel, in the dugout, staring over at the team that had evicted them so scandalously two years ago. But there was another, more valid tension to be tasted; one sensed that this game was a crisis for the Mets—their first chance to discover, against the all-conquerors, whether they were truly a ball team. A rout, a laugher, a comedy of ineptitude might destroy them before the season ever began.

St. Petersburg fans are elderly, all right, but they are noisier, keener, and more appreciative than their counterparts to the south. For one thing, they know more baseball. Al Lang Field has for years been the late-winter home of two good teams, the Yankees and Cardinals; when the Yankees moved to new quarters at Fort Lauderdale this year, the Mets moved in to take their place. I had guessed that this switch of home teams might cause some confusion of loyalties, but I was wrong. There was a respectable burst of applause when Mickey Mantle stepped up to the plate in the second inning, but this was almost immediately smothered by a full roar of pleasure when Charlie Neal collared Mantle's streaking grounder in short right and threw him out. Groans and headshakings followed when the Yanks collected three singles and a run off Roger Craig's pitching, but the Mets failed to collapse. Frank Thomas hit a double in the Mets' half of the inning—the first hit given up by Bill Stafford, the Yankees' starting pitcher, all spring—and there was another startled shout a few minutes later when Hodges and Chacon pulled off a 3-6-3 double play on Maris's bouncer. The Mets not only belonged, they were winning converts every minute.

The Mets are an attractive team, full of echoes and overtones, and one must believe that George Weiss has designed their clean, honest, but considerably frayed appearance with great care. Gus Bell, Frank Thomas, Eddie Bouchee, and Richie Ashburn are former headliners whose mistakes will be forgiven and whose accomplishments will win sentimental affection. Coach Cookie Lavagetto and pitchers Roger Craig and Clem Labine will bring the older Dodger fans up to the Polo Grounds this summer. Neal and Zimmer looked unchanged—Neal intense, withdrawn, talented,

too tightly wound for an ideal infielder, and Zimmer eager and
competitive, angrily trying to make pugnacity compensate for
what he lacks in size, skill, and luck. Gil Hodges still cannot hit
pitches over the outside corners, but his stance and his manner-
isms at the plate are a cup of limeflower tea to those with memories: The bat is held in the left hand while he fiddles with his eye-
lashes with his right hand, then settles his helmet, then tucks up
his right pants leg, then sweeps the hand the full length of the
bat, like a duelist wiping blood off a sword, and then at last he
faces the pitcher. Finally, there is Casey himself, a walking pantheon of evocations. His pinstripes are light blue now, and so is
the turtleneck sweatshirt protruding above his shirt, but the short
pants, the hobble, the muttering lips, and the comic, jerky gestures are unaltered, and today he proved himself still capable of
the winning move.

The Mets went ahead, 3-2, in the sixth inning, on two Yankee errors, two walks, and Zimmer's single. After that, the St. Petersburg fans began a nervous, fingers-crossed cry of "Keep it *up*,
Mets!" and welcomed each put-out with shouts of incredulity
and relief. In the ninth, though, the Mets' second pitcher, a thin
young Negro named Al Jackson, up this year from Columbus,
gave up four singles and the tying run after Neal messed up a
double play. With the winning runs on base, Stengel showed
how much he wanted this game for his team, for he came out to
the mound and relieved Jackson. (Pitchers are almost never
yanked in mid-inning in spring training.) The relief man, Howie
Nunn, retired Blanchard on a pop behind second for the last out.
More wonders followed. Joe Christopher, another unknown, led
off the Mets' ninth with a triple, and after Zimmer had fouled
out, Stengel looked into his closet of spare parts, which is far less
well stocked than his old Yankee cornucopia, and found Ashburn
there. Richie hit the first pitch into right field for the ball game,
and George Weiss nodded his head, stood up in his box, and
smiled for the first time today.

I doubt whether any of the happy six thousand-odd filing out of Al Lang Field after the game were deluding themselves with dreams of a first-division finish for the Mets this year. The team is both too old and too young for sensible hopes. Its pitchers will absorb some fearful punishment this summer, and Chacon and Neal have yet to prove that they can manage the double play with any consistency. Still, though, the Mets will be playing in the same league with the Houston Colt .45s, another newborn team of castoffs, and with the Phillies, who managed to finish forty-six games out of first place last year and will have eight more games this year in which to disimprove that record. The fight for the National League cellar this summer may be as lively as the fight for the pennant. What cheered *me* as I tramped through the peanut shells and discarded programs and out into the hot late sunlight was not just the score and not just Casey's triumph but a freshly renewed appreciation of the marvelous complexity and balance of baseball. Offhand, I can think of no other sport in which the world's champions, one of the great teams of its era, would not instantly demolish inferior opposition and reduce a game such as the one we had just seen to cruel ludicrousness. Baseball is harder than that; it requires a full season, hundreds and hundreds of separate games, before quality can emerge, and in that summer span every home-town fan, every doomed admirer of underdogs will have his afternoons of revenge and joy.

Tampa, March 24

The population of Tampa is 275,000. I looked it up this morning, but I could have saved myself the trouble. Anyone attending a game in the big, modern reinforced-concrete-shell grandstand of Al Lopez Field (named for the White Sox manager, who is a Tampa native) could figure out that this is the big town in these parts; he could tell it by the sound of the crowd alone—a steady, complex, cosmopolitan clamor made up of exhortation, laughter, outright booing, the cries of venders, and the hum of garrulous city talkers. Today the old people in the stands were outnumbered. There were young women in low-cut sun dresses, children of all ages (two boys near me were wearing Little League uniforms with "Western Fertilizer" emblazoned on the back), and Negroes and Cubans in the grandstand. The sun was hot and summery, and I felt at home: this was July in Yankee Stadium. Nevertheless, I had trouble concentrating on the first few innings of the game, which was between the Cincinnati Reds, who train here, and the visiting Dodgers. My mind kept returning to an incident—a sudden visual snapshot of a scene—in the game I saw yesterday in Bradenton, where Milwaukee had beaten the Yankees.

Bradenton yesterday was nothing like Tampa today. The weather was cold early spring, with low clouds and a nipping wind blowing in from left field. The stadium might have been a country fairgrounds, and the elders who had come early and filled up the park to see the mighty Yankees had the gravity, the shy politeness, and the silence of a rural crowd at a tent show. A rain the night before had turned the infield into a mudpie, and while we waited patiently for it to dry, three bearded men wearing plumed Spanish helmets, silvery chest plates, short striped pants, and high boots trooped out in front of the dugout, carrying swords, to have their picture taken with Mickey Mantle. They were local citizens participating in Bradenton's annual de Soto celebration. Mickey grinned and brandished one of the swords for the photographer, and the conquistadors looked awed. At last, the game began, in tomblike silence. No one complained when Mantle, Howard, Boyer, and Berra failed to appear in the opening lineup. Hardly anyone cheered when the Braves got to Jim Coates for a run in the third. A man standing in front of the scoreboard in deep center field hung up a numbered placard for each ball, strike, and out. When the sun began to break through, another employee came out of the Braves' clubhouse beside left field and hung a dozen sweatshirts—white, with black sleeves —out to dry on a clothesline strung between two palm trees. The game turned out to be a good one; there was some small shouting when the Braves came from behind to tie the score in the bottom of the ninth on a home run by Tommie Aaron, Hank Aaron's kid brother, and some guffaws when the Yanks lost it on an error in the tenth. In spite of the score, and perhaps only because of the peacefulness and stolidity of the fans, I came away with the impression that the Braves have become a middle-aged team, now somehow past the point of eagerness and energy that has made them champions or fearsome contenders for the last nine years.

The incident that startled me at Bradenton was one of those astonishing juxtapositions that are possible only in spring training. In the seventh inning, with the sun now fully out and the grass turning soft and emerald as it dried, Whitey Ford came in to pitch for the Yankees. At the same moment, in the Braves' bullpen in deep left field, Warren Spahn began throwing—not warming up but simply loosening his arm. Suddenly I saw that from my seat behind first base the two pitchers—the two best left-handers in baseball, the two best left- *or* right-handers in baseball—were in a direct line with each other, Ford exactly superimposed on Spahn. It was a trick photograph, a *trompe-l'oeil:* a 158-game winner and a 309-game winner throwing baseballs in the same fragment of space. Ford, with his short, businesslike windup, was all shoulders and quickness, while, behind him, Spahn would slowly kick his right leg up high and to the left, peering over his shoulder as he leaned back, and then deliver the ball with an easy, explosive sweep. It excited me to a ridiculous extent. I couldn't get over it. I looked about me for someone to point it out to, but I couldn't find a recognizable fan-face near me.

The Tampa crowd this afternoon would have spotted it. They knew their baseball, and they were tough and hard to please. Joey Jay, the Reds' top starter, was having all kinds of trouble on the mound. His control was off, he had to throw too many pitches, and he kept shaking his head disgustedly. After the first two innings, the Dodgers were waiting for him to get behind and come in with a fat pitch. They batted around against him in the third inning, scoring five runs; two of them came on a home run by Daryl Spencer, and then in the fifth Spencer knocked another pitch over the fence. Manager Hutchinson left Jay in, letting him take his punishment while he got the work he needed. The fans, though the Reds are their team, seemed to enjoy it all. They booed Jay lightly; they didn't mind seeing him suffer a little—not with that $27,500 salary he won after a holdout this spring. They applauded Koufax, the Dodger pitcher, who was working easily and impressively, mixing fast balls and curves and an occasional changeup, pitching in and out to the batters, and hitting the corners. Koufax looked almost ready for opening day.

There were fewer rookies and scrubs in the lineups today; the season begins in just over two weeks. These two teams will almost certainly fight it out with the Giants for the pennant, and I was tempted to make comparisons and private predictions. But then I reminded myself that baseball would be competitive and overserious soon enough. The city crowd around me here, the big park, and the approaching time for headlines, standings, and partisanship had almost made me knowing and Northern again. Already I had begun to forget the flavor of Florida baseball—the older, easier pleasures of baseball in the spring in the country.

The Short Season

Baseball has begun. East and west, this is the week of the unfurled bunting, the flexed mayoral or gubernatorial wing, the restored hope, the repainted seat, the April fly ball falling untouched on resodded turf, the windblown shout, and the distant row of pitchers and catchers huddling deeper into their windbreakers as the early-spring sunlight deserts the bullpen. Now everything counts; from now until October, every pitch and every swing will be recorded. In another month, some order will begin to emerge from the standings. Infields will have hardened, some arms and expectations will have gone bad, and enormous crowds will pour out for the first weekend doubleheaders. The long season will engage us once again. Before this happens, however, there may still be time to set down some notes about the other, shorter baseball season that is just past—the time of spring training. I know, of course, that spring ball games in Florida and Arizona are meant to be forgotten. March standings and averages are written in the sand; winning is incidental. Many ballplayers hate spring training—rookies because of the anxieties of trying to win a job, the regulars because of the immense labor and boredom of physical conditioning, the fear of injury, and the threat, heavier each year, of losing a starting position. Only the fan—and perhaps only the big-city fan, at that—is free to savor the special taste of this time and place. After a recent week in Flor-

ida, spent mostly in the company of the White Sox and Red Sox,
I came home with the curious feeling that I had been retrained,
too—that the short season had renewed my fondness for small
ballparks and small crowds and the country quiet of afternoons
given over without regret to the sunshine game.

Spring baseball is all surmise. This year, of course, the pleasures
of comparison and speculation were sharpened by the memory of
last summer's extraordinary baseball events, which concluded
with the closest pennant race in history—a four-way struggle
won by the Red Sox on the last afternoon of the season—and a
brilliant World Series, won by the Cardinals in the seventh game.
On my first mid-March afternoon at Payne Park, the wooden,
old-timey stadium of the Chicago White Sox in Sarasota, the Red
Sox were the visiting team, and the warm, windy air was instantly full of hints and auspices. Pitching for the home side was
Cisco Carlos, a young right-hander who had run up a slick late-
season record with the White Sox last year, when he gave up a
bare five runs (and no extra-base hits) in forty-two innings, for an
earned-run average of 0.86. "Cn. Crls. kp. it up?" I scribbled on
the margin of my scorecard—a note suggesting that Carlos
might be a formidable additional starter for the Chicago pitching
staff, already the best in the league, which kept the club in contention with Boston, Minnesota, and Detroit until the last three
days of the 1967 race. Carlos gave up a wrong-field triple by José
Tartabull, the Boston lead-off man, who scored a moment later
on an infield out—a chopper that was briskly charged and
flipped by Luis Aparicio, the quick and admirable shortstop who
has returned to the White Sox after a five-year absence with the
Orioles. "Apar. to glue Chisox i.f.?" I wrote. Next up was Carl
Yastrzemski, the Boston demigod who won the American League
titles for batting, home runs, and runs batted in last year. He was
welcomed by awed applause from the Sarasota old folks, and a
full shift by the Chicago infield. He grounded out to Aparicio,
who was playing a good ten feet on the first-base side of second.
"Yaz rbbd.," I noted. "Tgh. yr. ahead." Tony Conigliaro then

lined out quickly, offering no immediate evidence about the results of the terrible injury he suffered last August, when he was
struck in the face by a pitch and was finished for the season.
"Tony C. gnshy?" I asked myself. "Wt. & see."

The Boston battery in the bottom half was Dick Ellsworth, a
competent but unstartling left-hander picked up from the National League last winter and now counted on to bolster the thin
Red Sox pitching ("Ex-Phil Elsie no Lonbrg"), and Elston Howard, who will be the top Boston catcher this summer, at the age
of thirty-nine (*"Eheu fug!"*). The game moved on. The White
Sox tied it in the third, on two singles and an error, and an inning later Tommy Davis pulled a low two-base screamer just inside the bag at third, apparently fossilizing Joe Foy, the young
Boston third baseman. Davis, a lifetime .300 hitter who twice
won the National League batting title, came over to the White
Sox from the Mets in a major trade last winter ("Mets ckoo!"),
and Foy, who swings a strong bat, was being offered another
crack at the position he lost last year because of weak fielding
("Foy nonch. glove—Bost. 3b still up air?").

My list of scribbled guesses lengthened excruciatingly, and I
was glad to abandon it in the middle innings, when most of the
starters gave way to rookies and other figures of lesser omen. The
game fell apart in the sixth, when a Chicago pitcher named Fred
Klages could not find the plate, and six runs scored. The day's
final entertainment was a legal discussion between a subsequent
Chicago pitcher, Bob Shaw, and the home-plate umpire, Bill
Kunkel, centering on this year's new spitball rule—a landmark
ruling, already twice modified, which is apparently destined to
become as controversial as *Escobedo*. Its central provision prohib-
its the pitcher on the mound from placing his bare hands anywhere near his mouth, even to cover a giggle. Shaw, a thirty-
four-year-old veteran of six major-league clubs, is known to be a
student of pitches and pitchers' rights. He was making a hard,
outside fight for a place on the White Sox staff and one more
year in the majors; his name did not appear on the back of his

uniform shirt, or even in the program. Now, working against Elston Howard with men on base, he heaved a sigh, passed his
gloved hand briefly across his sweaty brow, and leaned in to get
his sign. As he went into motion, Umpire Kunkel sprang out
from behind the catcher, uttering shocked noises, and pointed
first at heaven and then at the pitcher. "What, *me?*" cried Shaw.
"What'd I do?" Kunkel, in a piece of vivid mime that would
have done credit to Marcel Marceau, imitated a veteran right-
hander spitting on his left wrist while apparently wiping his
brow, and then craftily transferring the hideous moisture to his
right fingertips. Out on the mound, Shaw threw his arms apart,
displaying innocence, disgust, and dry paws. These two turns received loud, predictably mixed notices from the Chicago and
Boston dugouts. In time, baseball resumed ("Spit horrid wd"),
and Shaw got out the side. Boston won, 7–1.

  The following evening, at the Yankees' bijou ballpark in Fort
Lauderdale, the only vestige of drama came an hour before the
game with the White Sox, when a storm blew in from the east
just as night was falling. A watery wash of indigo clouds hung
lower and lower over the field during batting practice, deepening
the greens of the box-seat railings, the infield grass, and the tall
hedges in center field, and for a time the field, a box of light in
the surrounding darkness, resembled an aquarium full of small,
oddly darting gray and white fish. The game, played in a chilly,
moaning wind and occasional showers, was curious, for the two
teams had evidently agreed to switch their traditional styles of
baseball—the Yankees bunting, sacrificing, and stealing bases,
and Chicago bashing the ball. Neither appeared comfortable in its
new role. In the bottom of the first, the Yankees craftily combined a bunt, a perfect hit-and-run single, a stolen base, a wild
pitch, another single, and a walk to produce one run, while the
Sox, after eight innings, had rapped out eleven hits good for a
total of one run. The baseball was unedifying. In the fourth inning, for instance, Tom Tresh played Pete Ward's fly to left into

a double, and Ward scored when four Yankees gathered under Tim Cullen's fly and watched it fall to earth; in the Yankee half, Horace Clarke singled, stole his third base of the night, and came around when a rookie Chicago infielder named Reichenbach dropped a double-play ball at second and then threw the ball over the catcher's head. There were eight errors in all, and the night of windy foolishness concluded, in almost total privacy, with the Yankees on top, 4–2.

Back at Sarasota the next day, the White Sox managed some less fidgety fielding and beat the Tigers, 3–1. Among the spectators was a pathetic little band of Detroit sportswriters, utterly orphaned by the five-month-old newspaper strike in their home town. The only consolation for their plight that I could think of was that it might spare them the embarrassment of once again having to predict a pennant for the Tigers, a team endowed with muscular batters, fine pitchers, and habitual late-summer neurasthenia. On this warm, glazy Saturday, Al Kaline, Willie Horton, Jim Northrup, Norm Cash, and the other visiting long-ball hitters could do nothing much against Tommy John and Joel Horlen, who are both celebrated Chicago starters, and the game ticked slowly along in a deepening afternoon silence. I began studying the Payne Park crowd, which must be the oldest sporting audience in the world, and I wondered sleepily whether a demographer could discover why the capital of Gerontia seemed to have slid south in recent years from St. Petersburg to Sarasota. (One holder of a season ticket in Payne Park had informed me that he would request a seat away from the aisle next spring; too many tottery elders had been falling on him on their way out in the late innings.) Perhaps it was the winter presence of the Sox, themselves the oldest team in baseball, that had brought on this senectuous stampede.

As if to confirm this theory, there was a stirring and some thin cries in the stands as the oldest Chisock of them all—the oldest active player in the majors, in fact—approached the mound and prepared to demonstrate his celebrated parlor trick. It was

Hoyt Wilhelm, of course, who is, at forty-four, the best knuckle-ball pitcher in baseball. Last year, he won eight games and lost three for the White Sox in relief, and his earned-run average of 1.31 was his lowest in sixteen years in the majors. After forty-two more mound appearances—perhaps some day late this summer—he will break Cy Young's all-time record of pitching in 906 big-league games. Here, in the top of the ninth, he cocked his head to one side to pick up his sign (a quirk caused by his poor vision), stretched languidly, and threw his knuckleball past the hitter. There was no surprise in it, and very little speed. The ball sailed up, made a sudden small swerve, like a moth in a hallway, and flumped feebly into the catcher's glove, as the fans cried, "Ah-*hah!*" in unison. Wilhelm does not have to think too hard about his work, since he has no more idea than the batter which way the spinless ball will jump, and he delivers the pitch with approximately the same effort as a man tossing a pair of socks into a laundry hamper. He set down the Tigers on a handful of pitches—three weak infield taps and a scratchy single—and sent the old folks home happy.

Mornings are the best time at a winter ballpark. After calis-thenics, the players scatter—pickups and pepper, outfield wind-sprints, batting for the scrubeenies, infield practice for the regulars. The batting-practice pitcher throws and, with the same motion, drops his head below the low screen just in front of him; the man in the cage swings away, the ball flies over second, and, an instant later, coaches on the first and third baselines tap grounders that cross each other on the way to opposite sides of the infield. A couple of sportswriters, wearing T-shirts, shades, and team caps, emerge from the dugout carrying cardboard con-tainers of coffee. The smell of coffee fills the air, mixing with the smell of freshly mown grass. From right field comes a curious, re-peated pattern of sounds—a pitching machine. There is a slow hum and squeak as the machine's metal arm gravely rotates, se-lecting a ball from the trough on its upward path; a quick,

springy "Thwongg!" as the ball is released; then the crack of the
bat and a whir as the ball skids along the rope netting that en-
closes machine and batter. Sometimes there is a muttered curse
instead of the whir: pop-up.

At Payne Park one morning, Marv Grissom, the Chicago
pitching coach, was working on a sinker-ball with Bob Locker, a
tall, right-handed relief man. Locker was wearing an uncomfort-
able-looking canvas vest buttoned over his uniform shirt; the vest
was loaded with bird shot, and Locker was sweating heavily,
which was the whole idea. He was throwing from a mound along
the right-field line, and down at the other end a large dummy in
full uniform stood stiffly up to the plate, holding a bat and batting right-handed. The dummy had a painted face and mustache,
making him look like a ballplayer from the nineties. Locker
threw at three-quarter speed, keeping the ball low and inside.
The catcher fired the ball back to him without rising out of his
squat. "Turn it more," said Grissom after a few minutes, leaning
across and taking Locker's wrist in his hand. "You got to turn it
over. Open these two fingers a little." He rotated Locker's hand
to the left.

Locker wound and threw, and the ball came in just under the
dummy's left elbow. "Hey!" the young catcher called. "This batter really hangs in there, don't he?"

Now Grissom threw the pitch, and the ball seemed to dip off
to the right just as it crossed the plate. "Don't force it," Grissom
said. "You got to keep that wrist loose."

Locker kept at it, the sweat running down his face under his
cap. The catcher whipped the ball back to him easily and precisely, not making him work at catching the ball. "This guy digs
in at the plate better than anybody I ever seen," the catcher said
happily.

Grissom watched each pitch, his arms folded. "Now you're
getting it," he said. "Don't hold it too tight." Locker's next pitch
broke down and in, struck the dummy on the knee, and bounced
in the dirt, and the catcher sprang after it quickly. "Look out,

stupid," he said, and hit the dummy in the stomach with the back of his glove. Then he threw the ball back and squatted down again.

There was an overflow, standing-room crowd at Al Lang Field in St. Petersburg for the Sunday game between the Red Sox and the Cardinals on St. Patrick's Day. I got to the park a bit late, in the bottom of the first, just in time to see Bob Gibson throw a fast ball with his familiar flailing, staggering delivery and Yastrzemski slice it to left field, to score a run from third. The deep, sustained wave of noise that followed was startling and sweet; we were back in October, just where we had left off, and that unforgettable World Series had somehow been extended. Now here on the mound for Boston was José Santiago, who had started the first Series game against Gibson, and here, too, was that instant, reflexive Cardinal response—a double to left by Curt Flood and a single by Maris, to tie the game. There was nothing to choose between the two teams after that, and the tension and pride and almost visible mutual dislike on the field produced marvelous baseball. Santiago, displaying utter cool, pitched quickly into trouble and quickly out again. Gibson poured in his fast ball, shoulder-high, defying the hitters; he struck out George Scott and Reggie Smith in succession, both swinging. In the third, Curt Flood went back to the fence and jumped high for Joe Foy's drive in front of the 398-foot sign, saving a homer. Later, Scott, the enormous Boston first baseman, went far to his right to scoop up Tim McCarver's low shot, bobbled the ball, and then threw in time to Santiago while falling away from the bag. The sport was riveting and autumnal, but between innings there were subtropical distractions. My seat in the auxiliary press box offered a vista of a considerable section of nearby Tampa Bay, all ruffled and glittery and, on this day, cluttered with a heavy traffic of power yachts, water-skiers, and runabouts. A good distance out, the white sails of a gigantic Lightning-class regatta clustered thickly, and then, after the distant bump of the starting gun, the boats strung themselves out on their first reach like a line of drying wash. A series of racing hydroplanes appeared just inside a nearby seawall, threw themselves around a pylon in a snarl of noise and spray, and went bucking off to the west. I began to think I was watching the afternoon show at the Florida Pavilion in some World's Fair.

The best exhibit, however, was the one I had come for. In the sixth, Gibson and Santiago gave way to two other starters, Steve Carlton and Lee Stange, and the Cardinals quickly put together two singles around an error by Mike Andrews to go ahead, 2–1. Carlton, a left-hander, looked even more resolute than Gibson, throwing low and staying well ahead of the hitters, so there was no preparation for what happened in the Boston ninth, when Tony Conigliaro led off with a double to deep right center and moved along to third on Scott's even deeper fly to the same spot. Reggie Smith tripled off the center-field wall, to tie it up in a crescendo of yawping from transplanted New Englanders. Reggie then scored on Petrocelli's fly, sliding under McCarver's spikes as the catcher leaped for the throw, and that was enough. A line-drive double play finished the champions in their half, and the whole thing was over in an hour and fifty-five minutes. Great game.

Frank Robinson, the celebrated Baltimore outfielder, wears the highest cutouts in the American League. Ballplayers' outer stockings are cut away at heel and toe, leaving a stirrup under the arch and exposing a scallop of white understocking fore and aft. Custom-made stockings can bring the cutouts halfway up the shin and calf, giving the wearer's legs the unmistakable look of white-wall tires. Robinson's late-Gothic cutouts soar to within an inch or so of his long, skin-tight pants, and the stocking stripes have disappeared under the pant legs. Last year, league executives tried to limit the length of cutouts, but nothing came of it, of course. What does affect the fad is the opinion within the trade that .250 hitters and other noncelebrities look silly in high cutouts. Robinson's cutout rival in the other league is Willie McCovey.

Watching Robinson in a game against the White Sox, I could sense that he was ready to challenge Yastrzemski this year for every one of those batting titles. Robinson missed a month of the season last year after a base-path collision but still wound up with thirty homers and an average of .311. He does not conceal his bitterness over the fact that nothing like the total celebrity that has descended on Yastrzemski came to him in 1966 after *his* triple crown, fine World Series, and Most Valuable Player award. The Yaz-Robby race would have to wait, but in the Sarasota game there was an absorbing contrast of baseball styles and instincts between Robinson and Tommy Davis. Robinson, who is a threat to break up a game each time he comes up, attempts to dominate the plate, but Davis wants only to dominate the bat. Twice already in Florida I had seen him stroke a hit-and-run ball to exactly the spot just vacated by the second baseman, and now, in the first inning against the Orioles, he singled straight up the middle on another hit-and-run. In the third inning, with Aparicio on third base after a triple, Davis swung away twice and then, on a 1–2 count, shortened his swing almost to a half-stroke and slapped an outside pitch to right for a dinky single and the run batted in. This kind of batting is sometimes underestimated, especially if the hitter plays for a team perpetually in need of catch-up homers in the late innings, which was Davis's lot with the Mets last year. Davis is not fast or particularly aggressive in the field, and this spring he has required cortisone shots in his throwing shoulder. (His manager, Eddie Stanky, wanting that bat in his lineup, told him to *kick* the ball back to the infield if he had to.) The outcome of the White Sox' adventures this summer will depend in good part on the margin between Davis's success at the plate and his deficiencies in the field, and the other contending teams conducted probing operations this spring. In the fourth inning of the Orioles game, Robinson hit a low drive to left field, and then challenged Davis by steaming along to second, drawing only a weak and perfunctory throw. A moment later, there was another hit to left, and Robinson loped confidently around third, only to be nailed at the plate by Davis's high-backed but dead-accurate peg. Robinson got up laughing and shaking his head.

Eddie Stanky, a famously sharp-tongued and combustible manager (last summer he called Yastrzemski a "Most Valuable Player from the neck down") has promised his wife to limit himself this year to "three or four aggravations." He also told reporters in Florida that he would not attempt much lineup tinkering (in one game last September he used twelve pinch batters and base-runners in one-third of an inning), but would merely play his best hitters ("my big buffaloes") every day. He has benefited from a series of remarkable trades in the past year, which has brought him such estimable senior buffaloes as Ken Boyer, Russ Snyder, Davis, and Aparicio while keeping his pitching intact, and it may be that he will at last be able to count on winning some ball games on base hits, instead of on nerve, defense, and opponent-baiting. When I last saw the White Sox—they beat the Orioles that day—Aparicio was batting .428 for the spring, Davis was at .417, the team average stood at .302, and Manager Stanky had not yet used up one of his aggravations.

The most significant moment of preseason athletics for the Boston Red Sox took place not in Florida but on a mountain slope at Heavenly Valley, California, late in the afternoon of last December 24, when Jim Lonborg, taking a last run down an expert trail through heavy, crusty powder, crossed his right ski tip over his left while making an easy right-hand turn and fell slowly forward, snapping the anterior cruciate ligament of his left knee. The Knee, subsequently operated on and now slowly on the mend, was the object of intense daily ministrations, rituals, aspersions, invocations, and solemn preachments observed and participated in by the sixty-odd reporters at the Bosox camp in Winter Haven. Lonborg won twenty-four games last year, including the famous pennant-clincher and two World Series games, but his importance to the Sox may be even greater this year; most of his fellow staff members have shown only a minimum competence this spring, sometimes absorbing terrific pastings at the hands of such lightweights as the Senators and the Astros, and Lonborg's value has seemed to rise every day, even though he has not yet thrown a pitch. When I saw him in March, he was lifting twenty-five pounds of weights strapped to a boot on his left foot, and had only slight flexibility of the leg. When he could lift forty pounds, he would be allowed to start throwing. He may be ready to pitch early in June, maybe later. Nobody knows, because baseball medicos have never had to study a skiing injury before, and ski-injury orthopedists rarely meet pitchers. The only person in Winter Haven who seemed interested in this socio-medical paradox (and the only one apparently able to look at the knee with something less than Trappist gloom) was Lonborg himself, a young man who is intensely interested in almost everything. He is even interested in skiing again. "You can understand the thrill of baseball," he said, "but there's something *mysterious* about skiing." He told me that he could hardly wait to get back on skis, but added thoughtfully that there was an unspoken agreement between him and the Red Sox management that this moment should be postponed until after his baseball days were finished. This agreement is unspoken, I discovered, because Dick Williams, the Red Sox manager, can barely bring himself to say anything about Lonborg's injury, the effect of Lonborg's absence, the date of Lonborg's return, or the permanence of Lonborg's Killy-cure. Williams has spent his life in baseball, and the idea of a Cy Young Award winner's risking his future for the mystery and joy to be found on a ski slope is beyond his experience. The generation gap is everywhere.

Morning training sessions at Chain-O'-Lakes Stadium, in Winter Haven, were studied with a mixture of excessive optimism and unjustified despondency by the immense Boston press corps, which has traditionally been made uneasy by success. Soft breezes carried a festive, wedding-cake fragrance across the diamond from an orange grove beyond the outfield, and three large cardboard golden crowns, suspended by wires and marked "BA .326,"

"HR 44," and "RBI 121," swayed in the bright air above the boxes behind home. Yastrzemski, the inspiration for this impermanent trophy, seemed unconcerned by the almost visible rays of speculation that fell on him wherever he went in the field. Mostly, he was glad that the winter of his celebrity was over. He had been to too many banquets and benefits, once making seventeen appearances in the span of two days, and he told me that he now felt grateful when strangers in a restaurant waited until he had finished eating before coming up to introduce themselves. In Florida, he took long extra turns in the batting cage, sometimes staying for another hour of batting after playing a full game. He was admittedly tired, and he was having trouble with his timing. He knew, of course, that every pitcher in the league would have special plans for him this summer, that he would be the victim of shifts and stratagems and bases on balls, and, most of all, that even another great year at the plate could not bring him the same emotions and rewards. Yet as I watched him set himself again and again in the cage—settling his helmet and tugging at his belt and touching the bat to the ground and leveling his shoulders in exactly the same series of gestures, and then unleashing that flat, late, perfect swing—it came to me that all this was not just preparation for what was to come but that here, strangely, was a place where he could find privacy. Inside the cage, inside the game, he was alone, approachable only by his fellows and subject only to the demands of his hard profession.

Surrounded by more elders (the freshwater, or blue-gilled, geezer is almost indistinguishable from the Gulf variety), I watched the Red Sox split two games in Winter Haven, losing to Detroit by 13–3 and then beating the Phillies the next afternoon, 6–1. In the eighth inning of the game against the Tigers, while the visitors were batting around against a succession of unhappy Boston pitchers, I left the ballpark and walked back to the clubhouse, which lies beyond the stands in deep right field. Here, on a patch of grass in front of the locker rooms, in the midst of a smaller crowd, José Santiago was enjoying a moment of absolute triumph as a pitcher. Dressed in slacks and a short-sleeved shirt, his hair combed after his shower, he was tossing underhand to his four-year-old son, Alex, from a range of about ten feet. Alex was wearing a miniature Red Sox uniform, with his father's number, 30, on the back, and he was swinging a plastic bat. As I counted, Alex took fourteen successive swings at the ball without even managing one foul tip. Watching this game were perhaps a dozen other players—some in uniform, some not, some in stocking feet or with towels draped around their necks—and a good many wives and children and babies. Several of the wives were pregnant, and all of them were very young. They had driven over to the park to pick up the husbands at the end of the day's work. Now, at last, Alex Santiago hit the ball, and everybody cheered. His father let the ball roll through his legs and across the lawn, and Alex ran excitedly around an imaginary set of base paths, fell down once, and then made it safely home.

PART 2

Amazin'

The "Go!" Shouters

Through April and May, I resisted frequent invitations, delivered
via radio and television, to come up to the Polo Grounds and see
"those amazin' Mets." I even resisted a particularly soft blandish-
ment, extended by one of the Mets' announcers on a Saturday afternoon, to "bring the wife and come on up tomorrow after
church and brunch." My nonattendance was not caused by any
unwillingness to attach my loyalty to New York's new National
League team. The only amazement generated by the Mets had
been their terrifying departure from the runway in a full nosedive
—the team lost the first nine games of its regular season—and
I had decided it would be wiser, and perhaps kinder, to postpone
my initial visit until the novice crew had grasped the first princi-
ples of powered flight. By the middle of May, however, the Mets
had developed a pleasing habit of coming from behind in late
innings, and when they won both ends of a doubleheader in
Milwaukee on May 20, I knew it was time to climb aboard. In the
five days from Memorial Day through June 3, the Los Angeles
Dodgers and the San Francisco Giants were scheduled to play
seven games at the Polo Grounds, and, impelled by sentiment for
the returning exiles, who would be revisiting the city for the first
time since 1957, and by guilt over my delayed enthusiasm for the
Mets, I impulsively bought seats for all five days. The resulting
experience was amazin', all right, but not quite in the manner

expected by the Mets or by me or by any of the other 197,428 fans who saw those games.

I took my fourteen-year-old daughter to the opening double-header, against the Dodgers, and even before we arrived at the park it was clear that neither the city subway system nor the Mets themselves had really believed we were coming. By game time, there were standees three-deep behind the lower-deck stands, sitting-standees peering through the rafters from the ramps behind the upper deck, and opportunist-standees perched on telephone booths and lining the runways behind the bleachers. The shouts, the cheers, and the deep, steady roar made by 56,000-odd fans in excited conversation were comical and astonishing, and a cause for self-congratulation; just by coming out in such ridiculous numbers (ours was the biggest baseball crowd of the 1962 season, the biggest Polo Grounds crowd since September 6, 1942), we had heightened our own occasion, building a considerable phenomenon out of the attention and passion each of us had brought along for the games and for the players we were to see.

It must have been no more than an hour later when it first occurred to me that the crowds, rather than the baseball, might be the real news of the two series. The Dodgers ran up twelve runs between the second and the sixth innings. I was keeping score, and after I had jotted down the symbols for their seven singles, two doubles, one triple, three home runs, three bases on balls, and two stolen bases in that span, the Dodgers half of my scorecard looked as if a cloud of gnats had settled on it. I was pained for the Mets, and embarrassed as a fan.

"Baseball isn't usually like this," I explained to my daughter.

"Sometimes it is," she said. "This is like the fifth grade against the sixth grade at school."

For a time, the long, low "Oooh!" sound and the accompanying thunderclap of applause that greeted the cannon shots by Ron Fairly, Willie Davis, Frank Howard, and the other visitors convinced me that I was in an audience made up mostly of veteran Dodger loyalists. The Mets' pitchers came and went in si-

lence, and there were derisive cheers when the home team finally
got the third out in the top of the fourth and came in to bat trailing 10–0. I didn't change my mind even when I heard the explosive roar for the pop-fly homer by Gil Hodges that led off the
home half; Hodges, after all, is an ex-Dodger and perhaps the
most popular ballplayer in the major leagues today. Instantly,
however, I learned how wrong I had been. Gil's homer pulled
the cork, and now there arose from all over the park a full, furious, happy shout of "Let's go, *Mets!* Let's go, *Mets!*" There
were wild cries of encouragement before every pitch, boos for
every called strike. This was no Dodger crowd, but a huge gath-
ering of sentimental home-towners. Nine runs to the bad,
doomed, insanely hopeful, they pleaded raucously for the impossible. When Hickman and Mantilla hit a double and a single for
one run, and Christopher singled for another, the Mets fans
screeched, yawped, pounded their palms, leaped up and down,
and raised such a din that players in both dugouts ducked forward and peered nervously back over the dugout roofs at the vast
assemblage that had suddenly gone daft behind them.

The fans' hopes, of course, *were* insane. The Dodgers got two
runs back almost instantly in the fifth, and in the top of the ninth
their lead was 13–4. Undiscouraged, the spectators staged another screaming fit in the bottom half, and the Mets responded
with four singles, good for two more runs, before Sandy Koufax,
the Dodger pitcher, grinning with embarrassment and disbelief,
got the last man out. It was the ninth successive victory for the
Dodgers, the ninth successive defeat for the Mets, and the Mets
had never been in the game, yet Koufax looked a little shaken.

The second game was infinitely better baseball, but the fans, either wearied by their own exercise or made fearful by legitimate
tension, were noticeably more repressed. A close, sensible game
seemed to make them more aware of reality and more afraid of
defeat. The Mets spotted the Dodgers three runs in the first on
Ron Fairly's second homer of the afternoon, and then tied it in
the third on homers by Hodges and Hickman. It was nearly

seven o'clock and the lights had been turned on when Hodges, who was having a memorable day, put the Mets in the lead with still another home run. Suddenly convinced that this was the only moment in the day (and perhaps in the entire remainder of the season) when the Mets would find themselves ahead, I took my fellow fan reluctantly away to home and supper. This was the right decision in one respect (the game, tied at 4–4 and then at 5–5, was won by the Dodgers when Willie Davis hit a homer in the ninth) but the wrong one in another. A few minutes after we left the park, the Mets pulled off a triple play— something I have never seen in more than thirty years of watching big-league baseball. Sandy Koufax and I had learned the same odd lesson: It is safe to assume that the Mets are going to lose, but dangerous to assume that they won't startle you in the process.

In the following four days, the Mets lost five ball games—one more to the Dodgers and all four to the Giants— to run their losing streak to fifteen. Some of the scores were close, some lopsided. In three of the games, the Mets displayed their perverse, enchanting habit of handing over clusters of runs to the enemy and then, always a little too late, clawing and scratching their way back into contention. Between these rallies, during the long, Gobi stretches of home-team fatuity, I gave myself over to admiration of the visiting stars. Both the Dodgers and the Giants, who are currently running away from the rest of the league, are stocked with large numbers of stimulating, astonishingly good ballplayers, and, along with the rest of their old admirers here, I was grateful for the chance to collect and store away a private visual album of the new West Coast sluggers and pitchers. Now I have them all: Frank Howard, the six-foot-seven Dodger monster, striding the outfield like a farmer stepping through a plowed field; Ron Fairly, a chunky, redheaded first baseman, exultantly carrying his hot bat up to the plate and flattening everything thrown at him; Maury Wills, a skinny, lizard-quick base-runner. In the Thursday-night game, Wills stole second base twice in the span of three minutes. He was called back after the first clean steal, because Jim Gilliam, the batter, had interfered with the catcher; two pitches later, he took off again, as everyone knew he would, and beat the throw by yards. Willie Davis, the Dodger center fielder, is the first player I have ever been tempted to compare to Willie Mays. Speed, sureness, a fine arm, power, a picture swing—he lacks nothing, and he shares with Mays the knack of shifting directly from lazy, loose-wristed relaxation into top gear with an instantaneous explosion of energy.

I cannot understand how Orlando Cepeda, the Giants' slugger, ever hits a pitch. At the plate, he stands with his hands and the bat twisted back almost behind his right shoulder blade, and his vast riffles look wild and looping. Only remarkable strength can control such a swing. In one game, he hit a line drive that was caught in front of the center-field screen, 425 feet away; in another, he took a checked half-swing at an outside pitch and lined it into the upper right-field stands. Harvey Kuenn, by contrast, has the level, controlled, intelligent swing of the self-made hitter. He is all concentration, right down to the clamped wad of tobacco in his left cheek; he runs with heavy, pounding determination, his big head jouncing with every step. Mays, it is a pleasure to say, is just the same—the best ballplayer anywhere. He hit a homer each day at the Polo Grounds, made a simple, hilarious error on a ground single to center, and caught flies in front of his belt buckle like a grocer catching a box of breakfast food pulled from a shelf. All in all, I most enjoy watching him run bases. He runs low to the ground, his shoulders swinging to his huge strides, his spikes digging up great chunks of infield dirt; the cap flies off at second, he cuts the base like a racing car, looking back over his shoulder at the ball, and lopes grandly into third, and everyone who has watched him finds himself laughing with excitement and shared delight.

The Mets' "Go!" shouters enjoyed their finest hour on Friday night, after the Giants had hit four homers and moved inexorably to a seventh-inning lead of 9–1. At this point, when most sensible baseball fans would be edging toward the exits, a man sitting in Section 14, behind first base, produced a long, battered foghorn and blew mournful, encouraging blasts into the hot night air. Within minutes, the Mets fans were shouting in counterpoint— *Tooot!* "Go!" *Tooot!* "Go!" *Toooooot!* "GO!"—and the team, defeated and relaxed, came up with five hits and five runs that sent Billy Pierce to the showers. It was too late again, even though in the ninth the Mets put two base-runners on and had the tying run at the plate. During this exciting foolishness, I scrutinized the screamers around me and tried to puzzle out the cause of their unique affliction. It seemed statistically unlikely that there could be, even in New York, a forty- or fifty-thousand-man audience made up exclusively of born losers—leftover Landon voters, collectors of mongrel puppies, owners of stock in played-out gold mines—who had been waiting years for a suitably hopeless cause. Nor was it conceivable that they were all ex-Dodgers or ex-Giant rooters who had been embittered by the callous snatching away of their old teams; no one can stay *that* bitter for five years. And they were not all home-town sentimentalists, for this is a city known for its cool and its successful teams.

The answer, or part of the answer, came to me in the lull during the eighth inning, while the Giants were bringing in a relief pitcher. Two men just to my right were talking about the Mets.

"I tell you, there isn't one of 'em—not one—that could make the Yankee club," one of them said. "I never saw such a collection of dogs."

"Well, what about Frank Thomas?" said the other. "What about him? What's he batting now? .315? .320? He's got thirteen homers, don't he?"

"Yeah, and who's he going to push out of the Yankee outfield? Mantle? Maris? Blanchard? You can't call these characters *ball-*

players. They all belong back in the minors—the *low* minors."

I recognized the tone. It was knowing, cold, full of the contempt that the calculator feels for those who don't play the odds. It was the voice of the Yankee fan. The Yankees have won the American League pennant twenty times in the past thirty years; they have been the world's champions sixteen times in that period. Over the years, many of their followers have come to watch them with the stolidity, the smugness, and the arrogance of holders of large blocks of blue-chip stocks. These fans expect no less than perfection. They coolly accept the late-inning rally, the winning homer, as only their due. They are apt to take defeat with ill grace, and they treat their stars as though they were executives hired to protect their interests. During a slump or a losing streak, these capitalists are quick and shrill with their complaints: "They ought to damn well do better than *this*, considering what they're being paid!"

Suddenly the Mets fans made sense to me. What we were witnessing was precisely the opposite of the kind of rooting that goes on across the river. This was the losing cheer, the gallant yell for a good try—antimatter to the sounds of Yankee Stadium. This was a new recognition that perfection is admirable but a trifle inhuman, and that a stumbling kind of semi-success can be much more warming. Most of all, perhaps, these exultant yells for the Mets were also yells for ourselves, and came from a wry, half-understood recognition that there is more Met than Yankee in every one of us. I knew for whom that foghorn blew; it blew for me.

The Mets saved their best effort for the final game of the two series. They led the Giants 1–0 for five innings, gave up the tying run in the sixth, and then fell apart in the seventh and lost 6–1. The crowd, which had been beery and raucous toward the end of Saturday's long doubleheader, was smaller and more subdued—a polite Sunday audience, full of children, enjoying a warm, lovely spring day and too absorbed in the game to indulge in much yelling. The Mets scored their run in the first, on a single, an infield out, and a nubbed, wrong-field looper by Frank Thomas that just eluded Cepeda's glove. After that, the Mets played good ball—for a while—and everyone settled down to watch the first real pitchers' duel of the week. Young Bob Miller, who hadn't won a game this year, was matching the Giants' ace, Juan Marichal, pitch for pitch, and looked almost quicker; he struck out eight Giants in the first six innings. The contrast in their styles was pleasing. Marichal has the exaggerated windup, the deep body-bend, the mighty leg-kick of a scatter-armed twelve-year-old fast-baller; he reminded me of Joe E. Brown's old pantomime of a cocky bush-league pitcher. Miller's motion is economical. His pitches are more sidearm than Marichal's, and his deceptive speed comes from a big twist of the torso toward left field just before he delivers the pitch. He was keeping the ball low, which is something the Mets' pitchers haven't been able to do often this spring, and the Giants were swinging late and hitting a lot of soft hoppers to the infield. In this brief interval, it was possible to look at the Mets as a ball team, rather than as a flock of sacrificial lambs, and to speculate about the causes of the chilly summer they face. Their regular lineup, which Casey Stengel has been tinkering with every day—an Edison working with rusty parts—contains three unexciting pros: Felix Mantilla, Charlie Neal, and Frank Thomas. Of these, only Thomas hits with power; he was purchased from the Braves because he pulls the ball consistently and the left-field upper deck of the Polo Grounds is only 279 feet away from home plate. So far, he has delivered handsomely, but his record in the majors does not suggest that he can keep up his current averages. Richie Ashburn and Gil Hodges are receding stars, only occasionally capable of the bursts of light that made them shine so brightly a few years ago. Ashburn, who has slowed down shockingly, has been used mostly as a pinch-hitter this year, and Hodges' legs apparently aren't up to the demands of daily play.

Two attractive youngsters have emerged from the Mets' kiddie corps. (The Mets, like France in the nineteen-twenties, have a missing generation between the too old and the too young.) Rod Kanehl, a lanky all-purpose infielder-outfielder, has been hitting and running bases with an opportunism and an energy that are conspicuous on this team, and the shortstop, Elio Chacon, although he cannot always make the double play, has the knack of getting on base with bunts, scratchy singles, and frequent walks. He is an eager, hilarious base-runner, for he runs almost exactly the way Casey Stengel walks—in a fast, bowlegged hobble, head twitching, elbows rotating.

In the six innings that the Mets were in the ball game on Sunday, I savored the tautness, the cleanness, the absorption in every detail of play that had been so glaringly absent before. Good pitching in a close game is the cement that makes baseball the marvelous, complicated structure that it is. It raises players to keenness and courage; it forces managers to think about strategy rather than raw power; it nails the fan's attention, so that he remembers every pitch, every throw, every span of inches that separates hits from outs. And in the end, of course, it implacably reveals the true talents of the teams on the field.

In the sixth, Miller, who had fanned Mays in his two previous trips to the plate, tried to blow another fast ball past him on the first pitch. It was his first mistake. Willie hit the ball against the upper façade of the top deck in deep left center, and the game was tied. A little disconsolate, Miller started the seventh by giving up a single and hitting the next batter. Chacon then hesitated a fraction of a second on Pagan's grounder and was too late with his throw, and the bases were loaded. Miller walked in one run, Kuenn singled in two, and after McCovey's out the infield botched a double play, and the Mets were finished. They had wasted the rarest of their meager assets—a good pitching performance.

Abysmal pitching, in the end, is what keeps the Mets on their knees. The Polo Grounds has become Coogansbad this year— the spa where ailing National League hitters come to get well

—and there is no present hope that its doors can be closed. Even when one of the team's better pitchers—Jay Hook, Al Jackson, Craig Anderson, or the Mets' own Cyrano, Roger Craig— achieves a few innings of competence or even brief brilliance, he is almost surely betrayed by egregious fielding or flabby hitting, and thus leaves the field with a fresh loss against his record and the deepened conviction that he is being punished for some un- forgivable misdeed in his past.

But for me, so far, the terrible performance of the Mets matters much less than the simple joy of their presence. When my daughter and I left the park on Memorial Day, with the second game of the doubleheader still in progress, we found a taxi on the Harlem Speedway. The cab swung west on 155th Street, and I glanced to my right, along Edgecombe Avenue, and saw a little crowd gathered on a path that runs through a scrap of park and down Coogan's Bluff toward the Polo Grounds. There were per- haps thirty or forty men and women there. Most were Negroes; many were carrying portable radios. Below them, the great bank of lights above the roofed horseshoe illuminated the bones of the absurd, doomed old stadium. The ticketless spectators stood im- mobile, staring down through the early dusk, although they could see no more of the field than the big scoreboard above the bleachers and a slice of emerald grass in deep center field. It seemed likely that some of them had been there all afternoon, lis- tening to the roars from below, smiling and nudging one another at each momentary bit of good news over their radio—a small standing committee gathered to welcome the new team and the old league to our city.*

* The boyish optimism of this dawn report on the Mets can be ex- plained partly because it was written too early in the year (the Mets didn't hit their real stride until July, when they won six games and lost twenty-three), and partly because, as a sometime, nonprofessional Mets-watcher, I often missed their most memorable performances. I missed the game of June 17, for example, against the Cubs, when Marv Throneberry, the new first baseman, began working on his own legend. Early in the game, the Mets caught a Chicago base-

runner in a rundown between first and second, and Throneberry managed to collide with him while not having the ball in his possession; reprieved by the interference call, the Cubs scored four times. In the bottom half, Marv attempted to make amends. With two mates aboard, he hit a drive to the right-field bullpen and chuffed happily into third, only to be called out because he had failed to touch first base. Ordinarily, there is hot protest over this kind of appeal play, but the Met bench did not exactly erupt, since it was perfectly plain that Throneberry had also failed to touch second. The Mets lost the game by one run.

S Is for So Lovable

The first man to bat at the Polo Grounds in 1963 was a right-handed outfielder named Curt Flood, who plays for the St. Louis Cardinals. As he stepped up to the plate shortly after two o'clock on the afternoon of April 9, he was studied by me and the 25,848 other spectators at the park with an almost palpable apprehension. Flood represented the first hazard of the new season to the New York Mets, who had begun the previous season, the first of their existence, by losing the opening game to the Cardinals; had then tied a National League record by losing eight more games in succession; and had gone on to establish an all-time record by losing a hundred and twenty of the hundred and sixty games they played. During the endless, turbulent summer of 1962, Met fans and Met players developed a needlelike sensitivity to omens and portents, a superstitious belief in historical inevitability, and a fondness for disaster that were positively Sicilian, and here, on opening day, we gave Curt Flood the same apprehensive, defiant glare that a farmer on the slopes of Mount Etna might cast toward the smoke plume on the summit just before he began his spring lava-plowing. Flood took his stance at the plate, looked over a couple of pitches from Roger Craig, the Mets' starter, and then swung at a curve. The pitch fooled him, and he barely managed to top the ball, which rolled slowly down toward third. Charlie Neal, the Met third baseman, dashed in, but Flood, who is fast, was only a step or two away from first when Neal snatched up the ball. At this instant, several appalling intuitions struck me simultaneously. Flood would beat out the hit, which was unfortunate but not especially serious. However, I also *knew* that Neal would make a useless, off-balance throw toward first, and then the ball would end up in right field, Flood would move to second, the Cardinals would score in this first inning, and the Mets would lose this first game. They might even be worse than last year; they might end up losing a hundred and fifty games. All these conclusions came to me—and, I'm sure, to most experienced Met students in the park—before Flood's foot came down on first base. Corroboration followed quickly. Neal's wild throw sailed into right field, and Flood proceeded to second. The Cardinals then added three singles, the Mets came up with another error, and two runs scored. The Cards won the game, 7–0. The Mets lost again the next day, and then left town and lost six more games in succession.

Last year, I took my first look at the Mets in late May and saw them drop seven games in a row to the Dodgers and the Giants; that losing streak eventually ran to seventeen. This year, hoping to change matters, I had planned an earlier spring reading period at the Polo Grounds, but the validity of my first-inning, first-game premonitions almost frightened me away from the team for good. Only the fact that I had already paid for the tickets brought me back to watch a doubleheader against Milwaukee on Sunday, April 21. It was a happy decision, for on that afternoon the Mets almost exorcised their past and for the first time relieved themselves and their supporters of some of the dead weight of superstition and doom. The subsequent adventures of this tattered band has been the most absorbing spectacle of the young season.

The Mets had snapped their opening losing streak at eight games—one short of last year's record—with a Friday victory over the Braves. They had won again on Saturday, but the significant Sunday doubleheader at first promised only a reburial. Jay Hook, a Met pitcher who seems to live under a permanent

private raincloud of misfortune, blew a two-run lead in the sixth
inning. Then, with the bases loaded and the score tied at 3–3,
he let fly a wild pitch. Another run scored from third. Hook hurried in to cover the plate, but his catcher, Choo Choo Coleman,
flung the retrieved ball between Hook's legs, and the fifth Brave
run came across. I entered the fiasco in my scorecard, nodding
my head sadly; same old Mets. A few minutes later, however, I
received a tiny premonition that this might be a different kind of
team after all. With two out in the top of the seventh, the Braves'
Hank Aaron ripped a low drive through the box, and Ron Hunt,
the Mets' rookie second baseman, made a sprint and a flying dive
to his right, landing on his belly in a cloud of dirt. He missed the
ball by about two inches—it went through for a single—but
he brought a gasp from the crowd. There was nothing meretri-
cious or flashy or despairing about that dive, even though the
team was behind. Hunt very nearly pulled it off, and I suddenly
realized that not once last year had I seen a Met infielder even attempt such a play. It gave me a curious, un-Metsian emotion—
hope. Then, in the bottom of the eighth, with the Mets still
trailing 3–5, Ed Kranepool, another home-team youngster, led
off with a triple to left. Coleman walked, and Neal drove in one
run with a double. Harkness, pinch-hitting, was walked, and Jim
Hickman hit a grand-slam home run and trotted around the bases
in a storm of screeching disbelief and torn-up paper. The Mets
then played errorless ball in the second game, kept their poise
when they fell behind 2–0, and jumped on Lew Burdette (*Lew
Burdette?*) for nine runs in their last three innings. The fans
trooping out into the darkness at the end of the long day chat-
tered ecstatically about the team's new power, its four-game winning streak, its imminent escape from the cellar. We had witnessed something like a jail break.

In the three weeks that followed the Braves series and the big
bust-out, the Mets won ten games, lost nine, and moved up

into eighth place. In this tiny euphoric period, Met followers
began to collect and exchange tidings, tidbits, and little moral
tales that seemed to confirm the new vigor and startling bour-
geois respectability of their old ne'er-do-wells. The team lost three
out of five games on a road trip and came home in last place
again; while in Chicago, however, they had won a game on a
Thursday—something they had never managed to do before
—and had thus slain the last of their foolish statistical dragons.
Back at the Polo Grounds, they took on the Dodgers in a night
game and came from behind to win, 4–2. It was a happy beginning against a team that had humiliated them sixteen times in
1962. The Giants, the defending National League champions, arrived a few days later and administered a fearful cannonading to
the outfield fences, winning three games in a row while scoring
twenty-eight runs on thirty-six hits. Was this the beginning of a
new collapse? No, it was not; Carlton Willey, a veteran pitcher
whom the Mets acquired from the Braves this spring, stopped the
Giants, 4–2, in the second game of a Sunday doubleheader,
while 53,880 "Go!" shouters shouted. Against the Phillies two
nights later, Ron Hunt ran down a bouncing single behind second base to save a run in a tight game, which the Mets won. The
Mets then took three games in a row, to achieve seventh place
and a five-game winning streak—both for the first time ever
—and to come within one game of the first division in the standings. More significant, perhaps, was the fact that these three
victories—two over the Phillies and one over the Cincinnati
Reds—all came on scores of 3–2. In the lore of baseball, the
ability to win one-run-margin ball games is a telling mark of team
maturity, pitching depth, and a cool defense; last year, the Mets
lost no fewer than thirty-nine games by one run. Finally, as the
home stand drew to a close, the Mets played three really bad
games against the Reds, looking slack in the field and foolhardy
on the bases; they were lucky to pull out a 13–12 victory in
the last one, after blowing two five-run leads. This year, the Mets
have often looked lucky; last year they were jinxed.

Watching baseball at the Polo Grounds this spring has made cruel demands on my objectivity. The perspiring earnestness of all the old and new Mets, their very evident delight in their own brief flashes of splendor, their capacity for coming up with the unexpected right play and the unexpected winning game, and the general squaring of shoulders visible around the home-team dugout have provided me with so much fun and so many surprises that my impulse is simply to add my voice to the ear-rending anthem of the Met grandstand choir—that repeated, ecstatic yawp of "Let's go, *Mets!*" backed by flourishes and flatted arpeggios from a hundred dented Boy Scout bugles. Caution forces me to add, under the yells, that this is still not a good ball team. Most surprising, in view of the Mets' comparative new success, is the fact that nobody is hitting. Last year, when the team trailed the entire league in batting (it also finished at the bottom in club pitching and club fielding, stranded the most base-runners, gave up the most home runs, and so forth), its team average was .240. So far this year, the Mets are batting .215, and a good many of the regulars display all the painful symptoms of batters in the grip of a long slump—not swinging at first pitches, taking called third strikes, lashing out too quickly at good pitches and pulling the ball foul. The batting will undoubtedly pick up someday, but Casey Stengel may not be able to wait. If the team begins to lose many close games for sheer lack of hits, he will be forced to insert any faintly warm bat into the lineup, even at the price of weakening his frail defense. This desperate tinkering can lead to the sort of landslide that carried away the citadel last year.

The Mets' catching is embarrassing. Choo Choo Coleman and Norm Sherry, the two receivers, are batting .215 and .119 respectively. Neither can throw, and Coleman, who is eager and combative, handles outside curve balls like a man fighting bees. He is quick on the base paths, but this is an attribute that is about as essential for catchers as neat handwriting. The Met outfield, by contrast, is slow. Duke Snider, although in superb condition, is thirty-six years old and can no longer run a country mile with his old pounding *élan*. Jim Hickman may be spryer, but he can be frighteningly uncertain in the field. More than one shallow fly has dropped in front of him because of his slow, thoughtful start in center field. (In a recent night game against the Reds, on the other hand, he got a fine jump on a line drive hit by Vada Pinson and thundered in at top speed; then he had to stop and thunder *out* at top speed as the ball sailed over his head for a triple.) Finally, to conclude this painful burst of candor, I must add my impression that the Mets' base-running is deteriorating—another indication of the character-sapping effects of low base-hit nutrition. A hitter who seriously doubts whether the man who bats behind him can get the ball out of the infield is tempted to try stretching a double into a triple in a close game, and quite frequently succeeds only in shooting a rally right behind the ear. I witnessed three such assassinations in the final days of the Mets' home stand.

The sun's brightest rays this spring have shone around the middle of the infield. Ron Hunt, a skinny twenty-two-year-old second baseman up from the Texas League, and Al Moran, a rookie shortstop snatched away from the Red Sox farm system, are the most impressive inner defense perimeter in the team's young history. Hunt has quick hands, excellent range to his left, and a terrierlike eagerness for a moving ball. Moran has made some dazzling stops at short, and his arm is so strong that he can almost afford his cocky habit of holding the ball until the last moment before getting off his peg. Together, they have pulled some flashy double plays and messed up some easy ones; more familiarity with each other's style is all that seems needed. The pair may not last long enough to acquire this polish, however, because Moran has not yet shown that he can hit big-league pitching. Hunt, by contrast, has kept his average close to .300. He reminds me of Pee Wee Reese at the plate—an unassuming, intelligent swinger who chokes up on the bat and slaps singles to all fields.

The remaining Met assets are harder to define. The disparity between bright-eyed youth and leathery age among the team's regulars seems, for reasons I cannot entirely fathom, a source of interest this season, where it was only grotesque in 1962. The contrast can be startling, though. In a game at Cincinnati in April, Duke Snider banged his two-thousandth major-league hit in the first inning; when he came up again in the fourth, looking for No. 2001, Ron Hunt was standing on first base, having just rapped his first major-league hit. And the big right fielder/first baseman who frequently bats right after Snider in the Met lineup is Ed Kranepool, who is eighteen years old and was playing baseball for James Monroe High School at this time last year. Collectively, the Mets are still both too young and too old to afford any but the most modest ambitions, but I think the time has arrived when they can look at each other with something other than pure embarrassment. They can at least admire their own hardiness, for they have survived. No fewer than thirty-two other Mets have vanished from the team in the past year—a legion of ghosts, celebrated and obscure: Richie Ashburn and Solly Drake, Gene Woodling and Herb Moford, Marv Throneberry and Rick Herrscher, R. L. Miller and R. G. Miller. That time of hopeless experiment and attrition is, in all likelihood, finished, and the Mets of the future—the squad that eventually erases the memory of these famous losers—will almost surely include some of the twenty-five men who now wear the uniform.* That is progress.

I am so aware of the attractiveness of this year's Met team, and I share so much of the raucous, unquenchable happiness of its fans, that I cannot achieve an outsider's understanding of this much-publicized love affair. I made a try at it during the long Sunday doubleheader against the Giants, when the biggest crowd of the baseball year imperiled its arteries with more than six hours of nonstop roaring, sat through a small rainstorm, threw enough

---

* Only one of the twenty-five survived until the Mets' championship of 1969, thus sustaining this brash prediction: Eddie Kranepool.

paper and debris to make the outfield look like the floor of the
Stock Exchange after a panic, and went home, at last, absolutely
delighted with a split of the two games. Met fans now come to
the park equipped with hortatory placards as well as trumpets
and bass drums, and during the afternoon one group unfurled a
homemade banner that read:

> M is for Mighty
> E is for Exciting
> T is for Terrific
> S is for So Lovable

Reason told me that the first three adjectives had been chosen
only for their opening letters; it was the *Giants* who looked
mightily, excitingly terrific. The day before, they had ripped off
six homers, a triple, and eight singles, good for seventeen runs,
and now Willie Mays settled the outcome of the Sunday opener
in the very first inning, when he hit a three-run homer that disappeared over the roof of the Polo Grounds in deep left center—
approximately the distance of six normal Met base hits laid end
to end. The Mets' boosters were unsilenced by this poke, or by
Jack Sanford's almost total mastery of the locals. In the fourth inning, when Choo Choo Coleman struck out with the bases
empty, amid deafening pleas of "Let's go, *Mets!*" I suddenly understood why Met fans have fallen into the habit of *permanent*
shouting. It was simple, really: Supporters of a team that is batting .215 have no heroes, no mighty sluggers, to save their hopes
for. The Mets' rallies fall from heaven, often upon the bottom of
the batting order, and must be prayed for at all times.

Another revelation came to me by degrees, from various Giant
fans who were sitting near me in the upper deck. Their team had
just gone into first place in the standings; on this day, with Mays,
McCovey, Felipe Alou, and Cepeda ripping off extra-base hits in
all directions, it seemed capable of winning the pennant by the
middle of August. Yet the Giant loyalists were burdened and irri-
table. "Look at that McCovey," one of them said bitterly, as

Stretch fielded a Met single in left. "He just won't run. He's no goddam outfielder. I tell you, Dark oughtta nail him onna goddam bench, save him for pinch-hitting." He was not watching the game before us; his mind was weeks and months away, groping through the mists of September, and he saw his team losing. The Giants' pennant of last year, the Giants' power of today had made a miser of him, and he was afraid. *I* had nothing to lose, though; I clapped my hands and shouted, "Let's go, *Mets!*"

Most of the identifiable Giant fans left before the end of the nightcap. They just couldn't take it. The Mets had stumbled into a first-inning lead on a pop-fly, wrong-field home run by Cliff Cook, good for two runs, and Carlton Willey was pitching carefully and intelligently, keeping the ball low and scattering the Giant hits. The absentees missed a Giant defeat, which might have done them in, and they also missed the last, tastiest bit of Met quirkiness. With two out in the top of the ninth, the bases empty, and the Mets leading 4–1, José Pagan hit a deep grounder to Al Moran, who heaved the ball away, past Harkness at first. Tom Haller then pinch-hit and scored Pagan with a monstrous triple. Willey sighed and went to work on Davenport, who now represented the tying run. Davenport hit another grounder to short. Moran cranked up and made good with his second chance, and the lovable Mets sprinted off to the clubhouse through snowbanks of trash and salvos of exploding cherry bombs.

The noisy, debris-throwing, excitable Met fans have inspired a good deal of heavyweight editorial theorizing this year. Sportswriters have named them "The New Breed." Psychologists, anthropologists, and Max Lerner have told us that the fans' euphoria is the result of a direct identification with the have-not Mets, and is anti-authoritarian, anti-Yankee, id-satisfying, and deeply hostile. Well, yes—perhaps. But the pagan *après-midi d'un Met fan*, it seems to me, also involves a simpler kind of happiness. The Mets are refreshing to every New York urbanite if only because they are unfinished. The ultimate shape, essence, and reputation of this team are as yet invisible, and they will not be determined by an architect, a developer, a parks commissioner, a planning board, or the City Council. Unlike many of us in the city, the Mets have their future entirely in their own hands. They will create it, and in the meantime the Met fans, we happy many, can witness and share this youthful adventure.

The dirt, the noise, the chatter, the bursting life of the Met grandstands are as rich and deplorable and heartwarming as Rivington Street. The Polo Grounds, which is in the last few months of its disreputable life, is a vast assemblage of front stoops and rusty fire escapes. On a hot summer evening, everyone here is touching someone else; there are no strangers, no one is private. The air is alive with shouts, gossip, flying rubbish. Old-timers know and love every corner of the crazy, crowded, proud old neighborhood: the last-row walkup flats in the outermost lower grandstands, where one must peer through girders and pigeon nests for a glimpse of green; the little protruding step at the foot of each aisle in the upper deck that trips up the unwary beer-balancer on his way back to his seat; the outfield bullpens, each with its slanting shanty roof, beneath which the relief pitchers sit motionless, with their arms folded and their legs extended; and the good box seats just on the curve of the upper deck in short right and short left—front windows on the street, where one can watch the arching fall of a weak fly ball and know in advance, like one who sees a street accident in the making, that it will collide with that ridiculous, dangerous upper tier for another home run.

Next year, or perhaps late this summer, all this will vanish. The Mets are moving up in the world, heading toward the suburbs. Their new home, Shea Stadium, in Flushing Meadow Park, will be cleaner and airier—a better place for the children. Most of the people there will travel by car rather than by subway; the commute will be long, but the residents will be more respectable. There will be broad ramps, no crowding, more privacy. All the accommodations will be desirable—close to the shopping centers, and set in perfect, identical curves, with equally good views of the neat lawns. Indeed, a man who leaves his place will have to make an effort to remember exactly where it is, so he won't get mixed up on his way back and forget where he lives. It will be several years, probably, before the members of the family, older and heavier and at last sure of their place in the world, indulge themselves in some moments of foolish reminiscence: "Funny, I was thinking of the old place today. Remember how jammed we used to be back there? Remember how hot and noisy it was? I wouldn't move back there for anything, and anyway it's all torn down now, but, you know, we sure were happy in those days."

Farewell

The Polo Grounds went under last week, and I had no wish to
journey up and watch the first fierce blows of ball and hammer.
The newspaper and television obituaries were properly melan-
choly but almost entirely journalistic, being devoted to the celebrated names and happenings attached to the old ballfield: John
McGraw, Christy Mathewson, Mel Ott; Carl Hubbell's five
strikeouts, Bobby Thomson's homer, Willie Mays' catch, Casey
Stengel's sad torment. Curiously, these historic recollections
played little part in my own feeling of sadness and loss, for they
had to do with events, and events on a sporting field are so brief
that they belong almost instantly to the past. Today's fielding
gem, last week's shutout, last season's winning streak have their
true existence in record books and in memory, and even the
youngest and brightest rookie of the new season is hurrying at almost inconceivable speed toward his plaque at Cooperstown and
his faded, dated photograph behind a hundred bars. Mel Ott's
cow-tailed swing, Sal Maglie's scowl, Leo Durocher's pacings in
the third-base coach's box are portraits that have long been fixed
in my own interior permanent collection, and the fall of the Polo
Grounds will barely joggle them. What does depress me about
the decease of the bony, misshapen old playground is the attendant irrevocable deprivation of habit—the amputation of so
many private, repeated, and easily renewable small familiarities.

The things I liked best about the Polo Grounds were sights and emotions so inconsequential that they will surely slide out of my recollection. A flight of pigeons flashing out of the barn-shadow of the upper stands, wheeling past the right-field foul pole, and disappearing above the inert, heat-heavy flags on the roof. The steepness of the ramp descending from the Speedway toward the upper-stand gates, which pushed your toes into your shoe tips as you approached the park, tasting sweet anticipation and getting out your change to buy a program. The unmistakable, final *"Plock!"* of a line drive hitting the green wooden barrier above the stands in deep left field. The gentle, rockerlike swing of the loop of rusty chain you rested your arm upon in a box seat, and the heat of the sun-warmed iron coming through your shirtsleeve under your elbow. At a night game, the moon rising out of the scoreboard like a spongy, day-old orange balloon and then whitening over the waves of noise and the slow, shifting clouds of floodlit cigarette smoke. All these I mourn, for their loss constitutes the death of still another neighborhood—a small landscape of distinctive and reassuring familiarity. Demolition and alteration are a painful city commonplace, but as our surroundings become more undistinguished and indistinguishable, we sense, at last, that we may not possess the scorecards and record books to help us remember who we are and what we have seen and loved.

A Clean, Well-Lighted Cellar

As the writer of two excessively vernal and optimistic previous dissertations on the New York Mets, I resolved this year to keep my distance after the home opener and not file a report until midsummer. This admirable plan lasted for three weeks, during which time the Mets lost sixteen of their first twenty games— exactly the same mark they achieved early in 1962 while rushing toward an all-time record, generally considered secure for the ages, of a hundred and twenty losses in a season. At this point, I reconsidered and hurried to the scene, and I am glad I did. After watching a dozen-odd home games and an equal number of tele- vised road encounters, I can report, almost without crossing my fingers, that the Mets are better than they were in 1962, and proba- bly not worse than they were last year, when they lost a hundred and eleven games. There will be greater joy in Endsville this summer.

Much of the local interest in the Mets this year will be archi- tectural rather than athletic or psychopathologic, for on April 17 the club finally moved into its long-promised new home, William A. Shea Stadium, which was built by the city (which owns it) at a cost of $25,500,000, seats 55,300 baseball fans, and is situated in Flushing, just across the elevated IRT tracks from the World's Fair. Indeed, on my first visit the new ballyard, with its cyclo- tron profile, its orange and blue exterior spangles, and its jelly-

bean interior yellows, browns, blues, and greens, looked to me remarkably like an extension of the Fair—an exhibit named
"Baseball Land," or perhaps "Stengel-O-Rama." To one nurtured
in the gray fortress of Yankee Stadium and the green barn of the
Polo Grounds (O lost!), the place came as a shock; luckily, the
Mets supplied a reassuring sense of continuity by giving up sixteen hits to the Pirates and losing, 4–3. On subsequent visits,
my feelings of outraged classicism grudgingly abated and I was
able to judge the park more coolly. Some complaints remain. The
acres of box seats—21,795 of them—in two ellipsoid scoops
on the field level, the entire loge circle, and much of the mezzanine and upper stand are probably a valid tribute to our affluent
times, but I wish that unmoneyed fans, who usually make up a
team's true loyalists, didn't have to climb to the top ten rows of
the upper level to find an unreserved seat. Those same top-rail-
birds must also be irritated to discover that the two bullpens are
out beyond the outfield fence in right and left field, thus making
it impossible for a spectator to identify and speculate about the
relief pitchers who are warming up. This could be remedied, no
doubt, if the gargantuan scoreboard in right center field provided
such useful information in lighted letters on its huge central message center, but so far that bulletin board has been largely employed to boost souvenir and ticket sales and (very unsuccess-
fully) song lyrics for between-innings sing-alongs. The bright
colors of the different stands are cheerful, I guess, but women in
the field boxes are not going to be pleased with their complexions
during night games, when the floodlights bouncing off those yellow seats make the section look like a hepatitis ward. The lights,
the most powerful in any ballpark, are bright enough to pick up
gleams from the shine on an outfielder's spikes, and most of them
have been set lower than usual, just above the upper tier of seats,
in order to make it easier for outfielders to follow fly balls. Shea
Stadium is built of reinforced concrete, and its banked seats, set
almost entirely within the foul lines, sweep around in a lovely
circle, offering everyone a splendid and unobstructed view of the

action. Unobstructed and, I should add, too distant. Only in the field-level seats—those two scooped sections that roughly parallel the infield foul lines—does one feel close to the action; the loge, mezzanine, and upper levels are all circular, and this imposed geometry keeps the elevated fan forever distant from the doings within the contained square of the infield. All this is because Shea Stadium (and all future big-city stadia) must also be suitable for professional football. The changeover will be achieved, come autumn, by sliding the two massive suspended field-level sections apart on their tracks and around the circle, until they face each other on opposite sides of the gridiron. This is an impressive solution to an old problem, but it has been achieved at the expense of the baseball fan, for the best ballparks —Ebbets Field, say, or Comiskey Park—have all been boxes. Many of the games I saw this spring were thickly attended, but again and again I had the impression that I had lost company with the audience. In the broad, sky-filled circle of the new stadium, the shouts, the clapping, the trumpet blasts, and the brave old cries of "Let's go, *Mets!*" climbed thinly into the air and vanished; the place seemed without echoes, angles, and reassurance. No longer snug in a shoebox, my companions and I were ants perched on the sloping lip of a vast, shiny soup plate, and we were lonelier than we liked.

The Mets this year have not exactly risen to historic occasions. On May 6, they returned from a disastrous road trip to play the Reds in the first night game at Shea. There were speeches, the new lights brought a massed "Aah!" from thirty-four thousand chilly fans, the organist played "When the Lights Go on Again All over the World," and the Mets performed like a pickup nine at a wiener roast. In the fifth inning, with the score tied at 2–2, various Met pitchers gave up two walks, three singles, two doubles, six runs, one wild pitch, two stolen bases, and one full windup with men on first and second, while the rest of the team chipped in a wild throw by the catcher, a wild throw by the center fielder, and an egregious play on what should have been a routine outfield fly. The bangs and thumps of the fireworks from the Fair were matched by the Cincinnati hitters, who came up with three rocketlike homers.

I went back the next afternoon and was well rewarded for my perseverance. Al Jackson, the Mets' little left-hander, was given a three-run lead by the second inning, and just managed to hold it, winning, 3–2, in spite of some uncertain defense in the outfield. This, to be fair, was a game much more typical of the 1964 Mets, who have frequently piled up small leads in early innings and then suffered ungodly difficulties in holding them. Casey Stengel was so tense about his club's minimal margin in the ninth that he summoned Galen Cisco in to pitch the last half-inning and then suddenly reversed himself and allowed Jackson to go to the mound and get the last three outs. The pattern was much the same the following night, against the Cardinals, but Jack Fisher, the Mets' starter, could not defend a painfully accumulated 4–1 lead in the eighth inning—a frequent failing of his this spring. Carl Warwick came in to pinch-hit with two men on and lined Fisher's first pitch into the left-field stands to tie it up. Experience now said that the Mets would lose, but with this new Met team experience is sometimes in for surprises; in the bottom of the ninth George Altman singled, was neatly sacrificed to second, and scored the winning run on Joe Christopher's pinch single. The homing fans on the IRT sounded like children returning from a birthday party that featured a good magician: "Did you see that!"

The next one was close but dull, for the Mets, who weren't hitting, looked doomed from the outset, even though some fool-hardy Cardinal base-running and some extraordinary throws by the Mets' outfield kept the Cards' lead to 1–0 until the seventh. In that inning, two Met relief pitchers—Wakefield and then Bauta—first walked the bases full and then gave up three ringing hits, good for four runs and the ball game. I spent much of the warm, blustery afternoon enjoying the sideshows in the stands—a teen-age bugle-and-garbage-pail-lid corps in the upper deck, a small boy near me who spread mustard on his hot dog with his ball-point pen, and a pretty airline stewardess next to me who wrote letters throughout the game, only rarely lifting her sleepy eyes to watch the action below.

The first half of the Sunday doubleheader with the Cards was perhaps the most pleasing regular-season game I have seen in five years, as the Mets' Tracy Stallard engaged Roger Craig, an old grad, in a stiff pitchers' battle that brought out the best in everyone. In the seventh, the Cardinals, down 1–0, had White on third base and Boyer on first, and tried to tie it with a double steal; Jesse Gonder, the Mets' catcher, whipped his peg to second, and Stallard, seeing White break for home, cut the throw off and nailed White at the plate in a rundown while Shea Stadium screeched in rapture. The Cards then tied it, 1–1, and the Mets untied it for good in the eighth, on homers by Rod Kanehl and Frank Thomas—exactly the way a pitchers' battle ought to end. In the second game, Casey Stengel, who has been desperate for a fourth starting pitcher, tried Jerry Hinsley, who is nineteen years old and had never pitched an inning of organized baseball until this season. Hinsley retired the first eight Cardinals in order, and then, as he was probably beginning to think long thoughts about his contract demands next spring, was socked for five straight hits and four runs; his teammates were commiserating but unhelpful, and the Cards won, 10–1.

In splitting their last eight games, against the Braves at home and the Giants on the road, the Mets have alternated dizzyingly between hopelessness and downright competence. Met pitching in this stretch has held the opposition to less than three runs per game. The hitting has been, to put it mildly, mixed; after rapping out forty-one hits in a span of three games, the Met sluggers, exhausted by the unexpected demands of base-running, reverted to form and failed to produce a single run in the ensuing thirty-two innings. Go figure it.* I sense at least a new resiliency, an occasional touch of professionalism, that has been lacking in previous Met squads. That is why I have only small hesitation in stating that this team will not fall victim to so many of those long stretches of ennui and botchery that so pained Met rooters the past two summers. At the same time, I think it unlikely the Mets will escape the cellar this season, if only because at least six of the other National League teams also look stronger than they did last year.

The Mets are short on heroes. Their gamecock, their small nova, is Ron Hunt, the second baseman. Now in his second season, Hunt appears to be one of those rare ballplayers who improve from year to year. Four years ago, he batted .191 in the low minors. Last year, as a major-league rookie, he hit a solid .272, and so far in this young season a stream of modest singles and doubles has kept him constantly above the .300 mark. Originally a third baseman, he now has mastered the pivot at second and he fields with assurance, if not brilliance. His new partnership with Roy McMillan, the veteran shortstop just purchased from the Braves, cements the Mets' infield. McMillan has slowed down a step or two and is having trouble at the plate, but he is a tough, tobacco-chewing, old-time pro and a boon to this young team.

This almost exhausts the good news. Rod Kanehl, Stengel's slick handyman, has filled in splendidly in the outfield during a series of injuries and is currently batting .333. Tim Harkness, at first base, had an early hot streak at the plate but has now plummeted below .250. Jesse Gonder, a catcher, can hit but cannot catch; Hawk Taylor, another catcher, can catch but cannot hit. Amado Samuel and Charlie Smith, who have shared third base, have both shown that they can make hard plays and butcher

* Excellent advice. A few days later, after this had gone to press, the Mets beat the Cubs, at Wrigley Field, by the score of 19–1. The last six runs were scored in the ninth inning, and Tracy Stallard said afterward, "That's when I knew we had 'em."

easy ones; their combined batting average is below .200. Frank Thomas is an earnest but deadly slow outfielder who occasionally hits a homer.*

The pitching staff, in spite of its recent parsimony, does not emerge much better from such a scrutiny. Al Jackson, its star, holds that spot only by default. On most teams, he would be the third pitcher in rotation, but as the Mets' No. 1 he is constantly matched against the league's best flame-throwers and consequently loses many low-run games. Carlton Willey, the best Met pitcher a year ago (his earned-run average was 3.10), suffered a broken jaw in spring training and has yet to pitch an inning this year. Larry Bearnarth and Tom Sturdivant, the relievers, have been uneven to date; the latter two might as well sleep with their rubber boots on, for they will be summoned to a lot of dangerous fires this summer. Stengel has also called on Jerry Hinsley and two other rookie pitchers, Bill Wakefield and Ron Locke, for spot duty. They have responded with eager gallantry—often of the kind once displayed by Eton sixth-formers taking to the air against Baron von Richthofen.

In 1963, the Mets, dead last all the way after their brief spring flurry, drew 1,080,108 spectators at the Polo Grounds, against a Yankee home attendance of 1,308,920. This season, the Mets have already drawn 21,128 more spectators to their home games than they had at this time last year, and even these figures do not tell the whole story, for the Mets have not yet played the Giants and the Dodgers at home, as they had last year before mid-May; those rich, nostalgic series will take place over the two weekends just

---

* Ed Kranepool was absent from the roster, having been sent down to the Mets' Buffalo farm club for seasoning. A couple of weeks later, on Saturday, May 30, he was summoned back, just after playing in both ends of a doubleheader for Buffalo. He traveled at night, arriving at Shea in time to play right through both games of a Sunday doubleheader against the Giants. The Mets lost the first game, 5–3, and the second, 8–6, in twenty-three innings. Welcome home, Eddie!

ahead, and, given decent weather, they should be good for at
least another two hundred thousand tickets. It is quite possible
that the perennial moles will outdraw the perennial champions in
New York this summer.

In my last report on the team, I speculated sadly that the move
from the banks of the Harlem River to the shores of Flushing Bay
might civilize the Met fans, transforming them into a cautious,
handclapping audience of suburban lawn-tenders. That alteration
may be taking place, but it is slower than I had anticipated.
There are more well-dressed, unexcitable, merely pleasant on-
lookers visible in the gleaming new stands, but a good many of
the men are wearing cowboy boots and a good many of the
women are carrying cameras, thus identifying themselves as Fair-
goers who have wandered in to rest their feet. Some of them
must have been startled during the night game with Cincinnati,
when a dozen or so of the New Breed—the *old* New Breed
—staged a rousing fistfight in the lower right-field stands, at-
tracting roars of encouragement and subsequent boos for the
fuzz.

Still, I doubt whether Shea Stadium will ever see the likes of
those steamy old midsummer doubleheaders at the Polo Grounds,
when visiting outfielders used to stare up in wonder at the
screaming sans-culottes, and had to brave summer thunderstorms
of trash and firecrackers while catching a fly. For one thing, the
loudest, most phenomenal Metsian roars used to come when the
team was at its very worst—eight runs down in the seventh inning, say. The Mets are too much improved to encourage that
kind of fanaticism with any frequency this year. Some of the
crazy pleasure has gone out of their games, for when they take
the field one no longer has the stimulating, if awful, impression of
watching a dotty inventor preparing to jump off the Eiffel
Tower with a parachute made of pillowcases. Better baseball has
also led to some disaffection. Unsuccessful pinch-hitters have
been getting stiff boos. During one game when the Mets were
having trouble hitting the ball beyond the pitcher's mound, I

overheard a new kind of remark from behind me about "our goddam sluggers." And on another occasion, when Stengel went to
the mound to yank a pitcher, I saw, to my shock, the first "Casey
Must Go" banner, flaunted by two malcontents.

As must befall all fanatical movements, self-consciousness and
formalization have overtaken the Met religion. Small pockets of
Met fans are now visible on television at out-of-town ballparks,
where they dutifully cry the old cry and wave banners identifying their cause and their home town. The thing is growing cute,
like those Pogo for President clubs. Formalization and self-consciousness are also detectable in many of the banners displayed
these days at Shea Stadium, which often look as if they had been
created by art students or advertising men. In the old days, banners were made up overnight, out of old sheets and towels, and
the messages were often misspelled or made jiggly by passion.
This year, I saw a neatly printed sign that could have been a
radio jingle:

> In Los Angeles, they wade through smog;
> Las Vegans lose their bets,
> But we New Yorkers aren't sad—
> We have our New York Mets!

Then, too, there were the eight forehanded fans who turned up
one afternoon with a group sign made up of eight separate letters.
When Roy McMillan came up to bat, they stood up in a row,
each holding one letter, and spelled out: "WE LUV ROY." When Rod
Kanehl appeared, the last letter had been changed and the sign
read: "WE LUV ROD," and a little later it was "WE LUV RON," for Ron
Hunt.* For a moment, I thought I had wandered into a California football game. And finally, to my dismay, I must report that
the signs this year seem to have been made for the television cam-

---

* This must have been inspired by a little band of Marv Throneberry
admirers—five of them—who once turned up at the Polo Grounds
wearing white T-shirts with different characters emblazoned on the
back. When lined up properly, they spelled out "MARV!" Sometimes, of
course, they spelled it "VRAM!"

eras rather than for the team; mostly they are unfurled when a foul ball, with its attendant TV eye, comes into the stands, instead of when the Mets desperately need a run.

All this, I suppose, is the inevitable result of the Mets' comparative maturity and comparative new success. The carefree unreality, the joyful bitterness, the self-identification with a brave but hopeless cause will become more and more difficult for Met rooters to sustain as their team draws closer to the rest of the league and faces the responsibilities and drudgery of an ordinary second-division team. As one sportswriter has observed, the only thing the Mets have to fear is mediocrity. This year, the Met cause reminds me of nothing so much as a party of young radical vegetarians who find they are on the point of being taken seriously and, somewhat anxiously, begin to understand that they are on the printed ballots at last and are thus capable of being beaten, instead of merely insulted and brushed aside. Without drawing any political parallel, it is my guess that reality will be postponed for the Mets at least for another year or two; they will be just bad enough to keep most of the "Go!" shouters shouting through this first summer in their new home.

PART 3

Classics and Campaigns—I

A Tale of Three Cities

Los Angeles, October 3

This afternoon, in the top of the ninth inning of the final playoff game between the San Francisco Giants and the Los Angeles Dodgers, Walter Alston, the Dodger manager, and Leo Durocher, his third-base coach, stalked slowly back and forth in their dugout, staring at their shoe tops and exuding an almost visible purple cloud of yearning; they wanted to have the National League season extended by a few more innings or a few more games. This wish, like so many other attitudes to be seen in this city, must be regarded as excessive. The teams on the field had already played more games in one season than any other two baseball teams in the history of mankind, and the quality of play demonstrated in the past three days by the twitchy, exhausted athletes on both squads was reminiscent of the action in the winter softball games played by septuagenarians in St. Petersburg, Florida. As everyone in this country must know by now, the newly elongated, hundred-and-sixty-two-game National League season proved insufficient to its purpose in its first year. The Dodgers, who led the Giants by four full games with a week to go, lost ten of their last thirteen games, including the last four in a row, and thus permitted their gasping pursuers to catch them on the final day. In the first playoff game, on Monday at Candlestick Park in San Francisco, the Dodger team displayed the muscle, the frightfulness, and the total immobility of a woolly mammoth frozen in a glacier; the Giants, finding the beast inert, fell upon it with savage cries and chopped off steaks and rump roasts at will, winning 8–0. The feast continued here for a time yesterday, and after five and a half innings the Giants led, 5–0. At this point, the Dodgers scored their first run in thirty-six innings, and the Giants, aghast at this tiny evidence of life, stood transfixed, their stone axes dropping from their paws, while the monster heaved itself to its feet, scattering chunks of ice, and set about trampling its tormentors. The game, which the Dodgers eventually won, 8–7, is best described in metaphor and hyperbole, for there was no economy in it. It lasted four hours and eighteen minutes—a record for a nine-inning game. There were twenty hits, thirteen walks, three errors, two hit batsmen, and a total of forty-two ballplayers in action (also a record), and the only positive conviction among the spectators when it was over was that the Mets could have beaten both teams on the same afternoon.

Today was a little different. For one thing, there was a noisy, shirtsleeve crowd of 45,693 on hand, in contrast with the embarrassing acres of empty seats yesterday, when the park was barely half full. Los Angeles calls itself the Sports Capital of the World, but its confidence is easily shaken. Its loyalists are made uneasy by a team that appears likely to lose. Today, with a final chance at the pennant restored, the Dodger rooters were back, and there was a hopeful violence in their cries. Fans here seem to require electronic reassurance. One out of every three or four of them carries a transistor radio, in order to be told what he is seeing, and the din from these is so loud in the stands that every spectator can hear the voice of Vin Scully, the Dodger announcer, hovering about his ears throughout the game. There is also a huge, hexagonal electric sign in left field, on which boosterish messages appear from time to time. The fans respond to its instructions with alacrity, whether they are invited to sing "Baby Face" between innings or ordered to shout the Dodger battle cry of "CHARGE!" during a rally. Today the sign also carried news flashes about the orbital progress of Walter M. Schirra, Jr., thus enabling the crowd to enjoy both national pastimes—baseball and astronaut-watching—at the same time. This giant billboard, protruding above the left-field bleachers like a grocer's price placard, was one of several indications to me that the new and impressive Dodger Stadium, which opened this spring, was designed by an admirer of suburban supermarkets. It has the same bright, uneasy colors (turquoise exterior walls, pale green outfield fences, odd yellows and ochers on the grandstand seats); the same superfluous decorative touches, such as the narrow rickrack roofs over the top row of the bleachers; the same preoccupation with easy access and with total use of interior space; and the same heaps of raw dirt around its vast parking lots. There is a special shelf for high-priced goods—a dugout behind home plate for movie and television stars, ballplayers' wives, and transient millionaires. Outside, a complex system of concentric automobile ramps and colored signs—yellow for field boxes, green for reserved seats, and so forth—is intended to deliver the carborne fan to the proper gate, but on my two visits to O'Malley's Safeway it was evident that the locals had not yet mastered their instructions, for a good many baseball shoppers wound up in the detergent aisle instead of in the cracker department, with a resultant loss of good feeling, and had to be ordered to go away and try again.

For a time today, it seemed that all the recent doubts and discomforts suffered by Dodger fans were finally to be rewarded, for their team, after handing the Giants two runs on three errors in the third inning, came back and took apparent command of the game, and in the happiest fashion imaginable. Duke Snider, the old demigod, led off the fourth with a double, and Tommy Davis, the young demigod and new National League batting champion, moved him to third with a single, from where he scored during an abortive double play. Then, in the sixth, Duke singled, and Davis, a batter who studies each pitch with the eye of a jewelry appraiser, hit a homer for the tying and the go-ahead runs. Duke jumped on home plate with both feet as he came

across. It was then appropriate for Maury Wills, the new base-
stealing champion and the ranking deity in Los Angeles this year,
to score the insurance run. He managed this because the Giants
forgot their newly discovered stratagem for getting Wills out; in
yesterday's game, Wills stole second, and the Giants' catcher, in
attempting to cut him down, relayed the ball to center field and
to the possessor of the best arm on the club, Willie Mays, who
then cut down Wills at third. In the seventh inning today, Wills
singled and stole second, but the ball didn't get out to Mays.
Wills then stole third, and Bailey, the Giants' catcher, angry at
having flubbed baseball's newest trick play, threw the ball into
left field, allowing Wills to score.

This was a movie ending, pat but satisfying. Unfortunately, the
game had two more innings to go. Matty Alou led off the Giant
ninth with a pinch single but was erased at second on Kuenn's
grounder. Ed Roebuck then walked the next batters, and Alston
and Durocher, sensing the onset of another ice age, suddenly
foresaw that the season might be too short after all. The clatter of
typewriters died away in the press box. Many of the sportswriters
had already departed for the victory celebration in the Dodger
clubhouse; those who remained fell silent, half hoping for more
drama, half praying that they would not have to rewrite their
leads so late in the day. The preposterous end came quickly. Willie Mays nearly tore Roebuck's glove arm off with a line single
that scored one run. Stan Williams came in to pitch, and Cepeda
delivered the tying run with a fly. With runners on second and
third, Williams walked one batter intentionally and another unin-
tentionally, and the game was untied. The final run scored on an
error, and the press-box loudspeaker announced that United Air-
lines would have a special flight leaving at seven o'clock for San
Francisco and the World Series. Billy Pierce came in to pitch for
the Giants and set the Dodgers down in order, and the visitors
went into the ritual autumnal dance of victory in front of their
dugout, leaping into the air like Watusi.

When I returned to my hotel, the Statler Hilton, I noticed for the first time that there was an art exhibit in one corner of the lobby. Ranged in a great semicircle were a dozen or so life-size pastel portraits of Dodger players, elegantly framed and each bearing a gold identifying plate. The exhibit was encircled by a velvet rope, like the one that protects the new Rembrandt in the Metropolitan Museum, and there was a uniformed Pinkerton on guard. No one was looking at the pictures.

San Francisco, October 5

On the evening of the day the Giants won the pennant, the circulation manager of the San Francisco *Chronicle* approached the news editor and said, "What's the headline?"

"It's 'WE WIN!'—white on black," the news editor said.

"How big?"

"Same size as 'FIDEL DEAD!' "

That evening, twenty-five thousand or perhaps five thousand celebrants tore down police barriers at the San Francisco airport and swarmed out onto the runways and taxiways, forcing several flights to delay their arrival or departure, and causing the team that they had come to greet to land at a distant maintenance runway. I arrived in San Francisco after eleven o'clock, but the jubilee was still in full swing. The gutters were awash with torn-up newspapers and office calendars, and Market Street, Geary Street, and Kearny Street were solid with automobiles crawling bumper to bumper, horns blasting. The faces inside all had the shiny-eyed, stunned, exhausted expression of a bride at her wedding reception. The police, who had planted red flares at intersections to guide the processions, were treating it all like cops in a college town after a big football victory—a little bored, a little amused, a little irritated. The San Francisco newspapers cannot get enough of the Giants. The team and the World Series cover the front pages, the sports pages (green and pink here), and most of the pages in between. There are human-interest stories about little boys who have run away from home with their piggy-bank savings in order to buy a Series ticket. In the papers, the name of the team is usually prefixed with the possessive pronoun—"our Giants."

The total identification of this attractive city with a baseball team is a sado-masochistic tangle. The gala this week has offended a good many proud old-time locals, who think the city should be less naïve. "Good God!" one of these said to me. "People will think we're like *Milwaukee*, or something!" One local sports columnist, Charles McCabe, of the *Chronicle*, has tried to stand against the river of heroic newspaper prose; he has characterized the Giants' style of play as "lovable incompetence" and has told San Franciscans that victory may be less cozy to live with than years of defeat. His warning will be considered, for this is a town fond of self-examination and afflicted with self-doubt. "We've had a lot of trouble in the past few years," a woman told me at a cocktail party, and for a moment I thought she was talking about some scandal or sickness in her family. She meant the Giants, who have frequently been favored to win the pennant in their five-year residence here but have staged a series of exaggerated pratfalls, sometimes in the final week of the season. As an old Giant fan, I was tempted to tell the woman that persistent ill luck and heroic failure, interspersed with an occasional triumph, had been characteristic of her team ever since Merkle's Boner in 1908. I thought of the Snodgrass muff in 1912; of the 1917 Series that was lost when Heinie Zimmerman chased Eddie Collins across the plate with the winning run; of the Series of 1924, when Hank Gowdy stumbled over his catcher's mask and a grounder bounced over Freddy Lindstrom's head and allowed Washington to win the last game; and of the last two games of the 1934 season, when the Dodgers dropped the Giants out of first place after Bill Terry had asked if they were still in the league. But I said nothing, for I realized that her affair with the Giants was a true love match and that she had adopted her mate's flaws as her own. The Giants and San Francisco are a marriage made in Heaven.

Candlestick Park is no supermarket; with its raw concrete

ramps and walkways and its high, curving grandstand barrier, it looks from the outside like an outbuilding of Alcatraz. But it was a festive prison yard during the first two Series games here. In order to beat the midafternoon Candlestick wind, which can blow pop fouls into triples and cause flags on adjacent outfield poles to flutter briskly in opposite directions, the games started at noon, and the fans arrived bearing picnic hampers and gin-and-tonic fixings. The crowd here is polite, cheerful, and gaily dressed; it has the look of a country horse-show audience. Some of the home-town exuberance wore off quickly yesterday afternoon, when the fans came in and found the Yankees waiting— Mantle and Berra, Ford and Howard and Maris, all instantly identifiable and suddenly menacing—on the field below. A few of the spectators gave up then and there. A man next to me in the lower stands watched Mickey Mantle hit four balls over the fence in batting practice, applauded politely, and then turned to his wife and said, "Well, at least we won the pennant." The Yankees started off just as he had feared they would, scoring two runs in the top of the first on three solid hits. The big crowd was restless and nervous until Mays came up to bat against Ford in the second. Willie Mays against Whitey Ford—this was worth the five-year wait! Willie singled, and came around to score the Giants' first run. An inning later, he drove in the tying run with another hit, and the San Franciscans whooped and screamed with elation and relief; every one of them, I was convinced, had harbored the secret fear that his heroes would perform like Little Leaguers against the all-conquerors. The Giants kept reaching Ford—nine hits in the first six innings—but they couldn't ruffle him or quite put him away. Ford stands on the mound like a Fifth Avenue bank president. Tight-lipped, absolutely still between pitches, all business and concentration, he personifies the big-city, emotionless perfection of his team. This was his seventeenth World Series game, and he was giving the young Giants a lesson in metropolitan deportment. O'Dell, the Giants' pitcher, was pitching better than Ford, but showing the strain. He was working too fast, striking out too many men, giving up walks, and running up high counts. Apprehension muffled the audience, and in the seventh Clete Boyer totally silenced the park with a home run over the left-center-field fence. It was all downhill from there. The champions got two more in the eighth and another in the ninth. With victory in his pocket, Ford retired the Giants on a handful of pitches and left the mound as if on his way to board the four-thirty to Larchmont.

The apparently inevitable outcome of yesterday's game seemed to afflict the home team and its fans deeply this afternoon. A man seated just in front of me was suffering from a severe case of the uh-ohs. "Uh-oh," he would murmur to his companion, "here comes Yogi Berra." . . . "Uh-oh, Mantle comes up this inning." Meanwhile, the Giants were clustering under pop flies like firemen bracing to catch a baby dropped from a burning building (they muffed one baby, right behind the mound), and wasting their substance in overexuberant base-running. In the seventh and eighth innings, they combined a home run by Willie McCovey, three singles, a walk, two successful sacrifices, and a Yankee error for the grand total of one run, which may be another Series record. Fortunately for everyone, Jack Sanford, a tough, hardworking right-hander, kept his courage and his presence of mind, and pitched a lovely, near-perfect game, shutting the Yankees out, 2–0, with three hits. After the last out, the massed San Franciscans expelled their breath in a shout, and then trooped out into the afternoon wind with the same relieved, "Still alive!" expression on their faces that they had been wearing all summer.

New York, October 10

This jet Subway Series moved three thousand miles east last Saturday, but in watching the reactions of the local crowds to the first of the three marvelous games in Yankee Stadium this week I had the recurrent impression that the teams' planes had overshot their mark, and that the Series was being continued before a polite, uncomprehending audience of Lebanese or Yemenis. New York is full of cool, knowing baseball fans—a cabdriver the other day gave me an explicit, dispassionate account of the reasons for the Milwaukee Braves' collapse this year—but not many of them got their hands on Series tickets. Before the first game here, on Sunday, the northbound D trains were full of women weighted down with expensive coiffures and mink stoles, not one of whom, by the look of them, had ever ridden a subway as far as the Bronx before. There was no noise in the stands during batting practice, and the pregame excitement seemed to arise from the crowd's admiration for itself and its size (a sellout 71,-431), rather than for the contest to come; ritual and occasion had displaced baseball. The only certifiable fans near me were among the standees packed three-deep behind the lower-grandstand seats. When Roger Maris came up to bat in the second, the box-holders gave him a dutiful spatter of applause, but the voice of the demanding, unforgiving Yankee fan came from behind me —a deep, rich "Boo!" and the cry "C'mon, bum!" During the long, austere pitchers' duel between Bill Stafford and Billy Pierce, which the Yankees finally pulled out, 3–2, the spectators near me who had radios were giving most of their attention to the football game between the New York Giants and the St. Louis Cardinals. (There are no low-scoring pitchers' duels in pro football.) By the sixth inning, when the game was still scoreless, spectators had begun walking out in twos and threes, surrendering their ticket stubs to the persevering verticals; the departees had accomplished their purpose, which was to be able to tell their friends they had been to a Series game.

Ignorance and moneyed apathy became less evident during the second and third games at the Stadium. I suspect that a considerable number of corporation seat-holders went home to Dallas and St. Paul after the weekend, in order to begin earning the money to buy next year's trip to the Series, and thus freed their tickets for resale to more knowledgeable resident fans. At the same time, the gallant, inflammatory, instructive baseball being played by both teams began to make believers and partisans among those who had come only for the show. To judge by my private decibel meter, most of the neutrals became Giant rooters. The San Francisco *équipe* is a genetically pure descendant of its dichotomous, death-loving, strong-jawed forebears. It is capable of appalling human fallibility, which it attempts to counteract with insane pluck. When one sees troops with such qualities brought into battle against the massed fieldpieces of the Yankees, one is filled with the same pride, foreboding, and strong desire to avert one's eyes that was felt by the late General Pickett. In yesterday's game, the Giants' pitcher, Juan Marichal, flattened a finger on his pitching hand while bunting in the fifth. Alvin Dark then called on Bob Bolin, an inexperienced twenty-three-year-old fast-baller, to hold the Giants' two-run lead. Bolin instantly pitched himself into and out of an appalling jam; apparently enjoying the tension, he tried the same thing in the sixth, walking Mantle and Maris in succession, but this time the bomb went off and the Yankees tied the game. Enemy scores are a tot of rum to this Giants team, however; in the past two weeks, they have usually responded to them with an instant retaliatory base hit. This time, Matty Alou hit a pinch double between two walks in the seventh, and the bases were loaded with two out when Chuck Hiller, the frail San Francisco second baseman, came up. Hiller had struck out in a similar situation in the fifth, but Dark merely told him to try harder this time, and Hiller hit a grand slam into the right-field stands for the ball game.

In today's encounter, the last Stadium game of the year, the same melodrama of error, reprisal, and retaliation was played, but with a different curtain. Jack Sanford, pitching powerfully again, held the Yankees to three hits through the seventh inning, but the score, instead of being 2–0 for the Giants, was 2–2, one Yankee run having scored on a wild pitch and the other on a passed ball. It is a poor idea to give the unsentimental Yankees a helping hand up, to dust their jackets and to set their caps straight after they have fallen into a ditch. In the eighth, Kubek and Richardson singled, and Tom Tresh, the Yankees' elegant switch-hitting rookie, hit a three-run homer. Willie McCovey started the reflexive Giant rally in the ninth with a single and came around on Haller's double, but Ed Bailey, pinch-hitting, missed his bid for the tying two-run homer by about fifteen feet, and the two teams trooped off toward the more impressionable audiences of the opposite coast.

What these ballplayers left behind, with at least one spectator, was not just an appreciation of their individual skills, courage, and opportunism but a refreshed admiration for the sport they pursue. Unlike the playoffs, each of the five World Series games to date has been taut, wholly professional, wholly absorbing. Each has been won by the team that deserved to win. Each, in fact, has revealed in early-inning whispers—a key strike delivered, a double play just missed—which team was a fraction sharper or luckier that day and would eventually win. This year, baseball's two best teams rose to the beloved, foolish, exciting autumn occasion, and did honor to their great game.

New York, October 14

The violent West Coast storm that has postponed the completion of the Series has bred in me the odd conviction that this championship can have no satisfactory conclusion. A victory by the Yankees will merely encourage smugness among their adherents, whose mouths are already perpetually stuffed with feathers, and will reinforce the San Francisco fans' conviction of their own fundamental insufficiency. (I can hear my friend from the cocktail party triumphantly crying, "I *told* you we always have trouble here!") A seven-game comeback win for the Giants, on the other hand, will lead to another horn-blowing and paper-throwing orgy out there, to the pain of the resident non-rubes. It will also cause San Franciscans to discover for themselves the gloomy truth in Charles McCabe's warning; total triumph is unsettling, for introverts can taste in it the thrilling, debilitating, and ultimately fatal virus of future defeat. Giant fans, like all neurotics, are unappeasable. I can see it now—the Dodgers should have won the playoff.*

----

* This account ended here, amputated by rain and deadline. As some dodderers may remember, the Series eventually resumed and went the full seven, the Giants winning the penultimate game, 5–2, after knocking out Whitey Ford, and losing the finale, 1–0, in a game whose gruesome denouement could have been foretold by every life-time Giant fan. In the bottom of the ninth, Yankee pitcher Ralph Terry gave up a bunt single to Matty Alou and, with two out, a double to Mays; McCovey then struck a low screamer toward right —a sure championship blow but for the fact that the ball flew directly into the glove of Bobby Richardson, at second. The ensuing speculation eventually hardened into the legend, "a foot either way, and the Giants win it," but I have recently re-examined the game film, which shows that "six feet either way" would be more like it; Richardson made the play without exertion. A. J. Liebling, who detested baseball, was in San Francisco at the time, waiting to see a prizefight that had been postponed in turn by the postponed Series, and he confessed himself dangerously bored by the endless public dissections of the play. "It may be noted," he wrote later, "that the Yankees are the least popular of all baseball clubs, because they win, which leaves nothing to 'if' about."

Taverns in the Town

Already, two weeks after the event, it is difficult to remember that there was a World Series played this year. It is like trying to recall an economy display of back-yard fireworks. Four small, perfect showers of light in the sky, accompanied by faint plops, and it was over. The spectators, who had happily expected a protracted patriotic bombardment culminating in a grand crescendo of salutes, fireballs, flowerpots, and stomach-jarring explosions, stood almost silent, cricking their necks and staring into the night sky with the image of the last brief rocket burst still pressed on their eyes, and then, realizing at last that there was to be no more, went slowly home, hushing the children who asked, "Is that *all?*" The feeling of letdown, of puzzled astonishment, persists, particularly in this neighborhood, where we have come to expect a more lavish and satisfactory autumnal show from our hosts, the Yankees, the rich family up on the hill. There has been a good deal of unpleasant chatter ("I always knew they were really cheap," "What else can you expect from such stuckups?") about the affair ever since, thus proving again that prolonged success does not beget loyalty.

By choice, I witnessed the Los Angeles Dodgers' four-game sweep at a remove—over the television in four different bars here in the city. This notion came to me last year, during the Series games played in Yankee Stadium against the San Francisco

Giants, when it became evident to me that my neighbors in the lower grandstand were not, for the most part, the same noisy, casually dressed, partisan, and knowing baseball fans who come to the park during the regular season. As I subsequently reported, a large proportion of the ticket-holders appeared to be well-to-do out-of-towners who came to the games only because they could afford the tickets, who seemed to have only a slipshod knowledge of baseball, and who frequently departed around the sixth or seventh inning, although all of last year's games were close and immensely exciting. This year, then, I decided to seek out the true Yankee fan in his October retreat—what the baseball beer commercials refer to as "your neighborhood tavern." I was especially happy about this plan after the Dodgers clinched the National League pennant, for I well remembered the exciting autumns here in the late forties and the mid-fifties, when the Dodgers and the Yanks, both home-town teams then, met in six different Series in what seemed to be a brilliant and unending war, and the sounds of baseball fell from every window and doorway in town. Those Series were a fever in the city. Secretaries typed only between innings, with their ears cocked to the office radio down the hall, and if business drew you reluctantly into the street (fingering your pool slip, designating your half-inning, in your pocket), you followed the ribbon of news via elevator men's rumors, snatches of broadcasts from passing taxi radios, and the portable clutched to a delivery boy's ear, until a sudden burst of shouting and laughter sucked you into a bar you were passing, where you learned that Campy or Duke had parked one, or that Vic Raschi had struck out Furillo with two on.

Even before Stan Musial had thrown out the honorary first ball to open the first game this year, I discovered that there would be no such attendant melodrama in the city. Just before game time, I walked west in the mid-Forties and turned up Eighth Avenue, searching for the properly athletic saloon in which I could, in Jimmy Durante's words, "mix wit' de *hoi pollew*" who had not felt inclined to plunk down thirty-two dollars for a block of four

home-game tickets at the Stadium. I stuck my nose in three or
four likely-looking bars, only to find no more than a handful of
fans who had staked out bar stools and were watching Whitey
Ford and Sandy Koufax complete their warmups. Finally, exactly
at game time, I walked into O'Leary's Bar, on the northwest corner of Fifty-third Street and Eighth Avenue, and found an audience of sufficient size and expectancy to convince me that it was
not about to watch an afternoon quiz program. There wasn't a
woman in the place, and the bar stools and nearly all the standing
slots along the bar were taken. It was mostly a young crowd—
men in their twenties, in sports shirts and with carefully combed
hair. There were some off-duty postmen in uniform up front,
with their empty canvas mailbags under their feet. I ordered a
beer and took up a stand beside the shuffle alley, near the front
door, from where I could see the television screen just above the
head of the bar. It was a color set, and I was appalled to discover
that Whitey Ford had turned blue since I last saw him; he and all
the other ballplayers were haloed in rabbit's-eye pink, like deities
in early Biblical color films. There was a black-and-white set at
the back of the bar, and from time to time during the afternoon I
turned around and watched that, just to reassure myself that Vic-
tor Mature was not kneeling in the on-deck circle.

It was a Yankee crowd at O'Leary's. There were winks and
happy nudges when Whitey struck out Maury Wills, the lead-off
man, and silence when Koufax fanned the side in the first. Frank
Howard's double off the center-field screen in the next inning
won an astonished "Oooh!" and a moment later, when Skowron
and then Tracewski singled, a man to my left shook his head and
said, "Whitey ain't got it today." I wasn't sure yet, but I had to
agree when Roseboro homered into the right-field stands, to
make the score 4–0; left-handed hitters do not hit homers off
Ford when he is pitching low and to the corners. Koufax stepped
up to the plate, and several watchers suggested to Ford that he
would do well to hit him in the pitching arm.

It was sound advice, though ignored. For a time, Koufax simply got better and better. He struck out Mantle and Maris in the second, and Pepitone in the third. With his long legs, his loose hips, his ropelike motion, and his lean, intelligent face, he looked his part elegantly—a magnificent young pitcher at an early and absolute peak of confidence, knowledge, and ability. In the fourth, facing the top of the order again, he struck out Kubek swinging, with a dipping curve that seemed to bounce on the ground in front of Roseboro, and got Richardson out on another big changeup curve; when he fanned Tresh, also for the second time, for his ninth strikeout, the men around me cried *"Wow!"* in unison. They had been converted; now they were pulling for Koufax. They knew their baseball—in the third, there had been expert admiring comment on a throw of Maris's that almost nailed Willie Davis at third base—and they knew they were watching something remarkable. What they had in mind, of course, was Carl Erskine's Series strikeout record of fourteen batters, which had been set exactly ten years before. Koufax, straining a bit now, struck out Mantle in the fifth, and then yielded three singles in a row before fanning Lopez, a pinch-hitter, for No. 11. In the sixth, he temporarily lost his poise; in spite of his 5–0 lead, he seemed edgy, and his motion had grown stiff and elbowish. He walked Richardson and Tresh in succession. There was a stirring under the TV set, a brief resurgence of Yankee hopes, but Koufax took a few deep breaths on the mound, went back to his fast ball, and got Mantle and Maris to pop up, ending the inning.

Two innings later, the strikeouts stood at thirteen, and there was much less interest in Kubek's single and Tresh's two-run homer than in Richardson's strikeout, which tied the old record. O'Leary's was jammed now; no one had left, and those who had wandered in stayed to watch Koufax. A middle-aged man came in and asked one of the men near the bar to order him a Fleischmann's whisky and a beer chaser. "I won't get in your way," he said apologetically. "I'm gonna *drink* it and then go right out." But he stayed, too.

Elston Howard led off the bottom of the ninth with a liner to Tracewski. Pepitone singled, and Boyer flied out to Willie Davis. Koufax's last chance—a pinch-hitter named Harry Bright— came up to the plate. The count went to two and two, and there was a mass expulsion of held breath when Bright hit a bouncer that went foul. Then Koufax stretched and threw, Bright swung and missed, and the young men in O'Leary's burst into sustained applause, like an audience at Lincoln Center. Up on the pink-and-blue stage, Koufax was being mobbed by his ac- companists. The sporting crowd left O'Leary's, blinking in the pale, unreal late-afternoon sunshine on Eighth Avenue and chat- tering about what it had seen. Not one of them, I was certain, was worried about what had happened to his team.

Oblivion descended on the Yankees after ten minutes of the second game. Maury Wills, leading off, singled, and was instantly trapped off first by Al Downing, the Yankees' young left-hander. But Pepitone's throw to second was a hair wide, and Wills skid- ded safely in on his belly. Gilliam singled to right, Willie Davis lined to right, and Roger Maris fell while going for the ball (or so Vin Scully, the announcer, told us—the camera missed the play), and the Yankees were down, 2–0. These rapid events were received with overpowering ennui in my second observa- tion post, a spacious restaurant-bar called the Charles Café, just west of Vanderbilt Avenue on Forty-third Street. I had chosen the spot as a likely sporting headquarters because of the dozens of jumbo-size baseball and boxing photographs that hang above the mirrors on its walls, but the customers had nothing in com- mon with the decor. These were youngish men too, but they were wearing dark suits and subdued neckties, and most of them were giving more attention to their hot-pastrami sandwiches and their business gossip than they were to the events on the televi- sion screens at either end of the long, shiny bar. One junior exec- utive next to me at the bar ordered a Beefeater dry martini on the rocks—a drink that has perhaps never been served in O'Leary's.

The only certifiable Yankee fan near me was a man who banged his palm on the bar when Maris tapped to the box in the second. His fealty was financially oriented. "Oh, God," he said. "For that they pay him seventy thousand a year." Subsequently, another railbird was unable to detect the considerable difference in appearance and batting style between two Yankee veterans. "Here's the man who took the catching job away from Yogi Berra," he said to me when Hector Lopez, an outfielder, came up in the fourth.

By the middle innings, shortly after two o'clock, these zealots were all back at their desks, the Yankees were down, 3–0, and I was lonely as a cloud in the Charles. Johnny Podres, the veteran Dodger lefty, was, unbelievably, pitching even better than Koufax had. He was less flashy but more efficient, working on the premise that it takes five or six pitches to strike a batter out but only two or three to get him to pop up or ground one to an infielder. This had become a nice, dull pitchers' Series. The TV announcers, Scully and then Mel Allen, tried to disguise the fact that the fall classic was laying an egg by supplying me with a steady stream of boiler-plate news. A dandruff of exclamation points fell on my shoulders as I learned that Dick Tracewski and an umpire named Joe Paparella came from *the same home town*, that Tommy Davis was the youngest batter to win the National League batting championship *two years running*, that Al Downing had been *twelve years old* when Jim Gilliam played in his first World Series, and that the Dodgers' Ron Perranoski and the Red Sox' Dick Radatz had *both attended Michigan State*! There was still another non-news flash from Mel Allen, but his peroration— "something that means nothing but is nonetheless interesting" —was so arrestingly metaphysical that I didn't catch the rest of the message.

Languishing, I studied the pictures on the wall—shots of Ketchel fighting Billy Papke, Dempsey knocking out Jess Willard—and wished I were at ringside. Then I found a framed motto and studied *that:*

> Life is like a journey taken on a train
> With a pair of travelers at each window pane.
> I may sit beside you all the journey through,
> Or I may sit elsewhere never knowing you.
> But if fate should mark me to sit by your side
> Let's be pleasant travelers, it's so short a ride.
>   —A Thought

I straightened my tie and looked about for someone to be pleasant to, but the nearest fellow-traveler was fourteen feet down the bar and totally occupied in making rings on the mahogany with his beer glass. I had to finish this particular part of life's journey, a longish one, alone with Mel Allen. Eventually, Podres ("The Witherbee, New York, Wonder!") won, 4–1, with a little help in the ninth from Perranoski, and the Series ("America's *greatest sporting spectacle!*") removed itself to California.

I was understandably anxious for company during the next game, and I found it at the Cameo, a Yorkville snuggery at Eighty-seventh Street and Lexington Avenue. The U-shaped bar, which enclosed two bartenders, two islands of bottles, and the TV set, was almost full when I came in, and everyone there seemed to know everyone else. It was a good big-city gumbo—men and women, Irishmen and Negroes and Jews and Germans, most of them older than the spectators I had encountered downtown. This was a Saturday afternoon, and the game, being played in Los Angeles, began at four o'clock, which is drinking time on Yorkville weekends. Boilermakers were the favorite, but there were interesting deviations, including one belt I had never seen before—a shot glass of gin with lemon juice squeezed into it. Everybody kept his drinking money out on the bar in front of him. With their club down two games, Yankee fans had grown reticent, but there was one brave holdout, a woman in her late

forties named Millie, who was relying on voodoo. She had fashioned a tiny Dodger image out of rolled and folded paper napkins
held together with elastic bands, and throughout the game she
kept jabbing it viciously and hopefully with toothpicks. When
Jim Gilliam came up in the bottom of the first, she stuck a tooth-
pick in each of the doll's arms. "He's a switch-hitter," she explained, "so I gotta get him both ways."

The arrows failed to reach Los Angeles in time, though. Gilliam walked and then took second when Jim Bouton, the
Yankees' sophomore fast-baller, threw a bullet all the way to the
foul screen behind home plate. Tommy Davis hit a ball that
bounced off the pitcher's mound and then off Bobby Richardson's shin, and Gilliam scored. The Yankees were again behind in
the very first inning (as it turned out, they never led in a single
game of the Series), and the Dodger glee club in the Cameo was
in full voice. "None of that sweet sugar for the Yanks *this* year!"
one man exclaimed.

In the next few innings, I evolved the theory that the Dodger
pitching staff had made a large pre-Series bet on their comparative abilities, because Don Drysdale, the handsome home-team
pitcher, was easily surpassing both Koufax and Podres. His fast
ball and his astonishing curves, pitched three-quarters overhand
from the apparent vicinity of third base, had the Yankee batters
bobbing and swaying like Little Leaguers. Even so, it was an exciting, lively afternoon, because Bouton, although in a lather of
nerves, kept pitching his way out of one jam after another, and
the game, if not the entire Series, now almost surely hung on that
one run. In the seventh, the Dodgers seemed certain to widen the
gap when they put Roseboro on third and Tracewski on second,
with none out. The combination of tension and boilermakers
proved too much for one fan at this juncture. "This Roseboro's
gonna blast one," he announced loudly. "Just watch and see."

"What's the matter with you?" his companion said, embarrassed. "Roseboro's standing on third. What are you—bagged
or something?"

"That's what I *said*," the other insisted. "He's gonna hit a homer. Roseboro's gonna hit a homer."

What did happen was almost as unlikely. Drysdale hit a sharp grounder between second and first, which Richardson ran down with his back to the plate and pegged to Pepitone for the out at first. Pepitone then jogged happily across the infield, having found both Roseboro and Tracewski hopefully toeing third base. Roseboro had held up, Tracewski had run, and it was a double play. The man on the bar stool just to my right, who had told me that he once played semi-pro ball, was disgusted. "What's the *matter* with that Roseboro?" he said in disbelief. "No outs and the ball's hit hard to right, you got to run. You don't even look—you just *go!* That's baseball. Everybody knows that."

As it turned out, the insurance run was unnecessary. With two out in the top of the ninth, Pepitone hit a high smash that seemed to be headed for the bleachers. The Cameo's Yankee fans gave their only yell of the afternoon, but Ron Fairly, with his back almost against the right-field wall, put up his hands and made the catch that ended the game. Millie shook her head slowly and then crumpled her doll into a wet ball on the bar.

The next afternoon, I witnessed the obsequies in the bar of the Croydon, a genteel residential hotel on Eighty-sixth Street just off Madison Avenue. Surrounded almost entirely by women, but joined from time to time by bellboys and doormen and waiters who dropped into the bar to catch the action, I saw Frank Howard, the Dodger monster, apparently swing with one hand as he hit a hyperbolic home run into the second tier in left field—a blow that Mickey Mantle almost matched with his tying poke in the seventh. Whitey Ford pitched perhaps the best of all his twenty-one World Series games, giving the Dodgers only two hits, but he was up against Koufax again, and the Yankee hitters remained hopelessly polite. In the seventh, Clete Boyer's throw to Pepitone went through the Yankee first baseman as if he had been made of ectoplasm, and Gilliam steamed all the way around to third on the error, immediately scoring on Willie Davis's fly. At this juncture, the talk in the bar, which had been pro-Dodger (when it was not concerned with *haute couture*, Madame Nhu, Elizabeth Taylor, and lower-abdominal surgery), took a sharp, shocked swerve toward disbelief and sadness. Even a lifelong Dodger fan who had come with me to the Croydon was affected. "I never thought the Yankees would go out like this, without winning one damned game," he said, shaking his head. He sounded like a tormented foretopman who had just learned that Captain Bligh was dying of seasickness. The demise came quickly. Richardson singled, but Tresh and then Mantle took third strikes with their bats resting comfortably on their shoulders. There was an error by Tracewski, but Lopez dribbled to Wills for the last out, and the Dodger squad galloped out and tried to tear souvenir chunks off their baby, Koufax.

As drama, the 1963 World Series was wanting in structure and development. This lack of catharsis was sensed, I am sure, even by Dodger supporters. The disappointment, the small, persistent resentment, about the outcome of the Series which is felt (or so I believe) by Yankee fans is at least partly a result of the fact that they had to wait through a long summer of vapid American League baseball, in which the Yankees walked over such feeble and acquiescent challengers as the Chicago White Sox, the Minnesota Twins, and the Baltimore Orioles. The only crucial series for the Yanks in 1963 was the last one, and they muffed it shockingly.

Those millions of us who saw the Series on television were left with the emptiest balloon of all. There is a small paradox here, because these were pitchers' games, and the television camera, hovering over the home-plate umpire's shoulder and peering down the back of the pitcher's neck, gives a far better view of each ball and strike than any spectator can get from the stands. But baseball is not just pitching. A low-scoring series of games is stirring only if one can sense the almost unbearable pressure it puts on base-running and defense, and this cannot be conveyed even by highly skilled cameramen. This World Series was lost by a handful of Yankee mistakes, most of which were either not visible or not really understandable to television-watchers. The cameras were on the hitter when Maris fell in the second game. The grounder that bounced off Richardson in the third game and Pepitone's astonishing fluff in the final game caused everyone near me to ask "What *happened?*" On the same two-dimensional screen, it looked as if the throw to Pepitone had hit the dirt, instead of skidding off his wrist, as it did. It is the lack of the third dimension on TV that makes baseball seem less than half the game it is, that actually deprives it of its essential beauty, clarity, and excitement.

Yankee fans grew increasingly invisible as the Series progressed, and now they must nurse their winter puzzlement and disappointment with whatever grudging grace they can muster; to do otherwise would seem ungrateful in the face of their team's nine world championships and thirteen American League pennants in the past fifteen years. But it must be clear to them now that this Yankee team is not the brilliant, almost incomparable squad that many baseball writers claimed it was. No team can be judged entirely on one series, and the Yankees were not disgraced, for all the games were close; this was nothing like the dreary one-sided pasting that the Yankees gave the Cincinnati Reds in five games in 1961. And the Dodgers' pitching, opportunism, and nerve were magnificent. But fine pitching inevitably means bad batting; the terms are synonymous. Hard luck and injuries notwithstanding, the Yankees' best and most publicized athletes have not been of much help to them in recent Octobers. Mickey Mantle has batted .167, .120, and .133 in his last three Series; Roger Maris has hit .105, .174, and .000 in the same span. Whitey Ford has failed to win one of the last four Series games he has pitched. There is something wrong here—too little day-to-day opposition, perhaps a tiny lack of pride, perhaps a trace of moneyed smugness.

Whatever it is, it probably explains this year's collapse and makes it certain that this Yankee team cannot be compared to the Ruffing-Gehrig-Dickey teams of the nineteen-thirties or the DiMaggio-Henrich-Rizzuto Yanks of the nineteen-forties and fifties. What made those Yankee teams so fearsome, so admirable, so hated was typified by the death-ray scowl that Allie Reynolds, their ace right-handed pitcher a decade ago, used to aim at an enemy slugger stepping into the box in a crucial game. I can think of no member of the current team capable of such emotion, such combative pride. I suspect that local Yankee fans sensed the absence of this ingredient almost unconsciously, even before the Series began. That would explain, most of all, why the deepest passions and noisiest pleasures of baseball were so conspicuously absent in the bars and streets and offices of the city this autumn.

Two Strikes on the Image

As we all know, when the typical American business executive
turns out his bedside light he devotes his next-to-last thought of
the day to his corporate image—that elusive and essential ideal
vision of his company which shimmers, or *should* shimmer, in the
minds of consumers. Do they like us, he wonders. Do we look
respectable? Honest? Lovable? Hmm. He sighs, stretches out,
and tries to find sleep by once again striking out the entire batting order of the New York Yankees. As he works the count to
three and two on Tom Tresh, it may suddenly occur to this
well-paid insomniac that baseball itself has the most enviable corporate image in the world. Its evocations, overtones, and loyalties,
firmly planted in the mind of every American male during child-
hood and nurtured thereafter by millions of words of free newspaper publicity, appear to be unassailable. It is the national
pastime. It is youth, springtime, a trip to the country, part of our
past. It is the roaring excitement of huge urban crowds and the
sleepy green afternoon silences of midsummer. Without effort, it
engenders and thrives on heroes, legends, self-identification, and
home-town pride. For six months of the year, it intrudes cheerfully into every American home, then frequently rises to a point
of nearly insupportable tension and absorption, and concludes in
the happy explosion of the country's favorite sporting spectacle,
the World Series. Given these ancient and self-sustaining attri-

butes, it would seem impossible that the executives of such a business could injure it to any profound degree through their own
carelessness and greed, yet this is exactly what has happened to
baseball in the past ten years. The season that just ended in two
improbably close pennant races and in the victory of the Cardinals over the Yankees in a memorable seven-game World Series
was also the most shameful and destructive year the game has experienced since the Black Sox scandal of 1919.

The fervent loyalties of baseball are almost, but not quite, in-
destructible. I know a New York lady, now in her seventies,
whose heart slowly bleeds through the summer over the misadventures of the Boston Red Sox, a team representing the home
town she left in 1915. With immense difficulty, I have sustained
something of that affection for the San Francisco Giants, once
my New York team, but I know that my attachment will not
survive the eventual departure of Willie Mays. Since 1953, six
teams have changed their homes and four entirely new teams
have been born, so exactly half of the twenty major-league teams
must count on a loyalty that is less than a dozen years old. Further expansion of both leagues is already being discussed, and at
this writing it seems entirely possible that faltering attendance
will cause three more franchises—Cleveland, Kansas City, and
Milwaukee—to shift to new cities within the next two seasons.
Another team, the Angels, will conclude its brief tenancy in Los
Angeles at the end of next year; starting in 1966, it will represent
Anaheim, California, which is the home of Disneyland.

The irritation and dismay that I share with most baseball fans
over this queasy state of affairs is not caused entirely by the appearance in our ballparks of so many semi-anonymous ballplayers
with unfamiliar insignia on their shirtfronts, or by the inept play
of so many of the new teams, or even by the ridiculously ex-
panded new schedules, which now require the majors to play
1620 games, as against the old 1232, before they can determine
two winners. Grudgingly, I can accept the fact that it was sensible for baseball to enlarge itself and to spread toward new centers

of a growing population. What I cannot forgive is the manner in which the expansion was handled. In 1957, Walter O'Malley, the owner of the Brooklyn Dodgers, abruptly removed his team to Los Angeles after making a series of impossible demands upon the City of New York for the instantaneous construction of a new ballpark. He was followed at once by Horace Stoneham, who took his Giants to San Francisco while piously denying that he had any understanding with O'Malley, although every schoolboy knew that National League schedules required the presence of two teams on the West Coast. Within a few days, the largest and most vociferously involved baseball audience in the country was deprived of its two oldest franchises and left with the new knowledge that baseball's executives cared only for the profits inherent in novelty and new audiences, and sensed no obligation whatever—not even the obligation of candor—to the fans who had built their business.

The subsequent operations of Mr. O'Malley, the other owners of big-league teams, the league presidents, and Commissioner Ford Frick have been watched by fans with growing cynicism. In 1961, O'Malley, supported by Frick, permitted the establishment of a rival team in Los Angeles only after imposing such punitive conditions and rental fees that the Angels could not possibly succeed. The result, of course, is Anaheim. In the 1962 draft creating two new teams, the National League owners, ignoring the much fairer system inaugurated by the American League the previous year, protected their player investment so carefully that the squads were manned entirely by a miserable collection of culls and aging castoffs, and the two teams—the Houston Colt .45s and the Mets—have been a disgrace to baseball. The perverse loyalty of the Met fans—the New Breed—is at least partly engendered by a hatred for the kind of cold-blooded success typified by Mr. O'Malley and by the owners of the New York Yankees.

In the past few years, baseball has staged such unedifying spectacles as the loud public wrangle carried on by Charles O. Finley, the owner of the Athletics, in his attempt to secure more favorable stadium-rental terms from the municipal government of Kansas City. At various times, since he purchased the club in 1960, Mr. Finley has threatened to move to Oakland, to Atlanta, or to almost any other city or hamlet that promised him a ballfield and the kind of profits he considers his due. Last winter, his negotiations with Louisville reached the point where the American League had to threaten him with expulsion before he accepted terms and signed a new lease for the Kansas City park. Mr. Finley, it should be added, is the man who had to be restrained by the baseball Rules Committee from enlivening the national pastime with orange baseballs and green-and-gold bats. His notion that baseball owes him a free, or almost free, municipal ballpark and the right to move wherever and whenever he chooses is neither eccentric nor atypical. Consider, for example, the fact that the Braves, who have been established in Milwaukee only since 1953, are now casting hungry eyes on Atlanta. This team—pennant winners in 1957 and 1958, and formidable contenders from 1952 through 1960—enjoyed four consecutive years in which their attendance topped two million, and in 1957 they established a league gate record of 2,215,404, so there can be no doubt about Milwaukee's enthusiasm for the sport. But now that the team is old and attendance is down, the chance to move on to new audiences, in the pattern established by O'Malley, may prove to be more tempting than the hard work involved in staying put and rebuilding the club. There is a powerful rumor that Milwaukee will move to Atlanta next year,* and other shifts, involving cities such as Cleveland, Kansas City,† Seattle,‡ Oakland,** and Dallas,†† are in the wind. If these shuttlings ever do take place, several million more fans will understand at last that baseball's executives view them as dimwitted louts who will automatically at-

* That was no rumor.
† ‡ ** †† Neither were these.

tach their attention and loyalty to the most recent second-rate team that happens to wear the home uniform.

The most significant event of the 1964 baseball season was the news on August 13 that the Columbia Broadcasting Company had bought control (80 per cent) of the New York Yankees for the sum of $11,200,000. The shabby and by now typical manner of the maneuver was as dismaying as its import. Charles Finley, of Kansas City, and Arthur Allyn, president of the Chicago White Sox, were both informed of the deal in telephone calls from the American League president, Joe Cronin, who in one breath told them that league rules required them to vote on the transaction and in the next that their votes were meaningless, since he already had the three-quarters majority necessary for it to pass. This call came only two days after the annual major-league executive meetings in Chicago, during which the deal was never mentioned to Finley, Allyn, or the public. Finley's and Allyn's subsequent shouts of rage and the astonished editorial protests of the press were so piercing that Cronin convened a league meeting in Boston to consider the possible antitrust violations implicit in the sale. The meeting turned into a whitewash, in which various proposals for reconsideration were ruled out of order or brushed aside and a tentative change of heart by the Baltimore owners (which could have killed the sale) was ruthlessly muscled down. A few facts about the inner councils of baseball may explain how this was possible. Dan Topping and Del Webb, the former owners and continuing managing executives of the Yankees, are as powerful in their league as Walter O'Malley is in his. Topping and O'Malley are both members of the majors' Executive Council, along with the two league presidents and Commissioner Frick. American League President Cronin is a brother-in-law of Calvin R. Griffith, the president of the Minnesota Twins. The Cleveland Indians are anxious to move their franchise, and would need the approval of the Yankees and other clubs in order to make the shift. Lee MacPhail, the president of the Baltimore Orioles, is the brother of Bill MacPhail, director of sports for CBS. Several American League executives own blocks of CBS stock; the owners of the Los Angeles Angels, who also needed league approval for *their* franchise move, operate CBS affiliates in California, and John Fetzer, president of the Detroit Tigers, operates CBS-affiliated stations in the Middle West.

Television now exerts the most intense pressure on all aspects of baseball. Since the war, its total exposure of major-league games has destroyed most of the minor leagues. The widely varying amounts of TV revenue enjoyed by the big-league clubs have made the rich teams richer and do much to explain why so many poorer clubs want to shift franchises. The potentialities of pay television, first attempted in California this year, are as yet unknown, but this new device may vastly increase the revenue of baseball, while causing further financial disruption in less-populated baseball territories. The Yankees, of course, already derive considerable money from their own telecasts and broadcasts— $1,200,000 from local stations, plus an additional $600,000 from CBS itself for their part in the nationwide *Game of the Week* telecasts. To drop CBS into the middle of this rich, untidy gumbo as the *owner* of baseball's No. 1 attraction may look like an engraved invitation for Congressional antitrust investigations, but it is an entirely appropriate symbol of television's enormous interest in the game.

The sports television business has never been happy with baseball, which so far includes only two big-revenue packages—the All Star Games and Series—each year.* Moreover, the old pastime does not produce tidy two-hour segments of marketable time; a nationally televised Saturday game may creep along into the early evening, and it cannot be puffed by much advance billing, since the meaning of its outcome may not be known until

---

* Now three, with the addition of the inflationary autumn playoffs, the so-called Championship Series, which constitute television's first contribution to the game.

late September. This is almost intolerable to the young men in blazers who run sports TV; their dream is fifty weekends of world championships—in football, in baseball, in surfing, in Senior Women's Marbles—that are *not to be missed* by the weekend watcher. Yet these sportsmen cannot be dismissed so easily, for they command an audience of millions and revenues that are almost immeasurable. It must be assumed that baseball executives will do almost anything to climb aboard this gaudy bandwagon, and that the ultimate shape of baseball in the next ten years or so—its size, its franchise locations, and even its rules—will be largely determined not by tradition or regard for the fans or regard for the delicate balances of the game, but by the demands of the little box.

These objections, I am certain, will cut no ice with most baseball magnates, whose instant response to criticism of this nature is to smile and say, "Well, I'm in this for the money, of course." Of course. Baseball is a commercial venture, but it is one of such perfect equipoise that millions of us every year can still unembarrassedly surrender ourselves to its unique and absorbing joys. The ability to find beauty and involvement in artificial commercial constructions is essential to most of us in the modern world; it is the life-giving naïveté. But naïveté is not gullibility, and those who persistently alter baseball for their quick and selfish purposes will find, I believe, that they are the owners of teams without a following and of a sport devoid of passion.

It is a breath of fresh air to emerge from those noisome back rooms and to report, if far too briefly, on the World Series just past. That Series and the two or three weeks of the season that preceded it constituted the happiest kind of surprise, for they demonstrated the vitality, unpredictability, and accomplishments of the game itself. This was the year in which a few dozen baseball players barely retrieved their sport from the indoor thinkers. As everyone but the most obdurate recluse must know by now, the Yankees, after stumbling futilely for most of the season, came

on to win thirty out of their last forty games, making up a six-
and-a-half-game deficit and climbing past the White Sox and the
Orioles to win the American League pennant on the next-to-the-
last day of the season. (This race, breathtaking as it was, would
have been even more dramatic if the league had not drawn up a
ridiculous schedule that left no games whatever between the Yankees and the two other contenders after the middle of August.)
Meanwhile, in the other league, the Phillies, a young, underprivi-
leged team of have-nots, had painstakingly compiled a six-and-a-
half-game lead of their own that looked absolutely unassailable
with two weeks of the season remaining. They then fell apart like
a dropped tray of dishes, losing ten straight, and first the Cincinnati Reds and then the St. Louis Cardinals drew even, with the
Giants hanging on by their fingernails just behind. On the last
Saturday of the season, the first four-way tie in the history of
baseball was entirely possible. That afternoon, though, the Giants
lost and dropped out of it, leaving the Phillies-Reds and Cardi-
nals-Mets games to settle matters on the last day. The Phils, loose
and angry now, took the Reds apart, 10–0, leaving it all for
the Cards, who had only to beat the most popular losers in history. For a few innings, a magnificent comic-opera ending
seemed possible, for the Mets, who had won the two previous
games from the Cards by scores of 1–0 and 15–5, were leading, 3–2, as late as the fifth inning, thus sustaining baseball's tradition of autumn embarrassments inflicted by last-place clubs
upon their betters. Class finally told, however, when three three-
run outbursts won the game, 11–5, and brought the Cards their
first pennant since 1946. The deep "Whew!" emitted by the na-
tion's fans sounded familiar; since 1946 the National League has
staged four pennant races that ended in a dead tie, four that were
determined on the final day, and six more that were settled only
in the final week of the season.

   That last afternoon, I discovered that I was being torn in three.
Part of me wanted the Phillies to win, because of their long,
teeth-gritting stand against superior forces. Part of me was pull-

ing for the Reds, if only because their admirable manager, Freddie Hutchinson, is suffering from lung cancer and deserved the present of another pennant. In the end, however, I was delighted about the Cardinals, because St. Louis is perhaps the most dedicated baseball town in the country, and eighteen years is too long for such worthy fans to wait for their reward. I must confess, too, to another, less noble feeling of joy: the Cardinals' pennant —and now their championship—is solid puck in the eye for contemporary baseball ownership and management. Over the years, the Cardinal organization has been a model of modest, intelligent planning and direction. Before the league expansion, theirs was the westernmost and southernmost franchise, and they drew swarms of players and fans from the vast stretches of baseball's heartland. Even in lean summers, their home attendance rarely fell below the million mark, although their park seats only thirty-odd thousand. Three or four years ago, Vaughn P. (Bing) Devine, the club's vice-president and general manager, began the moves that resulted in this year's flag. He installed Johnny Keane, a veteran member of the Cardinal chain, as manager; he put in Eddie Stanky as director of player development; and he negotiated a number of trades of such astuteness that he was named 1963's Major League Executive of the Year. Meanwhile, however, August A. Busch, Jr., the St. Louis brewer who purchased the Cards in 1953, was growing impatient. Two years ago, irritated by the club's sixth-place finish, Busch hired Branch Rickey, the octogenarian Grand Panjandrum of baseball, as "special consultant" to the club—a famously disruptive title in any business organization. Rickey arrived, heavily retinued, and began rumbling forebodings. He opposed Devine's pending Gotay-for-Groat trade with Pittsburgh—a deal, ultimately clinched, that nailed the Cardinals' infield together once and for all. The Mahatma was unappeased. As one Cardinal later said, "He sat in that damned box watching us and never smiled once. He didn't even smile when we won."

Last August, some weeks after Devine traded off an eighteen-game-winning pitcher, Ernie Broglio, for a .251-hitting Cub out-fielder, Lou Brock, he was summarily fired by Busch and Rickey, neither of whom noticed that the trade had transformed the Cardinals into the hottest team in the league. Eddie Stanky then resigned, and both Devine and Stanky were instantly hired by the New York Mets, who are unaccustomed to such strokes of fortune. It was also leaked to the press that Manager Keane, who had been a member of the Cardinal organization for thirty-five years, would be dropped at the end of the season and replaced by Leo Durocher. Thanks to his team's rush toward the pennant, Mr. Keane, a reflective, gentle-voiced Texan, received a public handclasp from Branch Rickey just before the end of the season, and the offer of a new one-year contract from August Busch. Keane looked Busch straight in the eye and said he'd think about it after the season was over—an act of character that may have taught Mr. Busch more about baseball than all of Branch Rickey's counselings.*

On the first two days of the Series, Busch Stadium—a seamed, rusty, steep-sided box that will be replaced within two years by a new ballpark on St. Louis's riverfront—reminded me of an old down-on-her-luck dowager who has been given a sur-prise party by the local settlement house; she was startled by the occasion but still able to accept it as no less than her due. The Cardinal fans around me were plainly and noisily delighted, but I detected none of the unbelieving hysteria with which San Fran-cisco greeted its first pennant, in 1962. These were veteran city and country loyalists. The parked cars around the stadium bore license plates from Iowa, Kentucky, Oklahoma, and Louisiana, and their occupants, approaching the gates, had to wade through a moat of trash, broken glass, and old beer cans left by the urban-ites who had camped outside the park for two cold nights while waiting for the bleachers to open. Inside, I noticed many specta-tors (and two young ushers) keeping score in their programs.

* Not, it turned out, an act of *pure* character; forehandedly, Johnny Keane had made other plans for the coming season.

Clearly, that new pennant would be at home here.

The Cardinals, it will be recalled, won the first game, 9–5, putting away Whitey Ford in the sixth inning and taking advantage of a startling number of Yankee errors and oversights. The Cards happily jumped on the Yanks' relief pitching, scoring seven runs in the last three innings—a procedure that the visitors reversed the next afternoon, when their seven hits and six runs in the last three innings broke up what had been a pitchers' game and brought them an 8–3 victory. What struck me during those two windy, cool, exuberant afternoons was not just the similarity of the games but the almost mirrorlike resemblance between the teams themselves. I cannot remember two Series opponents that were more closely matched in strength, weaknesses, and combative optimism.

To begin with, of course, there were the Boyer brothers, Ken and Clete, at third base. Then, both clubs had to play a substitute infielder—Phil Linz for the Yankees' Tony Kubek, and Dal Maxvill for the Cards' Julian Javier—through the entire Series. While the Cards' infield was far more threatening at the plate than that of the Yankees (361 runs batted in during the season, as against 263), the balance was redressed by the Yankee outfield power (289 RBIs, as against 200). The Yankees counted on the home run; the Cards were faster on the bases. Both clubs, it turned out, had no consistent relief pitching; by the end of the Series, the arrival of a fireman on the mound caused enemy partisans to grin with expectant relish. And, most remarkable of all, each team had won its pennant because of the performance of a pitcher straight out of the legends of baseball. Barney Schultz, a heavy-bodied thirty-eight-year-old veteran who had spent twenty years in the bushy environs of Terre Haute, Wilmington, Macon, Hagerstown, and Schenectady, joined the Cardinals at the beginning of August and then saved eleven games for the team with his knuckleball. At approximately the same time, Mel Stottlemyre, a cool, skinny-necked rookie pitcher with remarkable control, was called up from Richmond; he won nine key games for the Yankees in their stretch drive. Both of them, being creations of Ring Lardner, were a trifle unreal.

As it turned out, Schultz's only happy moments in the Series came in the first game, when he held the Yanks to four hits and a single run and saved the win for Ray Sadecki. Stottlemyre was the Yanks' starter in the second game, and he gave Bob Gibson, the Cardinals' ace, a rare lesson in pitching. Gibson started out like a Redstone missile, striking out eight men in four innings, and then ran out of fuel and was aborted. Stottlemyre, content merely to get men out on grounders, kept the ball low and concentrated on the tough hitters; he gave up exactly one hit to the top five men in the Cards' order and easily pitched his way out of three or four nasty jams while waiting for his team to put him ahead for good. He will be at home in New York for years—perhaps decades—to come.

The third game, at Yankee Stadium, was the only classic. For eight innings, Curt Simmons and Jim Bouton pitched marvelously—Simmons, the veteran, with a selection of soft, in-and-out sliders, curves, and other junk, and Bouton with a rearing fast ball delivered with such energy that his cap flew off on every second or third pitch. Yankee errors kept Bouton in trouble and cost him a run, but it was still 1–1 at the top of the eighth, when Simmons departed for a pinch-hitter. Barney Schultz walked in from the bullpen in the ninth and threw one pitch, which Mickey Mantle hit into the top right-field deck, instantaneously reconverting to Yankeedom several thousand of the 67,101 spectators, who had been rooting almost equally for the two teams.

What pleased me most at the three Stadium games was the fact that the fans in attendance, whatever their loyalties, *were* fans. During that lovely three-day holiday weekend, there were, for some reason, conspicuously fewer of the overdressed, uncomprehending autumn *arrivistes* who usually make up the World Series audience in New York; in their place were hundreds of children —boys with their fathers, teenagers in windbreakers—who screamed over every pitch, every foul. On Sunday, one of these, a youngster named Adam, made so much noise right behind me that his father tried to restrain him in the second inning. "Take it easy, Adam," he said. "You'll never make it through the game."

"I can't help it," Adam said proudly. "I'm tense. Listen to me —I'm hoarse *already*."

All his shouts couldn't help the Yankees, who started off in the first inning with five straight hits and three runs and then were able to manage only one more hit for the rest of the afternoon. They pitched Al Downing in place of Whitey Ford, whose sore arm had finished him for the Series. The Cards won it in the sixth, on Ken Boyer's grand slam, which had been set up by Bobby Richardson's error. Roger Craig pitched admirably in relief and got the 4-3 win, thereby easing some of the years of torment he had experienced as a blood sacrifice for the Mets.

Adam was absent the next afternoon—gargling at home, no doubt—which was just as well; I don't think he could have stood it. Gibson and Stottlemyre had at each other again, and this time Gibson remembered not to throw *all* strikes. Stottlemyre looked as icily effective as ever, but another error by Richardson led to two Cardinal runs in the fifth, and Stottlemyre was removed for a pinch-hitter in the seventh. In the ninth, a couple of outs away from a shutout, Gibson was nailed on the hip by Pepitone's line drive; the ball caromed toward third, but Gibson, a former member of the Harlem Globetrotters, leaped after it and made a looping, fallaway jump-shot to first base to nip Pepitone. It saved the game, because Tom Tresh then hit a two-run homer that tied it up. In the tenth, Tim McCarver hit a three-run homer after some further butterfingered work by the Yankee infield, and Gibson, who had struck out thirteen batters, had the victory he deserved.

The final two games, at Busch Stadium (which I watched on television), scarcely stand rational examination, for the starting pitchers for both clubs were so weary and the relief pitchers so ineffectual that the games were determined by sheer stamina. Simmons tired before Bouton on Wednesday, and Pepitone's bases-loaded homer scored the runs that reliever Schultz had put on base, the Yankees thereby tying the Series for the last time; the score was 8–3. On the final afternoon, Yogi Berra waited too long to remove the exhausted Stottlemyre, who was finally allowed to sit down after the fourth, when he trailed 3–0. Yogi's unwillingness to act became understandable at once, for Al Downing, the next Yankee pitcher, was bombed for a homer, a single, and a double on his first four pitches. Manager Keane, who has learned the virtues of patience this year, was thus able to stand with his own panting marathoner, Gibson, even after Mantle hit a three-run homer in the sixth. By the ninth, Gibson was ahead 7–3, but he was so tired that he could only heave his pitches right down the middle. Clete Boyer and Phil Linz each hit one of these into the left-field stands, but they were the last, dying salutes of this season. Bobby Richardson popped up to end it all, and five or ten thousand Cardinal fans tried to throw themselves into the home-team dugout in their ecstasy. I was sorry for the Yankees, pleased for St. Louis, happy for Johnny Keane, and delighted it was over. Another couple of innings of such attrition and somebody would have tried pitching underhand.

The day after the Series ended, Johnny Keane announced his resignation as manager of the Cards, and Yogi Berra was summarily dismissed as manager of the Yankees.* Berra, the last of the old Yankee demigods, was cast aside at the end of his first year at the helm for failing, after a hundred and sixty-nine games, by exactly three runs. The supporters of two baseball capitals have been deprived of their much-admired field leaders, and the pleasures of the World Series are already dimmed. The image-smashers are busy again.

* Keane, of course, was subsequently hired by the Yankees to succeed Berra, and disimproved on Yogi's managerial record. The Bronxian Dark Ages had begun.

West of the Bronx

The possibility must be entertained that the American baseball fan has grown insatiable. Consider his swollen expectations, his insane autumn *hubris*. Late in September, he confidently expects to find at least one of the two major leagues concluding its immense hundred-and-sixty-two-game season with two or three teams locked in exhausted contention for the pennant right up to the final weekend of play. This year, the National League obliged him again, when the Dodgers clinched on the final Saturday—a slip, nonetheless, from last year, when there were *four* National League clubs still in the fight on the penultimate day, and the Cardinals won the flag only on the last afternoon. Unappeased by the persistent recurrence of this statistical miracle (there have been thirteen final-weekend finishes in the majors since 1946), the fan then confidently looks forward to a long, bitterly fought World Series that will somehow produce the most brilliant baseball of the entire season. These expectations, too, are frequently rewarded. Seven of the past ten World Series have gone to the full seven games, and at least five of the past ten turned into classic baseball dramas that will be discussed and remembered decades from now. The World Series of 1965, in which the Dodgers defeated the Minnesota Twins in seven games, was no classic; it was, however, an entertainment of more than sufficient interest, and only the most thrill-surfeited fan could ignore its distinctive omens, curiosities, and pleasures.

To begin with, this was the first Series played between runaway orphans—the former Brooklyn Dodgers, who went west in 1958, vs. the former Washington Senators, who became the Twins in 1961. Both of them play before home crowds of less than ten years' loyalty. It should not be forgotten, however, that half the present twenty major-league clubs were born or have pulled up stakes since 1953, and that two of the rovers are changing homes again this year, which means that the Dodgers and the Twins are now among the more typical big-league teams, and that holdfast veterans like the Red Sox, the Cubs, the Pirates, and the Yankees are slipping into the minority. Attendance figures at all parks are memorized and whispered over with an almost rabbinical intensity by contemporary baseball executives, and the complex bond of loyalty, home-town pride, and critical favor that binds, or fails to bind, the man in the stands to the man at the plate has become the game's leading mystery. Two ghosts haunted the 1965 Series—the Yankees and the Braves. The Braves became the first modern team to move its franchise, when they left Boston for Milwaukee in 1953. In the ensuing five years, they won two pennants, set a major-league single-season gate record, and regularly enjoyed attendance in excess of two million per year. This same Milwaukee team is now defunct; it has just moved to Atlanta, leaving behind a mixed residue of indifference, bitterness, and lawsuits. At the Series this fall, at least a dozen Eastern fans, sportswriters, and baseball men separately described to me an identical experience—a sudden doubt, a momentary shivery silence, that they had felt when their plane paused in Milwaukee before carrying them on to Minneapolis and the noisy, unquenchable joys of another Series. I, too, had been chilled by that same cold breath at the Milwaukee airport: Perhaps baseball was not, after all, immortal.

The ghost of the Yankees was even more perceptible at the opening games of the Series; you could almost hear the distant rattle of IRT trains above center field. The Yankees are not dead,

of course—only their era is dead. The team collapsed and fell
to the second division this year, and there is only the smallest reason to believe that it can substantially improve its performance in
the seasons immediately ahead. This was only the third time in
the past seventeen years that the Yankees had failed to appear in
the Series, and the monstrous crash of this Ozymandian figure is
still shaking the ground. For a generation, the team was the premier attraction of its league, drawing more fans on the road than
at home and sustaining a good many clubs at the box office even
while in the act of destroying them on the field. The dilapidation
of the Yankees over the past four years can be seen not only in
declining attendance at the Stadium (it has fallen off by 280,000
in that period) but also in the entire league's loss of fans. American League attendance was down to 8,860,175 in 1965, a drop of
over a million in four years; the National League gained more
than two million spectators in the same span, and this year's attendance of 13,576,521 set an all-time record. The disparity can
be seen in other, even more painful comparisons. Those late-Sep-
tember dogfights in the National League recur, of course, because
there are generally four or five powerful teams in contention; six
different teams have won the NL pennant in the past eight years.
The National League has won five of the last seven World Series,
eight of the last dozen All-Star Games. This could be carried further, into an evaluation of the two leagues' individual players, but
the point is already clear. The incomparable Yankees are gone,
and their departure has at last permitted us to see the pitifully un-
dermuscled condition of the other members of their family,
whom they bullied over a period of decades into a condition of
hostile but abject dependency. The 1965 World Series, even if it
lacked the sense of moral drama that made the old autumn Yankee wars so exciting, at least began the essential and hopeful process of rebalancing the leagues.

The above, I must admit, is a most ungenerous way of intro-
ducing the Minnesota Twins, but politeness cannot cover the

curious fact that this team, which won the American League
pennant by seven games, went through its season without having
to survive a single game or set of games that might truly be
termed crucial. To put it plainly, no challengers appeared. The
Twins had the best batting in the league and the third-best pitching, but neither was overpowering. This was almost exactly the
same team that finished in a tie for sixth place in 1964, when it
led both leagues in home runs, with two hundred and twenty-
one; this year its homer output dropped to a hundred and fifty.
The Twins won largely because their manager, Sam Mele, hired
a new set of coaches last spring and taught his team a new kind
of ball. They eschewed the bomb and studied the hit-and-run,
the stolen base, the stretched single. Pitching coach Johnny Sain
put Jim Grant and Jim Kaat through a summer-long seminar on
spin ballistics, and they won twenty-one and eighteen games, respectively. Third-base coach Billy Martin persuaded the shortstop, a moody Cuban named Zoilo Versalles, that aggressiveness at
the plate, quickness on the bases, and a capacity for instantly getting rid of ground balls can make a star out of a small infielder.
Finally, no coaches at all were allowed near young Tony Oliva
when he approached the plate, and he wound up with his second
batting championship in as many years in the majors. Oliva, an
outfielder who bats left, has leopardlike reflexes and great speed
in the field, and he may become the best American League hitter
since Ted Williams.

The presence of the Dodgers in this year's Series was only
faintly more explicable, since they too had finished sixth in 1964,
and they won this year with a team batting average of .245 —
the lowest of any championship team since baseball's dark ages.
In May, the Dodgers lost *their* two-time batting champion,
Tommy Davis, who broke an ankle and was finished for the season. Unlike the Twins, they had to battle every day to survive in
their junglelike league, and they saw their carefully hoarded little
lead wiped out in September by a fourteen-game winning streak
of the Giants'. The Dodgers had great pitching and great cool,

however, and they responded with a thirteen-game streak of their own, which put them back on top. They clinched their pennant that last Saturday of the season with an almost typical performance—a 3–1 win by Sandy Koufax over the Braves in which the Dodgers collected only two hits. They won this year not just because of Koufax and Drysdale and Maury Wills but because of a combination of speed, pride, and managerial intelligence that enabled them actually to overturn the entire structure of modern offensive baseball, which had been built around the home run. The Dodgers hit only seventy-eight homers all year, but they stole a hundred and seventy-one bases, thereby inventing a brand-new sport—"tap-ball," perhaps, or "hot wheels"—which was more exciting and certainly more successful than the old game played by the rest of the league this summer.

No doubt there were some residents of Minneapolis and St. Paul in early October who were untouched by the impending clash of these oddly matched, oddly similar rivals, but I met none. On the eve of the opening game, the infection seemed absolute—perhaps not the loudest case of baseball fever I have observed but one of the happiest. Bunting and triple-life-size portraits of the Twins filled the windows of banks and department stores along Nicollet Avenue in Minneapolis, and homing automobiles bore exhortatory bumper stickers reading "Sam Mele for President" and "Twins A-Go-Go-Go!" At dusk, I saw cars with Iowa, South Dakota, Montana, and Manitoba license plates debouching fans at hotels and restaurants—country loyalists wearing platter-size Twins buttons, and straw boaters emblazoned with Twins heraldry. The local papers had made a brave try for balance, but they could not control their advertisers ("Homer after homer, Harmon Killebrew enjoys the Major League Benefit Plan underwritten by Equitable"), or even their headline writers ("Series Lures Recluse from Kentucky Cabin"). That evening, badge-wearing delegates to a recreation-industries convention wandered about in the lobby of the Leamington Hotel, nudging each other whenever they recognized a face— Red Schoendienst, Bobby Bragan, Eddie Lopat, Bill Veeck— among the cheerful, noisy knots of baseball people. Down at the Pick-Nicollet Hotel, a handful of students from the University of Minnesota danced in the Pic-Nic Locker Room, an impromptu cabaret that had been set up that afternoon right in the lobby and decorated in a hopeful attempt to resemble the Twins' clubhouse. The Fruggers were studied glumly by a cluster of tall teen-age boys in green blazers—members of the Charlotte Hornets' Nest Post No. 9 baseball team, from Charlotte, North Carolina, which had won the national American Legion baseball title in early September and thereby, a free trip to the Series. Late that night, I watched a taped TV show over WCCO–Channel 4 in which an announcer interviewed an almost interminable number of employees at the Twins' ballpark. "Tell me," he said to the grounds-keeper. "Are you responsible for putting down these nice straight lines?"

By midmorning the next day—a cool, burnished fall day— Minnesota had given up almost all pretense of civic equilibrium. In the State Supreme Court, in St. Paul, an attorney cut short his argument with "There are more important matters before us today!" He received grateful applause from both sides, court adjourned, and various jurists departed for their grandmothers' funerals. On Summit Avenue, also in St. Paul, a meeting of a ladies' study group was ruined when five members put down their copies of *Troilus and Cressida* and tiptoed out, off to meet their husbands at the ballpark. At about the same time, three suspected members of the Kansas City Cosa Nostra under surveillance by the Minneapolis Morals and Narcotics Squad aroused the darkest suspicions among their tailing detectives by *not* heading for the game. And on Minnehaha Drive the cabdriver who was taking me out to the game turned in his seat and said, "You know, five years ago we had nothing here but the Lakers, and they were bush. Now we got the Vikings, we got the Twins, we got the pennant, and Hubert is Vice-President!"

Hubert Humphrey—a Twins fan, of course—was there to throw out the first ball at Metropolitan Stadium, an airy cyclotron standing amid cornfields in Bloomington, precisely equidistant from Minneapolis and St. Paul. The most notable absentee that afternoon was Sandy Koufax, who was observing Yom Kippur. (Women's-page feature writers invariably refer to Koufax as "the world's most eligible Jewish bachelor.") The fans around me behind first base celebrated this bit of calendarial good fortune with hopeful yawps and bayings, even though Koufax's stand-in was Drysdale, a twenty-three-game winner and the world's most formidable No. 2 pitcher. Their cries died abruptly when Ron Fairly led off the Dodger second with a homer into the right-field bleachers (at least two spectators within my hearing muttered, "The Dodgers aren't *supposed* to hit homers!"), but the Twins' first baseman, Don Mincher, balanced matters with an almost identical poke a few minutes later. Then, in the bottom of the third, Swedish-American credulity and tonsils were imperiled by a swift succession of astonishments. Frank Quilici, the Twins' rookie second baseman, doubled just inside the left-field foul line. Pitcher Jim Grant bunted, Drysdale fell while fielding the ball, and both runners were safe. Versalles hit a three-run homer into the lower left-field deck. Two outs and two hits later, Drysdale walked Mincher, loading the bases, and Earl Battey, the Twins' catcher, popped a little Texas leaguer to right for his second hit of the inning, and Drysdale departed. When the side was out at last, the scoreboard operator had to try three times before he managed to put up the correct, incredible number of runs for the half-inning: six. That, of course, was the ball game, though the crowd sat tight through the rest of the affair, smiling in the afternoon sunshine. Versalles drove in another run and stole a base in the seventh, and Jim Grant, working quickly and perhaps a bit carelessly, permitted the visitors nine more scattered hits and one more run. The smiles remained as everyone trooped out to the parking lots. It was like a family wedding.

The following afternoon, a considerable number of those Twin-boosting straw boaters showed bitten-off brims—evidence of late celebrations of the famous victory. But it was a drizzly, sobering sort of day. Two roaring helicopters hovered just above the outfield grass, trying to dry out the surface, and when the game finally did start, amid light showers, there was Koufax. There, too, was the Twins' own ace left-hander, Jim Kaat, and for five full innings there was no way to choose between them—three hits for the Twins, two for the Dodgers, no runs at all. Tension and damp feet kept the crowd quiet until the Dodger fifth, when Bob Allison, in left field for the Twins, saved at least one run with a mad sprint to the foul line and a diving, cross-handed grab of Lefebvre's long drive. He slid a good fifteen feet into foul territory, and when he came up still holding the ball, I was suddenly persuaded that this, too, would be the Twins' day—a conviction that seemed to strike everyone else, even Koufax, at the same time. Versalles, leading off the sixth, slashed a grounder off third baseman Gilliam's glove for a two-base error. Nossek neatly sacrificed him to third, and Tony Oliva brought him home with a shot to left that he somehow stretched into a double. Killebrew scored Oliva with a single. Koufax steadied and pitched out of it, having actually given up only one earned run, but it was too late; he vanished, necessarily but uselessly, for a pinch-hitter in the seventh, when the Dodgers scored once on three singles. Versalles, who was now clearly running for governor, bashed a triple off Ron Perranoski in the same inning, and then scored, all unaided, when he feinted down the line so convincingly that Perranoski bounced a pitch past his catcher. The Twins, having devoured Drysdale and Koufax on successive afternoons, now disposed of Perranoski, the Dodgers' brilliant relief man; Kaat delivered the final two runs with a bases-loaded single in the eighth. The fans around me were laughing and hooting by now, and one next to me kept repeating, "It's all over now! It's all over now!" I hope he meant the game, and not the entire Series. After I had visited the clubhouse and heard Sandy

Koufax's precise, unapologetic, and totally unruffled analysis of the game, I came away with the curious impression that the Twins, after two straight victories, were only slightly behind in the World Series.

Rival baseball executives sometimes talk about Walter O'Malley, the owner of the Dodgers, with less than total admiration, but always with undisguised envy. For one thing, his Dodger Stadium, at Chavez Ravine, is the finest plant in baseball —a model of efficiency and attractiveness which is brightening the design of new ballparks across the country. For another, he has found in Los Angeles the perfect baseball audience. Dodger fans are numerous (attendance has averaged over two and a half million in the new park, by far the best in the majors), steadfast, and suffused with love. They need the Dodgers fully as much as the Dodgers need them, for the team seems to serve as a civic center or model home—a hearth to pull up to in a land of dusty patios. Caring about the Dodgers in Los Angeles is a form of mother love, and there were times during the three Series games in the Taj O'Malley when I had the feeling that I had wandered into a radio breakfast show for moms. It wasn't just the mass sing-alongs, encouraged by the electric signboard in left field—"Happy Birthday to You!" warbled, *cum* Wurlitzer, to a Dodger bat boy or a pitcher's father—but my growing conviction that the men and women around me, in their green stretch pants and russet golf cardigans, had, in some mild, innocent fashion, lost their marbles. They accepted the Dodgers' three one-sided and fundamentally unexciting victories at home as a source of continuous and uncritical self-congratulation, maintaining a nonstop high-decibel babble of joy ("Marvelous! Oh, marvie, marvie, marvie!" one woman cried after each Dodger base hit) during a span of twenty-seven innings in which the Dodgers outscored the Twins 18–2. It was a phenomenon; love of team had utterly eclipsed love of sport.

In the first Los Angeles game, Claude Osteen gave the National

Leaguers the best pitching they had yet enjoyed in the Series, allowing five lonely hits and keeping the ball so consistently low that the Twins managed only three flies to the outfield all afternoon. The Dodgers displayed some nifty base-stealing and sacrifices, but almost to no purpose, since they were hitting Camilo Pascual so energetically. Every home-team starter came up with at least one hit (there were ten hits in all), and the final score was 4–0. This outcome only nourished in me the belief that the next game, the fourth, would be the key to the Series; with a three-one lead, the Twins would be almost impossible to beat, but a two-two tie would require the Twins to beat Koufax once again—perhaps twice again. Both the Dodgers and the Twins played that fourth game as if they too had come to this conclusion—and the Twins, for all practical purposes, utterly blew the Series in six innings.

Wills, the very first Dodger batter, was knocked sprawling when various Twin infielders converging on first base failed to handle his infield bouncer. He got up and stole second, proceeded to third when Jim Grant forgot to cover first on a grounder by Willie Davis, and scored when Versalles messed up a double play. In the next inning, a second run scored on a bunt by the Dodgers' Wes Parker, another steal of second, another gift of third (on a wild pitch), and an infield error by Quilici. The Dodgers were playing their favorite kind of baseball on their favorite grounds (the infield grass there resembles shrunken worsted, and a chopped grounder sometimes bounces thirty feet in the air, like a golf ball landing on a highway), and the Twins grew badly rattled. They almost stayed in the game until the sixth, but then two high, useless throws by Minnesota outfielders allowed a Dodger runner an extra base, and the last vestiges of the Twins' poise vanished. Their subsequent butcheries are best forgotten; the game wound up 7–2, Los Angeles, and the Series was even.

It was unevened after the first two Dodgers had batted the next afternoon, when Wills doubled and steamed home on Gilliam's single. There were twelve more Dodger hits and six more runs, but that first score, as it turned out, would have been enough, for Koufax was back on the mound, and this time the W.M.E.J.B. was performing very close to his peak. By the end of seven innings, he had faced only one more than the absolute minimum number of batters, and he wound up with a four-hit shutout and ten strikeouts. It was the twenty-second time this year that he had struck out ten or more batters in a single game. There were other things to admire that afternoon (Willie Davis's three stolen bases, for instance, and the Twins' not falling apart again), but I concentrated on watching Koufax at work. This is not as easy as it sounds, for there is the temptation simply to discredit what one sees. His fast ball, for example, flares upward at the last instant, so that batters swinging at it often look as if they had lashed out at a bad high pitch. Koufax's best curve, by contrast, shoots down, often barely pinching a corner of the plate, inside or out, just above the knees. A typical Koufax victim—even if he is an excellent hitter—having looked bad by swinging on the first pitch and worse in letting the second go by, will often simply stand there, his bat nailed to his shoulder, for the next two or three pitches, until the umpire's right hand goes up and he is out. Or if he swings again it is with an awkward last-minute dip of the bat that is a caricature of his normal riffle. It is almost painful to watch, for Koufax, instead of merely overpowering hitters, as some fast-ball throwers do, appears to dismantle them, taking away first one and then another of their carefully developed offensive weapons and judgments, and leaving them only with the conviction that they are the victims of a total mismatch. Maybe they are right, at that; the records of this, Koufax's greatest year, suggest as much. In the regular season, he won twenty-six games, struck out three hundred and eighty-two batters (an all-time record), and pitched his fourth no-hit game—a perfect game, by the way—in as many years, which is also a new record. In the Series, he won two shutouts pitched within three days of each other, and gave up exactly one earned run in twenty-four innings. He was the difference between the two clubs; he won the Series.

I watched the last two games at home, on television, because I did not want to see or share the pain that I felt certain was waiting for the Minnesota fans. Besides, it had become clear that this was not to be a Series that would go echoing down the corridors of time. A curious, dissatisfying pattern to the games had emerged, for neither team had displayed the smallest ability to come from behind. In the first five games (in all seven games, it developed), the winning pitcher lasted the full nine innings, and no resolute power hitter stepped up to the plate to challenge him—to reverse matters with an explosion at a crucial moment. That pin-striped ghost remained; what I wanted—what we all wanted—was a moment of Yankee baseball. Still, my decision to stay away from Metropolitan Stadium was probably a mistake, because I missed some innings of rare tension and some sudden rewards for two or three ballplayers who deserved them wonderfully. There was, for instance, Jim Grant's slick, courageous 5–1 victory in the sixth game, in which he outpitched Claude Osteen, kept those Dodger sprinters off the bases, drove in three runs with his own sixth-inning homer, and generally restored the Twins to joy and self-esteem. Mudcat Grant himself is a singularly joyful and estimable young man, who has emerged this year as a pitcher of the first magnitude. He is a tall, self-possessed star who is also pursuing a second, cold-weather career as a singer and entertainer; he will make a nightclub tour this winter with a turn called "Mudcat and the Three Kittens." Even without those two big wins for the Twins, he would be notable for the most startling ballplayer's quotation to come out of this year's Series: "I was a member of the NAACP before it became Camp."

There were two more homers to remember with gratitude. Bob Allison's, in the sixth game, must have been at least a momentary salve for the unimaginable tortures he had suffered at the plate this year in his endless batting slump. And then, on the final afternoon, there was Lou Johnson's homer—a looping, dying blow to left that actually caromed off the foul pole. It came in the fourth inning, with no score and the bases empty, but it demolished Jim Kaat and the Twins, for Koufax had already struck out six batters and again appeared untouchable. Ron Fairly doubled on the next pitch, and Parker singled him home, but Johnson had really done the job. Lou Johnson is a somewhat shopworn Negro outfielder (he even looks a little tattered, because of an automobile accident years ago that cost him the top of his right ear) who has spent most of the past twelve years in the minors; he took over left field when Tommy Davis was injured, and hung on with the Dodgers as a regular by playing the best ball of his career. The sound, the weight, the feel and flight of that home run will stay with Johnson, I would bet, for at least twelve years to come.

Koufax's three-hit, ten-strikeout shutout in the final game was in many ways his finest feat, for he pulled it off without his curve ball. Discovering somewhere in the first or second inning that his curve was unreliable, perhaps because he was at last exhausted, he simply did without it; he threw the fast ball and challenged the Twin batters to touch him. Again he was too much. In the ninth, Killebrew reached first on a single, with one out, and the home-side zealots aroused themselves for some final, crepuscular yelling. Earl Battey struck out on three pitches. Bob Allison fouled one, took two balls, swung and missed, swung and missed, and winter descended on the northlands. As the Minnesotans filed out of Metropolitan Stadium in awful silence, I suddenly thought of the optimistic cabdriver who had driven me to the ballpark on the first day of the Series. I hope by now he has added another line to his little speech: "Anyway, we were beaten by the best— maybe the best pitcher in the whole history of baseball!"

PART 4

The Future, Maybe

The Cool Bubble

With two out in the top of the first inning on the afternoon of May 23, 1965, Jimmy Wynn, the center fielder of the Houston Astros, moved under a fly ball just struck by Jim Ray Hart, of the visiting San Francisco Giants. Looking upward, Wynn pounded his glove confidently, then anxiously, and then froze in horror. The ball had vanished into a pure Monet cloud of overhead beams, newly painted off-white skylights, and diffused Texas sunlight, and now it suddenly rematerialized a good distance behind Wynn and plumped to earth like a thrombosed pigeon. Three runs scored, the Giants eventually won, 5–2, and the next day a squad of workmen ascended the skies and, with paint guns, made the final severance between Houston baseball and the outdoors. Up to the moment of Hart's fly, it might have been assumed that the summer sport played last year in Houston's gigantic new air-conditioned Astrodome, which is the world's first indoor ballpark, was merely baseball under glass—the same old game, now happily sheltered from the voracious mosquitoes and dismaying swelter of the Texas Gulf Coast. However, the unexpected local discovery that sunshine had become inimical to the national pastime (in preseason practices and exhibition games, before the initial coat of paint was slapped on the skylights, a few players had begun wearing their batting helmets in the outfield) only completed what actually was a radical break

with baseball's past and hastened further changes. Through the
rest of last season, the grass in the crepuscular dome yellowed
and withered, was painted green in the infield, and finally had to
be replaced with new sodding, which fared no better. When ballplayers reconvened in the Astrodome this spring, they stepped
out onto an infield made of new green plastic carpeting called
AstroTurf.

It was not just the prospect of witnessing weatherless baseball
played on Chemstrand grass under an acrylic-painted Lucite sky
that induced me to travel to Houston last month to see the Astros
open their first 1966 home stand. There was also the fact that the
Astros' first indoor season had been a rousing success, in spite of
their customary ninth-place finish. Houston jumped from a 1964
home attendance of 725,773, smallest in the National League, to a
gate of 2,151,470, barely second to that of the World Champion
Dodgers, and more than six hundred thousand higher than the
best American League home draw. Since half of the majors'
twenty teams have been born or have moved to new cities in the
past twelve years, all in panting search of new audiences, these
figures were of remarkable interest; Houston seemed on its way
to becoming the capital of Baseball's Age of Alteration.

So it was that I found myself, early in the evening of April 18,
sitting in a cushioned deep-purple loge seat in left field of the
Harris County Domed Stadium (as the Astrodome is formally
named) and listening to the Jeff Davis High School band's pregame rendition of "The Good Old Summertime." The only good
and old object in view at the time was Robin Roberts, the erstwhile ace of the Phillies and Orioles and now the Astros' senior
mound statesman, who was warming up near the right-field
stands preparatory to taking on the Dodgers. He toiled earnestly,
though surrounded by distractions. A group of female scholars
from Tyler Junior College assembled along the foul lines and did
some high kicks in unison, wearing cowboy hats and peach satin
body stockings. The groundkeepers smoothing the base paths
were dressed in fake bright orange space suits and fake white

plastic space helmets. Each level of the stands was painted a different color—royal blue, gold, purple, black, tangerine, and crimson—and I had the momentary sensation that I was sinking slowly through the blackberry-brandy layer of a pousse-café. The AstroTurf infield was green, but more the shade of a billiard table than a lawn. Only the outfield grass (which will be replaced with AstroTurf later this year) was reassuring; it looked like any Westchester back yard after a five-year drought. The lacy overhead pattern of beams and cloudy panes arching up from the brilliant circle of field lights made a soft and surprising sky above me. Leaning back in my theater seat, I measured its height by eye and saw that it was far above the reach of any fly ball, and then I wondered why someone hadn't placed an altitude mark at the apex of the roof, to match the "340," "390," and "406" signs along the outfield wall and thus supply us with baseball's latest statistic.

The elegant stands slowly filled, the ceremonials slipped by (the National League president with a plaque, Dinah Shore with the anthem, a county judge with the first ball), and baseball was allowed to begin. It turned out to be the same old game, the same game as ever. I could tell, because there was Robin Roberts out on the mound fiddling with his right pants leg between pitches. There, too, were the Dodgers, the champions, instantly ripping off singles, bunting, scurrying for the extra base, taking charge of the game from the very beginning, just as they did in the World Series last fall. Only the fact that Maury Wills was thrown out stealing second kept them down to two runs in the first inning and sustained the hopes of the locals. I presumed that the Houston fans were hopeful, but it was hard to be certain. It was a thinnish turnout for an opening game—just over twenty-five thousand—and the spectators near me, who were remarkably well dressed, also appeared to be unaccustomed to indoor shouting. It developed, however, that they were merely waiting for directions. With two out in the home half of the first, Jimmy Wynn drew a base on balls, and the center screen of the Astro-

dome's huge, three-panel electronic scoreboard above the outfield
pavilion seats burst forth with a noisy, animated depiction of a
bugle bugling, followed by the lettered command "CHARGE!"
"*Charge!*" responded the crowd with one voice. The fans near
me were still laughing over this display of *a capella* ferocity
when Joe Morgan flied out and the tiny rally came to a close.

Several scoreboards in big-league parks are now wired for
bugle calls and CHARGE! injunctions (the device was born, I believe, in Los Angeles), but comic cavalry attacks are only the beginning of the Houston scoreboard's repertoire. The thing is
four hundred and seventy-four feet long and cost two million
dollars, and there is room on its various partitions for simultaneous presentation of the game's lineups and scoring, out-of-town
baseball results, messages of welcome to fan groups, plugs for
Astro souvenirs, and gigantic animated commercials. These last
flash on between innings—routine cartoon plugs for potato
chips, gasoline, an airline, and so forth, accompanied by sound effects but without a spoken message. This is the only mercy, for
the giant set is impossible not to look at, and there is no "off"
switch. Actually, there was plenty to watch and enjoy on the
field in that first game, in which Roberts, in search of his two-
hundred-and-eighty-second major-league win, was throwing a
potpourri of soft junk and being outpitched by a twenty-one-
year-old Dodger rookie named Don Sutton, who has been in organized baseball for exactly one year, but the scoreboard and its
busy screen seemed anxious to improve on the baseball. In the
second inning, second baseman Morgan and third baseman Bob
Aspromonte came up with successive brilliant stops for the Astros, to rob Jim Lefebvre and Lou Johnson of base hits; there
were shouts and applause in the stands, but the scoreboard commanded "OLÉ!" and was obeyed. By the middle innings, I found
that I was giving the game only half my attention; along with
everyone else, I kept lifting my eyes to that immense, waiting
presence above the players. In the eighth, with the Astros behind,
5–1, Sonny Jackson led off the home half with a nifty bunt,

and when Morgan singled him along, some fans began a hopeful, rhythmic clapping, instantly surpassed by the appearance on the screen of a giant female silhouette dancing the Frug, and then the words "GO-GO." The Astros went-went for two runs, but the Dodgers added another of their own and won the game, 6–3. As I walked down the broad ramps of the Astrodome and, oddly, stepped outdoors, I heard a good many Texans around me still talking about something that had taken place way back in the second inning, when Chuck Harrison had doubled off the left-field wall, for the Astros' first hit. The man in charge of the scoreboard evidently thought the ball had gone into the stands, for he pressed the button touching off the board's home-run celebration display—an immense, multicolor, forty-five-second extravaganza depicting an exploding ballpark, shooting cowboys, ricocheting bullets, a snorting steer with flags on his horns, a mounted cowboy with lariat, and a fusillade of skyrockets. This time, when it was all over Harrison was still standing on second, and the screen boffed the crowd with its next message, "OOPS." A minute or two later, catcher John Bateman also doubled, and the home team scored, but no one in the postgame crowd seemed to remember that. The board had been the big hit of the evening.

Baseball, of course, is not the only main event at the Domed Stadium. In the past year, it has put on such disparate attractions as Judy Garland, the Ringling Brothers circus, a rodeo, a boat show, a polo match, the home football games of the University of Houston, a bloodless bullfight, and a Billy Graham crusade. Some of these bombed and some did excellent business, but what emerged most startlingly was the fact that the Astrodome itself is its own best attraction. In the first year, close to four hundred and ninety thousand visitors paid a dollar apiece just to walk around inside the place. Most of these were out-of-towners, but in Houston itself the Astrodome seems to rank second only to the nearby Manned Spacecraft Center as a source of self-congratulation. Certainly there is far more conversational enthusiasm about the building than about the sport it was built to house; a local sportswriter told me he had never heard *anyone* say, "I'm an Astro fan." During my stay, I found that when I forced myself to look at the Astrodome as a work of art, my admiration for the improbable cool bubble grew with each visit. The exterior is especially pleasing—a broad, white-screened shell of such excellent proportions that you doubt its true dimensions until you stand at its base. The Astrodome is the world's biggest indoor arena, but its ramps are gentle, its portals and aisles brilliantly marked, and its various levels so stacked and tilted that immensity is reduced and made undiscouraging. There are almost no bad seats in the house, and the floors are so antiseptically clean that one hesitates before parting with a peanut shell or a cigarette butt.

Ballplayers like the Astrodome, too. Descending to the playing field during batting practices (I tried to pull up a blade of Astro-Turf to chew on while standing behind the batting cage, but the stuff is pluckproof), I talked to various Dodgers and Astros and found them unanimous in the view that the lighting is now excellent, the prefab infield very fast but perhaps not as fast as Dodger Stadium's brickyard, but the chilled, windless air profoundly unconducive to the long ball. Last year, only fifty-seven homers were struck in Houston, which is only a third of the total in most parks. Wes Parker, the young Dodger first baseman, said, "It's a park for singles-hitters. Hit the ball on the ground, *ffft*, and it'll likely go through. Good for our kind of team. I'll tell you, though, I just discovered something funny about this fake grass. Watch bunts on it. Watch what happens to them." I studied the next dozen-odd bunts laid down in practice, and each time, the spinning ball, catching the nap of the AstroTurf, suddenly veered off toward first base, like a marble dropped on the floor in a housing development. Later, after practice, I went out and walked around on the new surface, which has the consistency of an immense doormat. I dug down with my fingers and found the spine of one of the hidden foul-line-to-foul-line zippers that hold the new infield together; I had the sudden feeling that if I un-zipped it, I might uncover the world's first plastic worm.

The worst seats for baseball in the Astrodome are the most expensive—the narrow topmost ring of "Sky Boxes," which are sold on a season-long basis in blocks of twenty-four or thirty seats. Such an investment in the national pastime costs a minimum of $14,784 per season, and entitles the boxholder to approximately the same view of the ballplayers as he might have of a herd of prize cattle seen from a private plane. There are other perquisites, though, including membership in the Skydome Club, a private snuggery in the Astrodome that offers Lucite womb chairs, a pic-ture-window view of downtown Houston, and an Oriental res-taurant equipped with kimono-clad Japanese waitresses and elec-tric *hibachi* stoves. (Buyers of single season tickets have to make do with membership at the Astrodome Club, a capacious Tur-key-red lounge and restaurant, with beaded curtains, swinging sa-loon doors, and the longest bar in Texas.) Each Sky Box is connected to an individual small apartment containing a living room, bathroom, refrigerator, and closed-circuit TV set. These roomettes are heavily decorated in Texas provincial, motel Tu-dor, and other "themes," and I can only say I found them im-mensely glum—sad, soft caves for indoor sportsmen. The insti-tution is popular, however; women who are invited to a Sky Box dinner party and game can sometimes find their names in the so-ciety columns the next day, and a Texas businessman standing be-hind the Sky Box seats, with his foot on a railing, a glass of bour-bon in his hand, and a ball game in progress far below, is sometimes in the mood for a little wheeling and dealing with the other good old boys he finds up there at the top level of the big-gest new arena in the world.

Studying millionaires is Houston's favorite year-round enter-tainment, and Judge Roy Hofheinz, the Kublai Khan of the Domed Stadium, is the most entertaining millionaire in town. He has been, variously, a campaign manager for Lyndon Johnson, a boy-wonder jurist, mayor of Houston, a real-estate developer,

and a promoter and owner of radio and television stations. Hofheinz is not one of the big rich, like John W. Mecom, who seems
to have succeeded the late Jesse Jones as Houston's financial vizier,
but he talks more and gets into more fights than any other mon-
eyman in sight. Hofheinz's fallings-out are epochal. Among others, he has squabbled with Jesse Jones; with K. S. (Bud) Adams,
Jr., the owner of the American Football League's Houston Oilers
(the Oilers do not play their home games in the Astrodome); and
with R. E. (Bob) Smith, his former senior partner in Houston
Sports Association, Inc., the company that owns the Astros and
rents the stadium from Harris County for an annual payment of
three-quarters of a million dollars. This last blowup, a year ago,
ended with the Judge buying up most of Smith's interest, and he
now owns 86 per cent of the Astros. Hofheinz's experience in
baseball is minimal, and most of the club's field operations rested
in the hands of general manager Paul Richards, a former manager
of the Orioles and a widely admired baseball thinker. Experienced
Hofheinz-watchers predicted that there would be amity in the
organization until the day Hofheinz decided he had surpassed
Richards in baseball wisdom—a day that apparently arrived last
December, when Hofheinz abruptly fired Richards (whose contract had five years to run), along with farm director Eddie Robinson and manager Luman Harris. The new team manager is
Grady Hatton, and the Astros are now a pure Hofheinz fief.

Houston looks on Hofheinz with a mixture of awe, amusement,
and anxiety. There is the undeniable fact that the prodigious idea
of a domed year-round stadium was entirely the Judge's, and
without his plans for the new miracle park Houston almost certainly would not have been granted a franchise in the league expansion of 1962. It was also Hofheinz's energy and promotional
optimism that got the necessary bond issues approved and
launched, and his hand is recognizable in every corridor and cat-
walk of the finished marvel. Any remaining Houston doubts
about the Judge's genius are now centered on the awesome financial weight that is being balanced on top of the dome, and on the

recent population implosion of top executives at the Houston Sports Association. The precise break-even point of Astroperations has not been made public, but the stadium's financial overhead is known to be Texas-sized. The electric bill alone, covering lights and air-conditioning, comes to thirty thousand dollars a month. The best estimates of the amount of business required to keep the Domed Stadium afloat come down to about a hundred and twenty-five days of active operation at an average attendance of twenty thousand. This means that the Astros must continue to draw handsomely during their eighty dates at home, and that numerous additional attractions will have to be encouraged. No one in Houston doubts the Judge's energy and imagination, but Harris County voted in an investment of some thirty-one million dollars toward the success of the Astrodome—a sum that adds a certain sense of zesty involvement to each taxpayer's daily Hofheinz-watch.

I visited the Judge one afternoon in his famous Astrodome office—a two-story business pad of such comically voluptuous decor and sybaritic furnishings that I was half convinced it had been designed by, say, John Lennon. My awed gaze took in hanging Moorish lamps and back-lit onyx wall panels in His Honor's sanctum, a pair of giant Oriental lions guarding the black marble and rosewood judicatorial desk, a golden telephone awaiting the Hofheinzian ear, and, at the far end of the boardroom, a suspended baldachin above the elevated red-and-gilt magisterial throne. It would have been irreverent to talk baseball in these surroundings, but luckily the Judge received me in his box on an upper floor, which offered an expansive vista of the lofty, gently breathing dome and a distant view of some Astros working out in the batting cage. Hofheinz is a tall, thick-waisted man with lank hair, heavy black-rimmed spectacles, and small hands, in which he constantly rotates a giant cigar. We sat in gold plush swivel chairs overlooking the field and drank coffee out of gold cups, while the Judge talked about the long, tedious process of building a pennant contender from scratch. I asked about the Houston audience's devotion to baseball, observing that I had seen very few local patrons keeping score during the game, and Hofheinz said, "This park keeps 'em interested enough so they don't *have* to keep busy with a pencil and scorecard. Why, in most other parks you got nothing to do but watch the game, keep score, and sit on a hard wooden seat. This place was built to keep the fans happy. They've got our good seats, fine restaurants, and our scoreboard to look at, and they don't have to make a personal sacrifice to like baseball." He tapped the ash from his heater into a gold ashtray shaped like a fielder's glove, and went on. "We have removed baseball from the rough-and-tumble era, I don't believe in the old red-necked sports concept, and we are disproving it here. We're in the business of sports entertainment. Baseball isn't a game to which your individuals come alone just to watch the game. They come for social enjoyment. They like to entertain and *be* entertained at the ballpark. Our fans are more like the ones they have out in California. We don't have any of those rowdies or semi-delinquents who follow the Mets."

I started to put in a small word for rowdies, but Hofheinz continued. "We have by far a higher percentage of fans in the upper economic brackets than you'll find in any other park," he said, "but we *also* have the best seats and service at the dollar-fifty level. You're competing for attention in sports entertainment, and you've got to create new kinds of fans. We make a big effort to bring out the ladies. There are plenty of mothers and grandmothers who have just learned about the double play from some Little Leaguer, and now for the first time here's a ballpark where you would *want* to bring them and let them develop into real fans. And once they've seen what it's like here, they won't feel so bad about letting their husbands and boys go off to the ball game any old time they want."

For the remainder of my stay, I tried to concentrate on Houston baseball, instead of its setting, and I saw the Astros split a pair of lively games with the Dodgers. The first was one of those baseball rarities, a complete turnabout, in which the Astros, after giving up ten hits and five runs in the first four innings, suddenly bounced back with batches of runs of their own while entirely bottling up their tormentors, and won going away, 8–5. John Bateman's fourth-inning homer set off the scoreboard's steers and rockets for their first sanctioned gala of the year, and in the fifth the home side, assisted by some absent-minded Dodger fielding, batted around and drove Don Drysdale from the mound. This was perhaps less of a feat than it sounds, for Drysdale was far from sharp after his long, much-publicized dual holdout with Sandy Koufax, but it was popular; there is nothing like the public shaming of a hundred-thousand-dollar-a-year man to tone up a crowd. The Astros got some first-class pitching from a tough workmanlike reliever named Mike Cuellar, who struck out nine Dodgers with his down-breaking screwball. The next night, the Astros almost pulled out another, but they were up against Claude Osteen, the least publicized and perhaps the best No. 3 pitcher in the league, who fanned Jim Gentile with the tying run aboard in the ninth, and they lost a 3–2 squeaker.

The Astros are a curiosity, for they are a team without a star, present or past, unless one counts such mini-celebrities as Jimmy Wynn or Larry Dierker. Invented, along with the Mets, in the league expansion of 1962, they have consistently displayed a shabby competence that has kept them above New York in the standings every year, and has probably cost them much of the rich affection and attention generated by the Mets' anti-heroes.

There is no real doubt, however, that the Astros are on the way and will someday break into the tough, embattled territory of the National League's first division, but a healthy franchise, particularly in new baseball territory, also requires the building of a sizable body of young, resilient, and truly knowledgeable fans. No one knows much about the loyalties and passions of the Houston baseball audience, in spite of those enormous attendance figures of last season, for it is impossible to guess how many of the two million ticket-buyers came to see the Astros and how many to see the Astrodome. During the Dodger games, I kept moving about in the stands and changing neighbors, but I could not penetrate the placid bonhomie of those small, citified, early-season crowds or convince myself that we were watching a sporting event. There was applause at the appropriate moments, but not much tonsil-straining, and the scattered booing was mostly directed at the ball and strike calls of the home-plate umpire, which is bush. No one booed an Astro player. No one got into a fight; a fight at the Astrodome would be as shocking as fisticuffs in the College of Cardinals. And always, as before, the applause and attention of the fans around me would be interrupted, redirected, and eventually muffled by the giant scoreboard and its central screen. It commanded "CHARGE" and "GO-GO" for every Astro base-runner, it saluted a homer by the Dodgers' Wes Parker with the word "TILT," and when it broke in on a lively dispute at third base, the spectators forgot about the real thing and sat back in their armchairs to watch a cartoon umpire argue with a cartoon manager.

Toward the end of the last game, my irritation took me out to the pavilion seats in center field (Astropatrons, untouched by the sun, do not sit in bleachers), and here I found the first unscattered group of recognizable fans in Houston. It was a shirt-sleeved, short-sleeved crowd, Negro and white, full of young people. There were some big families, complete with sleeping babies, and a blond teen-age girl next to me wore a patch on the arm of her sweater that said "Future Homemaker of America." Some of the men wore straw cowboy hats, some were in city coconut straws. Shortly after I arrived, Dave Nicholson led off the Astro sixth with a triple off Osteen that almost landed in our laps, and at once the entire pavilion crowd was on its feet, shouting and cheering. The scoreboard, I remembered later, was behind us, but we didn't seem to need it. And then in the top of the seventh, when Houston pitcher Bob Bruce was in heavy trouble, first baseman Chuck Harrison speared a hopper by Maury Wills and then hesitated a moment over his play. I jumped up and yelled,

"Home! Throw home!," and it came to me suddenly that I had company: a hundred fans near me were screaming the same advice. Harrison got our message and threw to Bateman, who tagged out Nate Oliver at the plate, and we all sat down, grinning at one another.

Baseball is an extraordinarily subtle and complex game, and the greatest subtlety of all may well be the nature of its appeal to the man in the stands. The expensive Houston experiment does not truly affect the players or much alter the sport played down on the field, but I think it does violence to baseball—and, incidentally, threatens its own success—through a total misunderstanding of the game's old mystery. I do not agree with Judge Hofheinz that a ballpark is a notable center for socializing or propriety, or that many spectators will continue to find refreshment in returning to a giant living room—complete with manmade weather, wall-to-wall carpeting, clean floors, and unrelenting TV show—that so totally, so drearily, resembles the one he has just left. But these complaints are incidental. What matters, what appalls, in Houston is the attempt being made there to alter the quality of baseball's time. Baseball's clock ticks inwardly and silently, and a man absorbed in a ball game is caught in a slow, green place of removal and concentration and in a tension that is screwed up slowly and ever more tightly with each pitcher's windup and with the almost imperceptible forward lean and little half-step with which the fielders accompany each pitch. Whatever the pace of the particular baseball game we are watching, whatever its outcome, it holds us in its own continuum and mercifully releases us from our own. Any persistent effort to destroy this unique phenomenon, to "use up" baseball's time with planned distractions, will in fact transform the sport into another mere entertainment and thus hasten its descent to the status of a boring and stylized curiosity.

It seems to me that the Houston impresarios are trying to build a following by the distraction and entire control of their audience's attention—aiming at a sort of wraparound, programmed environment, of the kind currently under excited discussion by new thinkers of the electronic age. I do not wish them luck with this vulgar venture, and I hope that in the end they may remember that baseball has always had a capacity to create its own life-long friends—sometimes even outdoors. One Houston lady told me that she had been a fan for more than thirty years, beginning when she was a schoolgirl and the Houston Buffs were a Cardinal farm. "I remember a lot of players from back then," she said. "I saw them all before they went up to the majors and became famous. Howie Pollett and Danny Murtaugh were my *gods*. And I remember something else. Buff Stadium back in the old days used to be right next to a bakery—Fehr's Bakery, that's what it was called! I'll never forget sitting in the stands in the afternoon and watching the games, and the sweet smell of fresh bread in the air all around." *

* Now, six years later, the Astrodome remains our only domed ball-park, but newer and larger bubbles are on the way. The Astros' home attendance has leveled off in the neighborhood of 1,350,000—an extremely attractive neighborhood for a perennially noncontending club—so the park and its peculiar attributes are almost universally considered a success. Only the enormously increased costs of construction have delayed the erection of similar sports-tanks in other localities, but New Orleans has now sunk pilings for the 80,000-seat Louisiana Superdome, thus proving the American axiom that it is perfectly O.K. to go ape at the bank as long as you are drawing out the money for nuclear weapons or sports. Official estimates place the cost of the bayou balloon at one hundred and forty million dollars, but some irate taxpayers are suggesting final figures closer to three hundred million. This dome is promised for 1974, and will house the New Orleans Saints, of the National Football League; it is also expected that it will constitute an irresistible lure for some poor, heavily rained-upon baseball club, such as the Cleveland Indians.

The *next* roofed stadium will probably appear in Detroit, where the Tigers have already signed a forty-year lease on a projected downtown dome. A Buffalo dome has apparently been scrubbed, but the idea of the roofed field as a cure-all for many of the ailments of sport remains widespread. In New York last summer, the enlargement and doming-over of Shea Stadium was proposed by the customarily cautious *New York Times* as a solution to the decay of Yankee Stadium and the unhappiness of the football Giants. What the price of this roof would be and who would pay it were not specified. Neither did the paper wonder whether any New York fans wanted indoor baseball and football.

The Houston scoreboard has been surpassed, by the way, by a three-million-dollar double-panel job in Philadelphia's new Veterans Stadium. The home-run display, I am told, includes plashing fountains, the Liberty Bell, comical high-jinks by giant animated colonial dolls named Philadelphia Phil and Phyllis, and a guided tour of the downtown area, including Independence Hall, ending up with a lobster dinner at Bookbinder's. Something like that, anyway.

PART 5

Classics and Campaigns—II

A Terrific Strain

Spectators back from this year's minimum-sized World Series have been required to defend themselves against the repeated, baffled cry of "What *happened?*" The question, put by wives, office mates, cabdrivers, children, bartenders, and querulous grandfathers over the long-distance telephone, is at once redundant and very nearly unanswerable. Everyone knows what happened, of course: the American League's Baltimore Orioles, a young and almost purely untested team of exuberant hitters and indifferent pitchers, humiliated the defending champions, the Los Angeles Dodgers, possessors over the last decade of the best pitching staff and the best Series record in either league, in four straight games. The Dodgers scored no runs at all after the third inning of the opening game, thereby establishing a Series unrecord that may stand for the balance of the century. Contrariwise, two Baltimore starting pitchers and one relief man will now be able to open their contract negotiations next spring with the claim that their lifetime Series pitching records surpass those of Cy Young, Christy Mathewson, and Walter Johnson. The brevity and inscrutability of this year's Series were no less mysterious to eyewitnesses than to the millions who were done out of two or three happily wasted afternoons in front of their TV sets; fans and sportswriters straggling out of Baltimore's Memorial Stadium after the fourth game suggested theatergoers who had bought

tickets to a famous melodrama only to find that the bill had been
changed at the last minute to a one-acter by Samuel Beckett.
Baseball of the Absurd, however, invites criticism and after-
thoughts, and it is just possible that this Series will become more
intelligible in retrospect.

One must begin with the suggestion that the turning point in a
drama *can* appear three or four minutes after the curtain goes up.
The Orioles moved into first place in the American League after
the second week in June. By the end of July, they led the pack
by the debilitating margin of thirteen games, and though they
glided through the remainder of the season, winning twenty-
eight games and losing twenty-eight, they finished in front by a
comfortable nine without playing one game or series that could
be called crucial. In all those weeks, the team's numerous front-
line youngsters—including catcher Andy Etchebarren, second
baseman Dave Johnson, outfielders Paul Blair and Curt Blefary,
and pitchers Dave McNally, Jim Palmer, and Wally Bunker—
could only fill the languid hours with speculation about their
coming test in the World Series. To be sure, they owned a large
security blanket, made up of Frank Robinson, who was winning
every important batting title in the league, the incomparable
Brooks Robinson at third, and such unshakables as shortstop Luis
Aparicio, ace pitcher Steve Barber, and reliever Stu Miller. But
then Barber was lost with a sore arm, and Brooks Robinson fell
into a horrendous slump at the plate, and waiting in October
were the flutter and noise of the Series and the assured violence
of whichever National League team survived a summer of daily
warfare. The Dodgers, by contrast, won their race with the Pirates and the Giants in what has come to be obligatory style in
the National League—a September catch-up, some last-minute
stumbling, and the pennant on the final weekend (this time, in
the final game) of the season. The superlative Dodger pitchers
were perhaps a bit tired, but the champions walked onto the field
for the first game in Los Angeles like a synod of elders proceed-
ing to the front pews. For that matter, the only visible sign of

pre-Series nerves among the Orioles as they took batting practice might have been the excessive cheerfulness of their manager, Hank Bauer, who exchanged quips with a thick cluster of sportswriters while his eyes followed his athletes with a preoccupied, headmasterish flicker. But the tension was there; a full hour before the ceremonies and the anthem, Curt Blefary said, "If this damned thing doesn't start soon, I'm going to fly straight up into the air!"

The young Orioles' first flying, it developed, was delightful, being merely up out of their seats in the dugout. Don Drysdale, the Dodger starter, walked Russ Snyder in the top of the first, and then Frank Robinson hit his second pitch into the left-field stands. A minute later, the other Robinson, Brooks, sailed one even farther, into a descending cone of unbelieving silence, and the visitors were able to take the field with that best of all tension-dissolvers, a three-run lead. They added another in the second, less spectacularly but with admirable neatness, when Etchebarren walked, was bunted along by McNally, and came across on Snyder's single. McNally's bunt was his last sign of competence. In the Dodger second, he gave up a gargantuan homer to Jim Lefebvre, a double to Wes Parker, and four straight balls to Jim Gilliam, and was saved from disaster only by a nifty running catch in right center by Russ Snyder. No one could help him in the third, when his control entirely evaporated. Etchebarren was leaping and diving for his pitches, and in a matter of minutes McNally walked the bases full, with one out, and then disappeared, having thrown sixty-three pitches, more or less in the style of a wedding guest heaving rice, and thus destroyed the pace and pattern of the game. His successor, Moe Drabowsky, struck out Parker, walked in a run, and then got Roseboro on a foul. That, it turned out, was the ball game.

Might Have Been is dull sport, but the Dodgers, who have been frequently disparaged for being a lucky team, suffered such appalling bad luck in this space of two innings that fairness now calls for some second-guessing. In the second inning, with Parker

on second and Gilliam on first, Roseboro ducked away from a
McNally wild pitch that was headed straight for Cary Grant in
the celebrity boxes behind the backstop; the ball just ticked Roseboro's bat, behind his head, and the runners had to stay planted.
Without that freak, Parker would have scored easily from third
on Roseboro's long fly, which Snyder ran down. In the next inning, Drabowsky, after walking in one run, still had the bases
loaded when he threw a fourth ball, inside, to Roseboro, who
checked his swing but again saw the ball just tick his bat. Except
for these two kisses from providence, the game would have now
been tied, and—much more significantly—Drabowsky would
have joined McNally in the showers. Drabowsky, a tall, experienced middle relief man, is a streaky pitcher, and now, miraculously unhooked, he streaked in the other direction. After Roseboro's foul, he struck out the next six Dodgers in succession, to
tie a Series record, and then established a wholly new Series mark
for relievers by striking out a total of eleven Dodgers on the way
to his easy 5–2 victory. Within an inning or two after he settled down, his dominance over the home side was so evident that
I was free to wander about in the back aisles of the ballpark and
resume research on the monograph I may someday write about
Dodger fans. Someday, that is, if I ever begin to understand them.
The crowd that afternoon was the biggest in Dodger Stadium
history, and it had paid more money for its seats than any previous Series audience, and yet the spectators sat there, inning
after inning, in polite, unhappy silence, like parents at a rock
concert. They were mostly middle-aged or elderly—men with
long bellies and golf caps, women with elaborately waved white
or dyed hair, their mahogany hands crossed in their laps. Their
team was losing, but few hopeful or encouraging cries escaped
their lips, and there were few children among them to venture a
shout or two. Win was what they had come for, and, deprived of
that, they sat in silence and listened to an amplified play-by-play
description of the game that explained to them, by loudspeaker,

what they were seeing. The bright field below, the running players, the game of baseball seemed a hundred miles away.

By good fortune, I had brought along to Los Angeles the ideal
companion for a sometimes discouraging, sometimes embarrassing,
and undeniably historic World Series—an almost perfect new
baseball book called *The Glory of Their Times*, by Lawrence S.
Ritter. The author, a professor of economics at New York University, has spent all his recent vacations tracking down famous
old ballplayers and inducing them to reminisce about their youth
and their extraordinary companions and the long-flown summer
days they gave to the great game. The result is a vivid, gentle,
and humorous narrative, accompanied by marvelous photographs,
which is somehow both saddening and reassuring for the contemporary fan. That night, after the first game in Los Angeles, I read
Tommy Leach's account of the first World Series of all, played
in 1903 between the Pittsburgh Pirates and the Boston Red Sox,
then sometimes known as the Pilgrims. Leach, a small third baseman with that Pirate team, recalls, "That was probably the
wildest World Series ever played. Arguing all the time between
the teams, between the players and the umpires, and especially
between the players and the fans. That's the truth. The fans were
part of the game in those days. They'd pour right out onto the
field and argue with the players and the umpires. . . . I think
those Boston fans actually won that Series for the Red Sox." He
tells how the Red Sox partisans, who called themselves the Royal
Rooters, drove the Pirates to the edge of distraction by their endless bawling of a hit song called "Tessie," with extemporaneous
insulting variations. "Sort of got on your nerves after a while,"
Leach says. "And before we knew what happened, we'd lost the
World Series."

Today, of course, the gulf between the players and the every-
day fan is almost immeasurable, especially at the Series, and most
of the middle ground seems to be filled with distracters and

explainers—play-by-play announcers, beer and razor-blade commercials, stop-action TV shots, and battalions of sportswriters. Baseball is perhaps the most perfectly visible sport ever devised, almost never requiring us to turn to a neighbor and ask "What happened?" And yet our joy is no longer instantaneous. Scoreboards tell us when to cheer, and the incredible catch, the famous pinch-hit double are not entirely real to us until we have seen them confirmed on the late news show and in the morning columns. Years from now, we may find it difficult to remember whether we were really there at all. Inevitably, the fame and richness of the Series make it more and more difficult for most of us to make the scene, since large areas of the two autumn ballparks are occupied by moneyed boxholders, the press, and the immense bureaucracy of baseball. The *Times* estimated that thirty-two thousand Series seats at Dodger Stadium this year had been sold to season-ticket holders, and that twelve thousand more were reserved for baseball executives and their employees and friends. There were a thousand accredited reporters, cameramen, and radio and TV personnel in Los Angeles. The postgame crush in the clubhouses has lately grown so dense that most Series teams, including both the Dodgers and Orioles, now stage formal postgame press conferences in chair-lined rooms, where I have seen a slugger approach the microphones like an Under-Secretary of State, clear his throat, and murmur, "Well, in answer to that, I'd say it was a fast ball, high and inside." In the evenings during the Series week, the reporters and numerous, various-sized baseball wheels assemble at large cocktail-and-dinner gatherings thrown by the home club. These are loud, cheerful enough affairs, full of gossip and anecdote, old friends, and free provender, and yet I have never come away from one without a feeling of glumness. It is not just the annual presence there of so many down-on-their-luck baseball men—fired managers, superfluous coaches, and deterritorialized scouts—all looking for the fortuitous handshake, the whisky-warmed happenstance that will readmit them, however distantly, to the sunshine game. Concealed in the hoarse rumors, recollected heroics, and comical dugout yarns of the baseball writers there is also a simultaneous adulation and bitter patronizing of the young and lucky that reveals how out of it all we reporters are, how second-hand. We, too, are hangers-on of baseball.

The fearful happenings of the second game need not be lingered over, being now as well known as the circumstances surrounding the fall of Troy. Until the gods began their heavy-handed meddling, it was a fine, fast game, with the Dodgers having somewhat the better of it. Sandy Koufax, although making his third start in eight days, including the pennant-nailer on Sunday, looked quick enough to lengthen his string of scoreless World Series innings indefinitely, and it seemed only a matter of time before his teammates would mark up some runs against the unpuzzling fast balls thrown by his opponent, the twenty-year-old right-hander Jim Palmer. For half the game, the only sign of twitchy nerves came from the Orioles. In the second, Frank Robinson stumbled as he fielded Lou Johnson's hit to right field, and Johnson whizzed along to second; in the fourth, Robinson over-ran second on an error by Jim Gilliam and was thrown out easily. In the next inning, reality and the scoreless game came unstuck together. With Boog Powell on first and one out, Paul Blair lifted a high fly to center field, where Willie Davis, squinting up into the fierce, smog-glazed sun, allowed the ball to drop behind his left knee, and Powell and Blair each took two bases. The Dodgers thought so little of Andy Etchebarren, the next batter, that they decided to pitch to him, instead of putting him on and aiming for a double play. Their logic was perfect, but Etchebarren's short fly subjected Davis to further corona observation, and he dropped it. Still shuddering under the weight of so many footcandles, Davis now pounced on the ball and made his first really unforgivable play—an angry Little League heave into the Dodger dugout that scored the second run. Koufax, perhaps grieving for this teammate's sudden arrival in the record

books, gave up another run on a double by Aparicio, and disbelief was further stretched in the next inning, when Davis and
Ron Fairly allowed Frank Robinson's long drive to fall between
them for three bases, and Powell scored him with a single. Struck
dumb, the Dodgers stopped getting on base, and the game eventually ended with the score at 6–6—runs for Baltimore, errors for Los Angeles. It should be noted that the Dodger fans did
not remain silent this time; full of spunk, they cheered bitterly
every time Willie Davis caught the ball in the between-inning
warmups. The day's only display of gallantry came in the clubhouses after the game, where Willie Davis responded with grace
to a reportorial cross-examination that would have done credit to
Eichmann's prosecutors. Only ballplayers understand how hard
their game really is; over in the Oriole dressing room, Hank
Bauer closed the accident report on Davis when he said, "If the
Dodgers don't want him, I'll take him."

I could have provided further comfort for Willie Davis, had he
needed it, from the lively memoirs contained in *The Glory of
Their Times*, which I continued to read on the plane back to
Baltimore. The book is packed with disasters. I learned that
Roger Peckinpaugh, the Most Valuable Player in the American
League in 1925, committed *eight* errors for the Senators in the
World Series that year. I read several descriptions of the infa-
mous "$100,000 Muff" by Fred Snodgrass that cost the Giants
the 1912 Series with the Red Sox, and then Snodgrass's own assessment: "For over half a century I've had to live with the fact
that I dropped a ball in the World Series—'Oh, you're the guy
that dropped that fly ball, aren't you?'—and for years and
years, whenever I'd be introduced to somebody, they'd start to
say something and then stop, you know, afraid of hurting my
feelings. But nevertheless, those were wonderful years, and if I
had the chance I'd gladly do it all over again, every bit of it."
Snodgrass is stoutly defended by other witnesses, who point out
that he also saved the game with a magnificent running catch on

the next play and that the championship was actually lost when the Giant infield then misplayed a foul pop, thus permitting Tris Speaker to stay alive and drive in the winning run. Later, thinking back to Sandy Koufax and recalling the anxiety that stabs one when watching him pitch his flaring fast balls with an arthritic arm that may end his baseball days at any instant, I read Smoky Joe Wood's lacerating account of the sore arm that finished him as a pitcher after he had won thirty-four games for the Red Sox in 1912, and of his long struggle back to the majors and to the World Series as an outfielder with the Cleveland Indians. Half asleep during the soft, deadening trip from one unlovely city to another, I read about the dusty American small towns where so many of these past heroes had begun their baseball—Wahoo and Freemont, Nebraska; Princeton, Indiana; and Ness City, Ellis, Bazine, and Wa Keeny, Kansas. Sam Crawford, the old Tiger immortal, can remember when baseball was still a game for country boys:

> Every town had its own town team in those days. I remember when I made my first baseball trip. A bunch of us from around Wahoo, all between sixteen and eighteen years old, made a trip overland in a wagon drawn by a team of horses. One of the boys got his father to let us take the wagon. It was a lumber wagon, with four wheels, the kind they used to haul the grain to the elevator, and was pulled by a team of two horses. It had room to seat all of us—I think there were eleven or twelve of us—and we just started out and went from town to town, playing their teams. . . . We were gone three or four weeks. Lived on bread and beefsteak the whole time. We'd take up a collection at the games—pass the hat, you know—and that paid our expenses. Or some of them, anyway. One of the boys was the cook, but all he could cook was round steak. We'd get twelve pounds for a dollar and have a feast. We'd drive along the country roads, and if we came to a stream we'd go swimming; if we came to an apple orchard, we'd fill up on apples. We'd sleep anywhere. Sometimes in a tent, lots of times

on the ground, out in the open. If we were near some fairgrounds, we'd slip in there. If we were near a barn, well . . .

Two unexpected wins had Baltimore jumping. Airport redcaps,
cabdrivers, waitresses, storefronts, bank windows, and even a
church or two were decked out in buttons or banners exhorting
"Bomb 'em, Birds!" and indoor strippers and outdoor revivalists
in the downtown honky-tonk area known as The Block staged
extra shows Friday night for the visiting sports. Most of the
crowd turned up early at Memorial Stadium the next morning, in
plenty of time to watch batting practice, and the tootling of extemporaneous bands in the parking lots, the hawkers selling chry-
santhemums and orange-and-black pennants, and the excited faces
of young boys hurrying their fathers along to their seats made me
think for a minute that I was walking into Palmer Stadium. Out
on the field, it was the other side that was now trying to smother
its nerves. "I don't think any team can be really down for a Series," Ron Fairly said to me, but he seemed uncertain about it,
and then Maury Wills lost his famous cool for a moment and
threw angry imprecations at a sportswriter for an unfavorable
phrase in a column. The Robinson team, by contrast, posed arm
in arm for the photographers, laughing and hamming it up, and
when it was over, Frank Robinson, who is, of course, black, said
to Brooks, who was born in Arkansas, "If they print that down
home, man, you'll *never* get back." Noisy, elated fans streamed
into the stands wearing Oriole boaters and sunshades boosting a
gubernatorial candidate named Agnew, and outside the park, beyond the center-field scoreboard and the jammed parking lot, a
scattering of ticketless partisans had taken over a grassy knoll,
from which they might get a glimpse of an occasional fly ball
and hear the deep cries of the crowd.

It was a brisk game, marvelously enjoyable, and the innings
flew by to the accompaniment of hopeful toots on a hundred
horns in the stands and a flurry of witticisms in the press rows
about Willie Davis's attack of stone hands in Los Angeles. The

game was half gone after an hour, and there was nothing to
choose between the teams—no runs, two hits apiece, and identical football blocks thrown at second base by the Dodgers' Lou
Johnson and the Orioles' Luis Aparicio, which both spoiled double plays. If anything, I thought that the Dodger pitcher, Claude
Osteen, was throwing harder and lower than the Orioles' Wally
Bunker, and I went on thinking so even after Paul Blair, the
part-time Oriole center fielder, hammered a ball deep into the
left-field stands in the fifth. It was a good pitch, down and away
—the kind that any pitcher will occasionally see pickled even
on his best days. Any pitcher, that is, but an Oriole in October.
The Dodgers made agonized efforts to move their base-runners
along, but they now seemed to be guessing at the plate. Their last
flutter came in the eighth, with Tommy Davis on second, when a
committee of Orioles gathered under Parker's fly in left field and
almost tabled it. Aparicio made the grab, and minutes later the
Dodgers clumped wearily back to their clubhouse, their eyes still
all goose eggs.

The fourth game, before a cheerful, faintly incredulous shirt-
sleeved crowd, rematched Drysdale and McNally, but in tone
and flavor it much more resembled the previous day's game than
the slack opener—the same good pitching, the same fast, scoreless early innings, the same slick infield play. It was as if the two
teams had only knocked off for a tea interval before continuing
the same encounter. Drysdale, although his fast ball was not tailing off like a cast fishing plug, the way it does when he is at
his sharpest, was pitching with immense determination, and
McNally, on his home mound, had his control back and now
could share his fellow Orioles' mad conviction that the Dodgers
might not score another run until, say, late July in 1967. That remains a possibility to this day, of course, but this knowledge
should not keep anyone from remembering how close the Series
still looked early on that final afternoon. If Drysdale could win, if
the Dodgers could stop drowning in two feet of water, Koufax

would pitch the next game, and only members of the Flat Earth
Society are prepared to bet that Koufax can lose two Series
games in a row. Then the Series would move back to Los Angeles, surely at no worse than even odds. This quick, close, yet
one-sided Series was so mystifying that in the early innings on
Sunday the representatives of the magazine *Sport*, which
awards a sports car each year to the outstanding player in the Series, were helplessly asking for nominees in the press rows. The
most sensible suggestion, assuming a Baltimore victory that day,
was to permit each of the Orioles to drive it for a week and to
donate the safety belt to Willie Davis.

The resolver—of the game, the Series, and the *Sport* editors'
dilemma—was Frank Robinson, who hit a Drysdale fast ball
four hundred and ten feet into the left-field stands in the fourth
inning. Robinson, a tall, solidly built right-handed slugger with
long legs and gigantic forearms, stands in the batter's box with
his left foot almost touching the back corner of the plate; his
quick forward stride throws all his weight into the pitch, and he
swings with such violence that his third-base coach, Billy
Hunter, has learned to bail out rapidly on the frequent occasions
when Robinson's bat comes whirring through his place of business. Robinson's plate-crowding invites pitchers to throw at his
left ear—a game that Drysdale enjoys—but this was no occasion for games. Drysdale's pitch was a good, live fast ball, but
right over the middle, and after the explosive *whock!* of Robinson's bat Drysdale didn't bother to turn and follow the ball; instead, he kicked the mound violently, exactly the way he did in
the first inning of the first game. Robinson sailed around the infield, touching bases and counting his self-made blessings—
Series hero; league-leading batting mark of .316; forty-nine homers, and a hundred and twenty-two runs batted in; certain
attainment of the Most Valuable Player award; and, perhaps most
comforting of all, the knowledge that the Cincinnati Reds, who
sold him to the Orioles last winter after he had terrorized Na-

tional League pitchers for a decade, had been stuck with the most
foolish baseball trade in memory.

The game went on, instantly growing in omens and tension.
With two out in the same inning, Boog Powell, the immense
doorstop who plays first base for the Orioles, powered a drive to
deep straightaway center. I watched Willie Davis lope back until
he bumped into the wire fence at the 410-foot sign, and when he
dropped his arms I thought he had given up. He was merely coil-
ing himself, however, and at the last moment he sailed straight
up, hung in midair for an instant like a drip-dry shirt on a line,
and came down with the ball in his glove.

This kind of third-out catch is the classic baseball signal for a
turnabout, and the Dodgers reacted with alacrity. Lefebvre singled, and then Wes Parker hit a hard, high-bouncing hopper that
seemed headed through the infield between third and short. It
didn't get through. Brooks Robinson charged the ball and fielded
it, half staggering, just above his shoe tops, and then whipped it
over to second to start the double play. It was the second-best
fielding play of the Series (Davis made the best, and the worst),
and the Dodgers died right there. Drysdale pitched grimly, Lefebvre almost came up with a tying homer in the eighth, and the
Dodgers put two runners on base in the ninth, but they went
down in the end, sinking under a prodigal weight of zeros.

The Dodger collapse at the plate should not invite any corol-
lary murmuring to the effect that the Orioles do not deserve their
new status as champions. Although their own team batting average of .200 is a new low for a Series winner, they played perfect,
errorless ball, which is also a new team Series record. They had
excellent pitching, and the two Robinsons did what so few team
leaders accomplish in October: they led. Best of all, the Orioles'
victory restores prestige and interest to the recently flabby American League, and may help destroy the current misconception
that only National League teams are worth the price of a ticket.

At the same time, I doubt whether even the most Birds-mad Baltimore twelve-year-old would claim that the Oriole pitching was quite *that* good. The four pitchers who won three shutouts and ran up thirty-three consecutive scoreless innings in the Series managed only one shutout all season and pitched fewer complete games than Sandy Koufax alone. The only answer to that question "What *happened?*" is that the Dodgers stopped hitting, and the only explanation must be that baseball is still the most difficult, and thus the most unpredictable and interesting, of all professional sports. For all its statistics, the game does not yield itself readily to the form player or the expert; only two out of two hundred members of the Baseball Writers' Association of America correctly picked both pennant winners this year. There are so many surprises in baseball and so many precedents for this unexpected Series result that one must conclude that the only reliable precedent in baseball is surprise itself.

Old ballplayers know the game best, and the most appropriate autumn garland for the 1966 World Series comes from *The Glory of Their Times*.

Heinie Groh, of McGraw's Giants: "So much of baseball is mental, you know, up there in the old head. You always have to be careful not to let it get you. Do you know that I was scared to death every time I went into a World Series? Every single one, after I'd been in so many. It's a terrific strain."

Rube Bressler, of Connie Mack's early Athletics: "Baseball . . . is not a game of inches, like you hear people say. It's a game of *hundredths* of inches. Any time you have a bat only that big around, and a ball that small, traveling at such tremendous rates of speed, an inch is way too large a margin for error." And "[The Athletics] won four pennants in five years, and *three* World Championships. . . . The only one they lost was that 1914 one—to George Stallings' 'miracle' Boston Braves, of all teams. The weakest of them all. And we lost it in four straight games, too."

Sam Jones, of the Yankees, on the 1923 World Series: "Art

Nehf and I both pitched shutouts through six innings, but then in the seventh Casey Stengel hit one of my fast balls into the right-field stands. That was the only run of the game, and Nehf beat me, 1–0. Oh, that really hurt!"

Paul Waner, of the Pirates, on losing the 1927 Series to the Yankees in four straight: "Out in right field I was stunned. And that instant, as the run that beat us crossed the plate, it struck me that I'd actually played in a World Series. It's an odd thing, isn't it? I didn't think, 'It's all over and we lost.' What I thought was, 'Gee, I've just played in a World Series.' "

Waner was in his second year with the Pirates in 1927, and he batted .333 in that Series. He remained in the big leagues for twenty years more, with a lifetime average of .333, but he never got into another World Series. Baseball is a hard game.

The Flowering and Subsequent Deflowering of New England

The laurels all are cut, the year draws in the day, and we'll to the Fens no more. A great baseball season—the most intense and absorbing of our times—is over, the St. Louis Cardinals stand as champions of the world, and hundreds of thousands of New Englanders must winter sadly on a feast of memory. The autumn quiet that now afflicts so many of us has almost nothing to do with the Red Sox defeat in the last game of the World Series, for every Boston fan has grown up with that dour Indian-pudding taste in his mouth. New England's loss is not of a game or a Series but of the baseball summer just past—a season that will not come again, not ever quite the same. What will be remembered this winter, I think, is not so much a particular victory (Elston Howard blocking off the last White Sox base-runner at the plate one night in Chicago, Carl Yastrzemski's eleventh-inning homer at Yankee Stadium) or a nearly insupportable loss (all those Baltimore games in September) as the shared joy and ridiculous hope of this summer's long adventure. I resisted at first, but it caught me up, and then I was sorry for anyone who was too old or too careful to care. Almost everyone on the seaboard was caught up in the end, it seemed. Forty-four New England radio stations poured out the news from the Fenway, and home-game telecasts by Ken Coleman, Mel Parnell, and Ned Martin made for late bedtimes from eastern Long Island to the Gaspé. Maine lobstermen pulling their traps off Saddleback Ledge called the news of the previous night's game from boat to boat through the foggy dawn air. The moderator of an August town meeting in Andover, Massachusetts, interrupted a hot budget debate to cry, "The Sox are leading, 2–1, in the sixth!" Three hikers descending the Brook Trail on Mount Chocorua, in New Hampshire, caught the afternoon score from a transistorized ascending climber. Sunday sailors off Manchester Harbor, on Boston's North Shore, hailed a winning rally with foghorns and salvos of cherry bombs, and then cheered when a power yacht broke out a large flag emblazoned "THINK PENNANT!" Late in August, a patient recovering from surgery stood at the window of his room in the New England Baptist Hospital night after night, watching the lights of Fenway Park across the city and hearing the sudden double roar of the crowd—first over his radio and then, in a deep echo, through the warm night air. The sense of belonging was best in the crowded streets near the ballpark before game time. Up out of the subway on Commonwealth Avenue, up Brookline Avenue and over the expressway bridge, past the Pennant Grille, past the button-hawkers ("GO, Sox!") and the ice-cream wagons and the police horses; carried along in a mass of children and parents, old ladies in straw porkpies, pretty girls with pennants, South Boston and Dorchester youths in high-school windbreakers, a party of nuns; then pushed and jammed, laughing at the crush, through the turnstiles and into the damp gloom under the stands; and out at last to that first electric glimpse of green outfield and white bases—this is the way baseball is remembered, and the way it truly was, for once, in the summer of the Red Sox.

Even a restrained backward look at this season and this Series must appear hyperbolic; already there is the odd temptation simply not to believe one's recollection or the record. The Cardinals, sixth-place finishers last year, lost their best pitcher for half the season and still won their pennant easily, entirely dominating the other powerful contenders that had given the National League its recent reputation for late-season violence. The Red Sox, who finished the 1966 season one-half game out of the cellar, captured the American League pennant on the last afternoon of the year by winning the second of two consecutive essential victories over the Twins and then waiting for the Tigers to lose their last game. The Baltimore Orioles, who won the 1966 World Series in four straight games, fell to sixth place this year, while the Red Sox, Twins, Tigers, and White Sox clawed and clung to each other like rival mountain climbers at the topmost escarpment of the American League for more than two months, in the closest pennant race in baseball history. The White Sox fell only two days before the end, at a moment when it appeared that they had the best chance to take the flag and the Red Sox the worst. Finally, the World Series, which promised only to be a numb, one-sided anticlimax, went the full seven games, producing some of the best baseball of the year, and was won at last by the better team.

An appreciation of the Cardinals must be postponed in this account until their appearance, in due course, in the World Series. An appreciation of the Red Sox must begin with a look at their prospects last April, which seemed inadequate even to sustain the wild vernal hopes that leap every year, jonquil-like, in the hearts of their followers. The Sox were a young team, probably a better one than their ninth-place finish indicated, but a review of the troops suggested only that hostilities should somehow be postponed. The up-the-middle strength, the traditional spine of a ball team, consisted of an earnest but light-hitting young catcher named Mike Ryan and two rookies—second baseman Mike Andrews and center fielder Reggie Smith. Third baseman Joe Foy and shortstop Rico Petrocelli could hit an occasional fly ball into the Fenway's short left-field screen, but both were subject to fatal spells of introspection when approaching ground balls. The large, slick-fielding George Scott was set at first, but last year, after making the All Star team with his early slugging, he had apparently determined to hit every subsequent pitch out of the park, and wound up leading the league only in strikeouts. The two other outfielders—Tony Conigliaro in right and Yastrzemski in left—enjoyed star billing, but neither came close to .300 last year. Yaz, who had won the batting title in 1963, finished at .278, with sixteen home runs; he had never hit more than twenty homers in one season. There was, to be sure, a new manager— Dick Williams, up from two successful years with the Toronto farm—but a new manager in Boston has the same approximate hopes for tenure as a titled Balkan bridegroom in a Hollywood marriage. Any manager, however deep-browed, hates to do much thinking in the first two or three innings, and thus must own a pitching staff. The Red Sox had none, having failed in the winter to improve the corps that was the worst in the league last year. Their best starter, the youthful Jim Lonborg, could strike out batters but had proved too gentlemanly in the clutch ever to enjoy a winning season in the majors. There was one strong late reliever, John Wyatt, and some passable middle-innings men, but absolutely no other starters in sight.

Reasonable hope cannot be constructed out of such a sad pile of feathers, but the lifelong Red Sox fan is not a reasonable man. In him is the perpetual memory of a dozen seasons when the best of hopes went for nothing, so why is he not to believe that the worst of prospects may suddenly reward his fealty? If he is middle-aged, he remembers when, in the early nineteen-thirties, the team's owner, Tom Yawkey, acquired the Sox and almost bought a pennant within a few years, at an immense price, with a team built around such stalwarts as Jimmy Foxx, Joe Cronin, Lefty Grove, and a lanky young outfielder named Ted Williams. He remembers the home-grown squad of the mid-nineteen-forties, which included Williams, Dominic DiMaggio, Johnny Pesky, and Bobby Doerr. Those teams were wonderfully talented and exciting, but unfortunately they coexisted with two Yankee teams that were among the best in league history. There is one Boston pennant to treasure, in 1946, but that memory is accompanied by

the awful vision of Enos Slaughter, of the Cardinals, racing all
the way home from first on a double by Harry Walker and scoring the winning run of the Series while Johnny Pesky hesitated
with the relay at short. There was a tie for first with the Indians
in 1948, but the starting Red Sox pitcher for the one-game playoff was an aging journeyman named Denny Galehouse, who instantly unjustified the hunch. Since then, the Sox have been more
at home in the second division than in the first. There are other
interior daguerreotypes to sustain the New Englander—Ted
Williams towering over the plate and grinding the bat between
his fists before pulling an outside pitch into the bullpen, Dick Radatz fanning the side in relief—but these are matched by darker
plates: Williams hitting .200 in that 1946 Series, Williams never
hitting much against the Yankees, Walt Dropo and several other
immobile croquet wickets letting grounders bounce between their
legs at first, a dozen assorted infielders messing up a thousand
double plays. I have studied the diehard Boston fan for many
summers. I have seen the tiny, mineral-hard gleam of hope in his
eye as he pumps gas under the blighted elms of a New Hampshire village or sells a pair of moccasins to a tourist in the bal-
sam-smelling dimness of his Down East store, listening the while
to the unceasing ribbon of bad news by radio from Fenway Park.
Inside his head, I am sure, there is a perpetual accompanying
broadcast of painful and maddening import—a lifetime's amal-
gam of ill-digested sports headlines, between-innings commercials,
and Fenway Park bleacher cries:

"Hi, neigh-bor, have a Gansett! . . . DOUBLE-X 9 GAMES AHEAD
OF BABE'S SWAT PACE . . . Oh, God, *look*—Slaughter's going for
home! C'mon, Pesky, throw the ball, throw the *ball!* . . .
YAWKEY VOWS PENNANT . . . but the lowly A's, rising for three
runs in the eighth, nipped the Hose in the nightcap. . . . Hi,
neigh-bor. . . . SPLINTER DEFIES SHIFT . . . and now trail the Yankees by two in the all-important lost column. . . . *He's better
than his brother Joe—Domi-nic DiMaggio!* . . . RADATZ IN
NINETEENTH RELIEF STINT . . . and if Pesky takes the ball over his

right shoulder, Enos is dead, I'm telling you . . . GOODMAN NEARS BAT CROWN . . . Fenway scribes stated that Ted's refusal to doff his cap is nothing less than . . . HIGGINS SEES PENNANT WITHIN TWO YEARS . . . and Doc Cramer's shotgun arm *just* fails to cut down Averill at third . . . DID NOT SPIT, KID SWEARS . . . the aging shortstop-manager, lately known in the press box as The Ancient Mariner ('who stoppeth one in three') . . . ZARILLA TRADE STRENGTHENS O.F. . . . *better than his brother Joe —Domi-nic DiMaggio!* . . . HIGGINS, REHIRED, VOWS . . . A bright spot in the Bosox seventh-place finish was Pete Runnels' consistent . . . TED FIRST A.L. SLUGGER TO TOP .400 SINCE . . . but Schilling dropped the ball . . . delicious Narragansett Ale. So, *hi*, neigh-bor . . . and Keller matched Gordon's awesome poke over the inviting left-field screen with . . . MALZONE TRADE RUMORS DENIED . . . and Slaughter, running all the way, beat the startled Pesky's hurried . . . CRONIN, NEW MGR, VOWS . . . the hotly fought junior-circuit gonfalon . . . FOXX NEARS SWAT MARK . . . as Slaughter crosses the plate. . . ."

By Memorial Day, the Red Sox were only a game above the .500 level, but Manager Williams and the front office had seen enough signs of life on the field to decide that their young enlistees would benefit from the assistance of some experienced noncoms. Successive deals in June brought Gary Bell, a strong right-handed starter, from the Indians and infielder Jerry Adair from the White Sox. Later in the summer, Elston Howard was bought from the Yankees to help behind the plate, and then Ken Harrelson, a brash, hot-dog outfielder with the Kansas City Athletics, signed aboard for a large bonus, after having so enraged the owner of the A's, Charles O. Finley, during a squabble that Finley threw him over the side.

Just before the All Star Game, in mid-July, Lonborg ended a five-game losing streak with a 3–0 shutout over the Tigers. Dick Williams said that this game marked Lonborg's arrival as a great pitcher, but it is likely that Lonborg's immense subsequent season was more the result of his decision in spring training to throw an occasional fast ball in the direction of the hitters' chins. "Keep count of how many batters I hit this year," Lonborg whispered to a sportswriter in April. Lonborg also kept count himself, recording the plunkees in ink on the back of his glove, like a fighter pilot pasting confirmed-kill decals on his plane's fusilage. The final bag came to nineteen, with several dozen near-misses, and the message got around the league that Lonborg was no longer a fine, friendly fellow to swing against. He finished the year with twenty-two wins, nine losses, and two hundred and forty-five strikeouts. Meanwhile, pitchers like Bell, Lee Stange, and José Santiago began showing signs of equal obduracy. Petrocelli, Conigliaro, and Yastrzemski were all off to fine seasons, the rookies Andrews and Smith proved to be quick and unflappable, and Dick Williams established his directorship once and for all by benching George Scott during three essential games because he was overweight. Late in July, the Sox won ten straight games, came home from a road trip in second place, and were met at Logan Airport by ten thousand true believers.

I refused to believe what was happening. Unpleasantly cool, I told Boston friends to keep their eyes on the other teams—the White Sox, who were clinging to first place on the strength of nothing but a fine pitching staff and some hilarious needling of the opposition by their manager, Eddie Stanky; the Twins, obviously the class of the league, who were just beginning their move; and the Tigers, who showed signs at last of wanting the pennant they had seemed capable of winning for the past two years. Then, too, I was waiting for the Red Sox bad break—the moment of ill fortune, the undeserved loss, that so often cracks the heart of a young team playing over its head. The break came on August 18 and was infinitely worse than I had imagined. A fast ball thrown by the Angels' Jack Hamilton struck Tony Conigliaro on the cheekbone, finishing him for the season. In that instant, the Sox lost their right fielder, a bat that had already delivered twenty home runs and sixty-seven runs batted in, and the

only man on the team who could fill the key fourth spot in the
batting order. In a few days, I could see, the Red Sox would . . .
In the next few days, the Red Sox overcame an 0–8 deficit in
one game and won it, 9–8, jumped off on what proved to be a
seven-game winning streak, and climbed from fourth place to
within one game of the Twins and White Sox, at the top. I gave
up; from that week on, I belonged.

Even to neutralists, the last weeks of the American League race
must have seemed excessive. On any given evening late in August, knowing the leader often depended on which edition of the
papers one happened to buy. In the first week of September, the
four teams reshuffled themselves nervously, the Red Sox lost
three games without giving up much ground, and on Labor Day
at Yankee Stadium Eddie Stanky had to tackle one of his infielders, Pete Ward, to keep him from punching an umpire and thus
being ruled off the turf for the rest of the way. On September 7,
there was a four-way tie for first. My baseball nerves had grown
too raw to permit me to keep out of it, and a few days later I
flew west to see the four top teams in action. When I arrived in
Chicago on September 16, the Twins, Red Sox, and Tigers were
still even-up, and the White Sox, who had slipped a trifle, were
making up lost ground brilliantly. Two days before, they had
beaten the Indians with a tenth-inning grand-slam home run, and
the previous night they had won the first of a three-game series
with the Twins, which they had to sweep in order to stay alive.
That night, even the half-empty bleachers in White Sox Park (racial troubles on Chicago's South Side cut heavily into the White
Sox attendance this year) failed to diminish the wonderful baseball tension in the boxy old stadium. With two weeks to go, the
season had narrowed down to the point where each pitched ball
seemed heavy with omens, and spectators greeted the most routine enemy pop fly with nervous laughter and applause. The
Twins' ace, Dean Chance, was seeking his nineteenth win, and
after watching him jam the White Sox batters with his jumping

fast balls and low curves I concluded that I was in on a mismatch. Looking confident and workmanlike, the Twins loaded
the bases in the fifth on a hit batsman, a single, a sacrifice, and an
intentional walk. The White Sox pitcher, Tommy John, then
leaped anxiously after a hopper by Ted Uhlaender, managing
only to deflect it, and threw the ball past first, as two runs
scored. A third came in a moment later on a single, and a fourth
in the next inning on a home run by Bob Allison, which the Chicago outfielders studied in flight like junior astronomers. In the
bottom of the ninth, it was 4–1, Twins, and the crowd managed only a few imploring cheers for their dying banjo hitters.
The first Chicago batter, McCraw, singled, and took third on
Ron Hansen's single and Oliva's subsequent error in right. Cola-
vito then hit a perfect double-play ball, which manager Stanky or
some other deity caused to bound suddenly over the third baseman's head, scoring a run. Josephson, the catcher, now dropped
an unsurprising sacrifice bunt along the third-base line. Chance
pounced on it eagerly, dropped it, cuffed it, scuffled with it, patted it, and finally merely glared at it as it lay between his feet like
a kitten. The score was now 4–2, with none out and the bases
full, and wild bird cries rose into the night. Manager Stanky dispatched his third pinch-runner of the inning to first, and Wayne
Causey, batting in the pitcher's spot, came to the plate. Manager
Cal Ermer of the Twins called in Jim Kaat, who threw a wild
pitch, scoring a run and moving up the runners. Causey tied the
game with a fly to right. More strategy ensued. Worthington
came in to pitch. Smoky Burgess pinch-hit and was intentionally
passed, giving way to another pinch-runner. Buford was also
walked, to set up the force at all bases, and Pete Ward, the
twelfth Chicago player to appear in this one-third of an inning,
came to the plate. He had been hitless in his previous twenty-one
times at bat, but he lined the 2–2 pitch smartly off Killebrew's
glove and trotted to first, clapping his hands over his head all the
way, as the scoreboard rocket display went off. Afterward, in the
noisy Chicago clubhouse, I saw two Chicago coaches, Kerby Far-

rell and Marv Grissom, sitting silently side by side in front of their lockers. They had their pants and spikes off, their feet were propped up, and they were comfortably balancing paper cups of beer on their stomachs. Their seamed, down-home country faces were still alight with the game. As I passed, Farrell nodded his head once and said, "Hum-*dinger*."

The next day, a summery Sunday afternoon, Stanky got his sweep as Gary Peters shut out the Twins with four hits and won, 4—0. The cheerful family crowd got as much pleasure from the scoreboard as from the game; it showed the Tigers losing to Washington, and the Red Sox in the process of dropping their third straight to Baltimore. The Tigers now led Chicago by half a game and the Twins and Red Sox by one, and I passed the time during my flight to Detroit that night trying to fathom the recently announced schedule for postseason playoffs that might be needed to determine a winner; it listed eleven different possibilities for the teams and sites involved in two-way, three-way, or four-way playoffs. The World Series might never happen.

There was an enormous, noisy crowd the next night for the first of the Tigers' two-game series with Boston, and Tiger Stadium instantly justified its reputation as a hitters' park when the Red Sox jumped off to a three-run lead in the first. But no lead and no pitcher was safe for long on this particular evening; the hits flew through the night air like enraged deerflies, and the infielders seemed to be using their gloves mostly in self-defense. The Tigers tied it in the second with a cluster of hits, including a homer by Norm Cash, but the Red Sox instantly went one up, 4–3, after Yastrzemski's bullet-like single up the middle nearly nailed the second baseman on the ear. Cash's second homer retied it in the sixth, and then the rackety, exhausting contest seemed settled by Kaline's single and Northrup's double in the eighth, which put the home side in front for the first time. Just before that, though, in the Boston half of the eighth, there had been an extraordinary moment of baseball. With none out and Petrocelli at first and Dalton Jones on third, the Boston catcher, Russ Gibson, hit a sharp grounder to Dick McAuliffe at second. McAuliffe glanced over at third, freezing Jones there. Petrocelli, hoping for a rundown that would permit the run to score, stopped dead on the base path, and McAuliffe, ball in hand, ran him back toward first, tagged him, and stepped on the bag in time to retire Gibson for an unassisted double play at first base. No one in the park—at least, none of the ballplayers and none of the sportswriters—had ever seen a play like it.

Yastrzemski came up in the ninth with one out and none on. He already had two hits for the night, and was in the home stretch of an extraordinary season at the plate and in the field, which had made him the favorite to win the Most Valuable Player award in his league. Boston sportswriters, however, are famously unimpressionable, especially when the Red Sox are behind. "Go on!" one of them shouted bitterly from the press box at this moment. "Prove you're the MVP! Prove it to *me!* Hit a homer!" Yastrzemski hit a homer. In the tenth, Dalton Jones, a part-time infielder inserted in the Red Sox lineup that night only because he hits mysteriously well in Tiger Stadium, won it, 6–5, with another homer. There were some seven hundred members of the Polish National Alliance staying at my hotel, and the delegates' celebrations in the lobby that night made it clear that Yaz's homer, his fortieth of the year, had been voted the finest Polish-American achievement since Cornel Wilde wrote the "Polonaise Militaire."

The next evening's game, mercifully, was a more languid affair, in which the Tigers kept putting men on base and allowing them to die there. In the third, they hit three successive singles without issue. The Sox had managed one scratchy run in the early going, but the Tigers' fine left-hander, Mickey Lolich, was striking out Boston batters in clusters, and he seemed sure of his seventh straight win after Jim Northrup hit a prodigious two-run homer onto the roof, ninety feet above the right-field wall. Detroit loaded the bases in the eighth with none out but again failed to score, and its lead was somehow only 2–1 when Jerry Adair led off the Boston ninth with a single. Lolich, working like a man opening a basket of cobras, walked Yastrzemski, and then George Scott, after botching up two tries at a sacrifice, singled up the middle to tie it. Earl Wilson, the ace of the Detroit staff, came on in relief for the first time in the year, and gave up a sacrifice to Reggie Smith and an intentional pass to Jones. He then threw a wild pitch, and Yastrzemski sailed in from third. Gibson's fly scored Scott, who slid under Kaline's peg in a cloud of dust and unbelieving silence. Boston won the game, 4–2, and I came home with my first solid conviction about the pennant race: The Tigers could not win it.

No one, it appeared, wanted that pennant in the end. The four teams fell toward the wire in a flurry of failures, in one stretch losing ten out of twelve games against weaker clubs. With three days to go, the White Sox needed only wins against the Athletics and Senators to make up their one-game deficit. Chicago, pitching its two aces, Gary Peters and Joel Horlen, lost both ends of a doubleheader to Kansas City on Wednesday, and then fell out of the race when it lost to the Senators two nights later. That *coup de grâce* administered by the A's, a last-place club that had lost both its franchise and its manager in recent weeks, was an act of defiant pride that everyone in baseball, with the possible exception of Eddie Stanky, could admire. Three teams, then, for the final weekend. Minnesota, a game up on Boston, could eliminate the Red Sox by winning either of its two games at Fenway Park. The Tigers, facing two doubleheaders at home against the Angels, would gain at least a tie and a playoff by sweeping the four games.

There was perhaps less expectancy than gratitude in the enormous crowd that threw itself into Fenway Park that sunny Saturday. The possibility of winning two games from the Twins while the Tigers lost two looked to be beyond even New England hopes, but there was the plain joy of being there and seeing the old, low-roofed, country-style grandstand and the humpbacked bleachers choked with that enormous sitting and standing assemblage of zealots, all there to shout for the team that had given them such a summer. There was a flurry of governors and dignitaries behind the home dugout, and a much more interesting swarm of kids balanced precariously on top of an immense Old Grand Dad billboard across the street behind the left-field fence. That pale-green, too close fence looked dangerous today—a target for the Twins' Harmon Killebrew, who was tied with Yastrzemski for the home-run lead, at forty-three each.

Then the game began, and all the Twins looked dangerous. They scored an instant run off Santiago in the top of the first, and only a line drive out to the third baseman saved further damage. Jim Kaat, the Twins' enormous left-hander, struck out four of the first nine Boston batters, looking as formidable as he did two years ago, when he beat Sandy Koufax in a World Series game. Kaat's last strikeout, however, was an immense misfortune for the Twins, because he pulled a tendon in his pitching arm and was forced to leave the game. The import of this blow, however, was not immediately visible. Kaat's replacement, Jim Perry, went on fanning the home side, while Santiago continued his anxious-making practice of pitching into and barely out of fearsome difficulties.

It was still 1–0, Twins, when Reggie Smith led off the Boston fifth with a double to the left-field wall, and then Dalton Jones, pinch-hitting, was miraculously safe when his grounder to Carew suddenly leaped up and struck the second baseman in the face. Adair tied the game with a soft Texas leaguer. Yastrzemski then sent a low shot that went past the diving Killebrew but was fielded by Carew in short right. Perry, perhaps still brooding about Boston luck, failed to cover first, leaving no one for Carew to throw to, and the Sox led, 2–1. The Twins tied it in the sixth, but Perry vanished, necessarily, for a pinch-hitter, and George Scott bombed reliever Ron Kline's first pitch into the center-field stands. Baseball luck creates intolerable pressure in a close game, and in the seventh the pressure of the luck and the tie destroyed the Twins. Mike Andrews was safe on a topped roller that trickled about twenty feet toward third, and a moment later shortstop Zoilo Versalles dropped Kline's peg in the middle of an easy double play, making all hands safe. All hands then came home on Yastrzemski's homer off Jim Merritt, which landed beyond the bullpen, and the Red Sox players, leading by 6–2, attempted to pound their hero into biscuit dough as he returned to the dugout. The ensuing Fenway din was diminished only faintly when Killebrew hit a two-run homer over the screen in the ninth off Gary Bell, tying Yaz for the title and bringing the game back to 6–4. It ended that way, but I had to wait until almost nine o'clock that night before my hunch about the Tigers was rejustified, via TV, as they lost their second game. Now there was one day left.

There was no reticence in Boston the next day. A woman calling the Ritz-Carlton that morning suddenly found herself in conversation with the hotel telephone operator, who exclaimed, "What if the bases had been loaded when Killebrew hit that ball? My heart can't *stand* it!" Bad nerves took me to Fenway Park early, and on the way I spotted an empty hearse with a fresh "GO, Sox!" sticker on the rear bumper. At the ballpark, several hundred reporters could watch Ricky Williams, the manager's ten-year-old son, working out in uniform at first base during batting practice. I took this to be a last, brilliant managerial hunch by his father: Ricky had accompanied the squad during its all-winning road trip in July. "Look at him," Ken Harrelson said admiringly as the boy made a nifty, Gil Hodges pickup. "The kid has all the moves."

The big boys played the game, though—Chance against Lonborg—and the weight of it kept the crowd silent. The weight of it also seemed too much for the Red Sox. In the top of the first, Killebrew walked and Oliva doubled, and George Scott, relaying, threw the ball over the catcher's head for the first Minnesota run. In the third, there was another walk, and Yastrzemski let Killebrew's single into left field hop between his legs for an-

other error and another run. The Red Sox managed a hit in each
of the first four innings but could not advance the runners. Lonborg pitched on grimly, keeping the ball low. The immense
crowd was so quiet that one could hear the snarling and baying
of the Minnesota bench wolves between every pitch. The scoreboard reported Detroit ahead in its first game.

It was still 2–0 for the outlanders when Lonborg, leading off
the sixth, laid down a sudden bunt on the first pitch and hoofed
it out. Adair hit the next pitch through second. Dalton Jones
fouled off his first attempt at a sacrifice bunt and then, seeing Killebrew and Tovar, the third baseman, charging in like cavalry-
men, socked the next pitch past Tovar and into left, to load the
bases for Yaz with none out. The screeching in the park was almost insupportable: "*Go! Go!* GO!" Yastrzemski tied the game
with a single up the middle. When the count went to three and
two on Harrelson, Yaz took off with the pitch, arriving at second
just before Harrelson's high chopper got to Versalles behind the
bag; utterly unstrung, Versalles threw home, far too late to get
anybody. Dean Chance, unstrung, departed. Worthington, unstrung, came in and threw two wild pitches, letting in another
run. The fifth scored when Reggie Smith's hot grounder bounced
off the unstrung (or perhaps only unhappy) Killebrew's knee.

It was growing dark, but the dangerous season had one or two
moments left. Jerry Adair collided with the oncoming Versalles
on the base path in the eighth, but held on to the ball and flipped
out of the dust to first for a double play. The Twins, still fighting, followed with two singles. Allison then lined a hit to left;
Yastrzemski charged the ball, hesitated only an instant at the
sight of the runner racing for home, and then threw brilliantly to
second to cut down the flying Allison. You could see it all happening in the same twilight instant—the ball coming in a
deadly line, and Allison's desperate, skidding slide, and the tag,
and the umpire's arm shooting up, and the game and the season
saved. One more inning, and then there was nothing more to be
saved except Lonborg, who had to be extricated—sans sweat-

shirt, buttons, and cap—from the hands of the local citizenry, who evidently wanted to mount him in the State House beside the sacred cod.

The Boston locker room presented a classic autumn scene—shouts, embraces, beer showers, shaving cream in the hair, television lights, statements to the press. ("Never," said Lonborg, "do I remember a more . . . ecstatic and . . . *vigorous* moment.") But then it all sagged and stopped, for this was still only a half-triumph. Detroit had won its first game, and now we had to wait for the radio news of the second game to know whether this was the pennant or whether there would be a playoff with the Tigers the next afternoon.

During that long, painful interval in the clubhouse, there was time to look back on Yastrzemski's season. He had won the triple crown—a batting average of .326, a hundred and twenty-one runs batted in, forty-four homers—but this was not all. Other fine hitters, including Frank Robinson last season, had finished with comparable statistics. But no other player in memory had so clearly pushed a team to such a height in the final days of a difficult season. The Allison peg was typical of Yastrzemski's ardent outfield play. In the final two weeks at the plate, Yaz had hammered twenty-three hits in forty-four times at bat, including four doubles and five home runs, and had driven in sixteen runs. In those two games against the Twins, he went seven for eight and hit a game-winning homer. This sort of performance would be hard to countenance in a Ralph Henry Barbour novel, and I found it difficult to make the connection between the epic and the person of the pleasant, twenty-eight-year-old young man of unheroic dimensions who was now explaining to reporters, with articulate dispassion, that his great leap forward this year might have been the result of a small change in batting style—a blocking of the right hip and a slightly more open stance—which was urged on him in spring training by Ted Williams. There was something sad here—perhaps the thought that for Yastrzemski, more than for anyone else, this summer could not come again. He had become a famous star, with all the prizes and ugly burdens we force on the victims of celebrity, and from now on he would be set apart from us and his teammates and the easy time of his youth.

Detroit led for a while in its last game, and then the Angels caught up and went ahead, but the clubhouse maternity ward was an unhappy place. Players in bits and pieces of uniform pretended to play cards, pretended to sleep. Then, at last, it was the ninth inning, with the Angels leading, 8–5, and the Red Sox formed a silent circle, all staring up at the radio on the wall. The Tigers put men on base, and I could see the strain of every pitch on the faces around me. Suddenly there was a double-play ball that might end it, and when the announcer said, ". . . over to first, *in* time for the out," every one of the Boston players came off the floor and straight up into the air together, like a ballet troupe. Players and coaches and reporters and relatives and owner Yawkey and manager Williams hugged and shook hands and hugged again, and I saw Ricky Williams trying to push through the mob to get at his father. He was crying. He reached him at last and jumped into his arms and kissed him again and again; he could not stop kissing him. The champagne arrived in a giant barrel of ice, and for an instant I was disappointed with Mr. Yawkey when I saw that it was Great Western. But I had forgotten what pennant champagne is for. In two minutes, the clubhouse looked like a YMCA water-polo meet, and it was everybody into the pool.

Cardinal fans who have managed to keep their seats through this interminable first feature will probably not be placated by my delayed compliments to their heroes. The Cardinals not only were the best ball club I saw this season but struck me as being in many ways the most admirable team I can remember in recent years. The new champions have considerable long-ball power, but they know the subtleties of opposite-field hitting, base-running, and defense that are the delight of the game. Their quick-

ness is stimulating, their batting strength is distributed menac-
ingly throughout the lineup (they won the Series with almost no
help from their No. 4 and No. 5 hitters, Cepeda and McCarver,
while their seventh-place batter, Javier, batted .360), they are
nearly impregnable in up-the-middle defense, and their pitching
was strong enough to win them a pennant even though their ace,
Bob Gibson, was lost for the second half of the season after his
right leg was broken by a line drive. In retrospect, the wonder of
the Series is that the Cards did not make it a runaway, as they so
often seemed on the point of doing.

Fenway Park was a different kind of place on the first day of
the Series. Ceremonies and bunting and boxfuls of professional
Series-goers had displaced the anxious watchers of the weekend.
Yastrzemski, staring behind the dugout before the game, said,
"Where *is* everybody? These aren't the people who were here all
summer." The game quickly produced its own anxieties, however, when Lou Brock, the Cardinals' lead-off man, singled in the
first and stole second on the next pitch. Though we did not recognize it, this was only a first dose of what was to follow
throughout the Series, for Brock was a tiny little time pill that
kept going off at intervals during the entire week. He failed to
score that time, but he led off the third with another single,
zipped along to third on Flood's double, and scored on Maris's
infield out. The Cardinals kept threatening to extinguish Santiago, the Red Sox starter, but bad St. Louis luck and good Boston fielding kept it close. Gibson, hardly taking a deep breath between pitches, was simply overpowering, throwing fast balls past
the hitters with his sweeping right-handed delivery, which he finishes with a sudden lunge toward first base. He struck out six of
the first ten batters to face him and seemed unaffronted when
Santiago somehow got his bat in the path of one of his pitches
and lofted the ball into the screen in left center. It was a one-
sided but still tied ball game when Brock led off the seventh (he
was perpetually leading off, it seemed) with another single, stole
second again, went to third on an infield out, and scored on

Roger Maris's deep bouncer to second. That 2–1 lead was
enough for Gibson, who blew the Boston batters down; he struck
out Petrocelli three times, on ten pitches. The crowd walking out
in the soft autumn sunshine seemed utterly undisappointed. They
had seen their Sox in a Series game at last, and that was enough.

Five members of the Red Sox had signed up to write byline
stories about the Series for the newspapers, and Jim Lonborg, not
yet ready to pitch after his Sunday stint, kept notes for his column as he sat on the bench during the opener. He must have remembered to look at those earlier memoranda on his glove, however, for his first pitch of the second game flew rapidly in the
suddenly vacated environs of Lou Brock's neck. It was Lonborg's
only high pitch of the afternoon, and was fully as effective in its
own way as the knee-high curves and sinking fast balls he threw
the rest of the way. None of the Cardinals reached first until
Flood walked in the seventh, and by that time Yastrzemski had
stroked a curving drive into the seats just past the right-field foul
pole for one run, and two walks and an error had brought in another for the Beantowners. There were marvelous fielding plays
by both teams—Brock and Javier for the Cards, Petrocelli and
Adair for the Sox—to keep the game taut, and then Yaz, who
had taken extra batting practice right after the first game, hit another in the seventh: a three-run job, way, *way* up in the bleachers. After that, there was nothing to stay for except the excruciating business of Lonborg's possible no-hitter. He was within four
outs of it when Javier doubled, solidly and irretrievably, in the
eighth, to the accompaniment of a 35,188-man groan. (Lonborg
said later that it felt exactly like being in an automobile wreck.)
When Lonborg came in after that inning, the crowd stood and
clapped for a long, respectful two minutes, like the audience at a
Horowitz recital.

Everyone in St. Louis was ready for the third game except the
scoreboard-keeper, who initially had the Cardinals playing Detroit. More than fifty-four thousand partisans, the biggest sport-

ing crowd in local history, arrived early at Busch Memorial Stadium, most of them bearing heraldic devices honoring "El Birdos"—a relentlessly publicized neologism supposedly coined by Orlando Cepeda. Home-town pride was also centered on El Ballparko, a steep, elegant gray concrete pile that forms part of the new downtown complex being built around the celebrated Saarinen archway. I admired everything about this open-face mine except its shape, which is circular and thus keeps all upper-deck patrons at a dismaying distance from the infielders within the right angles of the diamond. The game, like its predecessors, went off like a pistol, with Lou Brock tripling on the first pitch of the home half. After two innings, Gary Bell, the Boston starter, was allowed to sit down, having given up five hits and three runs to the first nine Cardinal batters. That was the ball game, it turned out (the Cards won, 5–2), but there were some memorable diversions along the way. Nelson Briles, the Cards' starter, decked Yastrzemski in the first with a pitch that nailed him on the calf. Lou Brock, having led off the sixth with a single, got himself plunked in the back with a justifiably nervous pick-off throw by pitcher Lee Stange, and chugged along to third, from where he scored on a single by Maris. *L'affaire Yaz* was the subject of extended seminars with the press after the game. St. Louis Manager Red Schoendienst stated that inside pitches were part of the game but that his little band of clean-living Americans did not know how to hit batters on purpose. Pitcher Briles stated that the sight of Yastrzemski caused him to squeeze the ball too hard and thus lose control of its direction. (He had improved afterward, not walking a man all day.) Manager Williams pointed out that a pitcher wishing to hit a batter, as against merely startling him, will throw not at his head but behind his knees, which was the address on Briles' special-delivery package. This seemed to close the debate locally, but that night the publisher of the Manchester, New Hampshire, *Union Leader* wrote an editorial demanding that the Cardinals be forced to forfeit the game, "as an indication that the great American sport of baseball will not allow itself to be besmirched by anyone who wants to play dirty ball."

The great American sport survived it all, but it almost expired during the next game, a 6–0 laugher played on a windy, gray winter afternoon. The Cardinals had all their runs after the first three innings, and the only man in the park who found a way to keep warm was Brock, who did it by running bases. He beat out a third-base tap in the first and went on to score, and subsequently doubled off the wall and stole another base. Gibson, the winner, was not as fast as he had been in the opener, but his shutout won even more admiration from the Red Sox batters, who had discovered that he was not merely a thrower but a pitcher.

The Red Sox, now one game away from extinction, looked doomed after that one, but Yastrzemski pointed out to me that most of his teammates, being in their early twenties, had the advantage of not recognizing the current odds against them. "Lonborg goes tomorrow," he said, "and then it's back to Boston, back to the lion's den." Lonborg went indeed, in a marvelously close and absorbing game, that I watched mostly through Kleenex, having caught a pip of a cold in the winter exercises of the previous day. The Red Sox won, 3–1; two former Yankees settled it. In the Boston ninth, Elston Howard, who can no longer get his bat around on fast balls, looped a dying single to right to score two runs—a heartwarming and, it turned out, essential piece of luck, because Roger Maris hit a homer in the bottom half, to end Lonborg's string of seventeen scoreless innings. Maris, freed from his recent years of Yankee Stadium opprobrium, was having a brilliant Series.

Laid low by too much baseball and a National League virus, I was unable to make it back to the lion's den, and thus missed the noisiest and most exciting game of the Series. I saw it on television, between sneezes and commercials. This was the game, it will be recalled, in which the Red Sox led by 1–0, trailed by 2–1, rallied to 4–2, were tied at 4–4, and won finally, 8–4, burying the Cardinal relief pitchers with six hits and four runs in the seventh. Brock had a single, a stolen base, and a home run. Yastrzemski had two singles and a left-field homer. Reggie Smith hit a homer; Rico Petrocelli hit *two* homers. This was the first Series game since the Cardinal-Yankee encounters in 1964 in which any team rallied to recapture a lost lead, which may account for the rather stately nature of most of the recent fall classics. My admiration went out not only to the Red Sox, for evening the Series after being two games down, but to Dick Williams, for having the extraordinary foresight to start a young pitcher named Gary Waslewski, who had spent most of the season in the minors, had not started a Boston game since July 29, and had never completed a game in the major leagues. Waslewski didn't finish this one, either, but he held the Cards off until the sixth, which was enough. Williams' choice, which would have exposed him to venomous second-guessing if it had backfired, is the kind of courageous, intelligent patchworking that held his young, lightly manned team together over such an immense distance. In the opinion of a good many baseball people, his managerial performance this year is the best since Leo Durocher's miracles with the Giants in the early nineteen-fifties.

Nothing could keep me away from the final game of the year, the obligatory scene in which Lonborg, on only two days' rest, would face Gibson at last. Fenway Park, packed to the rafters, seemed so quiet in the early innings that I at first attributed the silence to my stuffed-up ears. It was real, though—the silence of foreboding that descended on all of us when Lou Brock hit a long drive off Lonborg in the first, which Yastrzemski just managed to chase down. Lonborg, when he is strong and his fast ball is dipping, does not give up high-hit balls to enemy batters in the early going. After that, everyone sat there glumly and watched it happen. Maxvill, the unferocious Cardinal shortstop, banged a triple off the wall in the third and then scored, and another run ensued when Lonborg uncorked a wild pitch. In time, it grew merely sad, and almost the only sounds in the park were the cries and horns from Cardinal owner Gussie Busch's box, next to the St. Louis dugout. Lonborg, pushing the ball and trying so hard that at times his cap flew off, gave up a homer to Gibson in the fifth, and then Brock singled, stole second, stole third, and came in on a fly by Maris. A fire broke out in a boxcar parked on a railway siding beyond left field, and several dozen sportswriters, looking for their leads, scribbled the note, ". . . as Boston championship hopes went up in smoke." Manager Williams, out of pitchers and ideas, stayed too long with his exhausted hero, and Javier hit a three-run homer in the sixth to finish Lonborg and end the long summer's adventure. The final score was 7–2. Gibson, nearly worn out at the end, held on and finished, winning his fifth successive Series victory (counting two against the Yankees in 1964), and the Cardinals had the championship they deserved. I visited both clubhouses, but I had seen enough champagne and emotion for one year, and I left quickly. Just before I went out to hunt for a cab, though, I ducked up one of the runways for a last look around Fenway Park, and discovered several thousand fans still sitting in the sloping stands around me. They sat there quietly, staring out through the half-darkness at the littered, empty field and the big wall and the bare flagpoles. They were mourning the Red Sox and the end of the great season.

A Little Noise at Twilight

Some years ago, during a spell of hot-stove mooning for summer and baseball, I jotted down on a slip of yellow paper the names and batting averages of the top National League hitters in the year 1930. I have carried the slip in my wallet ever since, and on occasion, when comfortably surrounded with fellow baseball bores, I produce it. While being unmemorable in every other way, 1930 was a hitters' year. The combined National League batting average was .303, and the top finishers, all full-time regulars, were:

Bill Terry	.401
Babe Herman	.393
Chuck Klein	.386
Lefty O'Doul	.383
Freddy Lindstrom	.379
Paul Waner	.368
Riggs Stephenson	.367
Lloyd Waner	.362
Kiki Cuyler	.355

During the season just past, which concluded with the Detroit Tigers' stimulating seven-game, come-from-behind victory over the Cardinals in the World Series, I reread this list often, with a deepening incredulity; once an oddity (attributable in part to the jackrabbit ball), it suddenly had become a document of almost paleographic significance—a record of another sport, now clearly gone forever. The 1968 season has been named the Year of the Pitcher, which is only a kinder way of saying the Year of the Infield Pop-Up. The final records only confirm what so many fans, homeward bound after still another shutout, had already discovered for themselves; almost no one, it seemed, could hit the damn ball any more. The two leagues' combined batting average of .236 was the lowest ever—four points below even the .240 compiled by the Mets in 1962, their first year of hilarious ineptitude. This year, there were three hundred and forty shutout games, as against a hundred and ninety-nine in 1962, and 1994 home runs, as against 3001. Only five National League batters finished over the .300 mark, and only one batter—Carl Yastrzemski—in the American; his average of .3005 was the lowest ever to win a batting title. Baseball owners and other positive thinkers will find more joy in studying these statistics from the pitcher's mound, from which direction 1968 becomes a year of triumph. Denny McLain, of the Tigers, won thirty-one games and lost six, thus becoming the first thirty-game winner since 1934. Bob Gibson's earned-run average of 1.12 was the lowest in the history of the National League. Don Drysdale ran off a record fifty-eight and one-third scoreless innings; a Mets rookie named Jerry Koosman pitched seven shutouts; Gaylord Perry, of the Giants, and Ray Washburn, of the Cardinals, threw no-hitters on consecutive days in the same ballpark; and there was only a minimal stir when a journeyman hurler, Catfish Hunter, of Oakland, achieved that ultimate rarity, a perfect game—no runs, no hits, no one on base, twenty-seven up and twenty-seven out.

Adding up zeros is not the most riveting of spectator sports and by mid-July this year it was plain to even the most inattentive or optimistic fans that something had gone wrong with their game. Why were the pitchers so good? Where were the .320 hitters? What had happened to the high-scoring slugfest, the late rally, the bases-clearing double? The answers to these questions are difficult and speculative, but some attempt must be made at them before we proceed to the releasing but somewhat irrelevant pleasures of the World Series. To begin with: Yes, the pitchers are better—or, rather, *pitching* is better. All the technical and strategic innovations of recent years have helped the defenses of baseball; none have favored the batter. Bigger ballparks with bigger outfields, the infielders' enormous crab-claw gloves, more night games, the mastery of the relatively new slider pitch, the persistence of the relatively illegal spitter, and the instantaneous managerial finger-wag to the bullpen at the first hint of an enemy rally have all tipped the balance of this delicately balanced game. Less obvious, perhaps, is the fact that that young relief pitcher motoring in from the bullpen in a golf cart is significantly different from the man who walked the same distance twenty or thirty years ago, and so is the pitcher he is replacing on the mound. Like all young athletes, they are an inch or two taller and twenty or thirty pounds heavier than their counterparts of a generation ago, and they throw the ball harder. The batter waiting in the on-deck circle is also enormous, but all that heredity and orange juice are going to be of no help to him if he can't meet the ball with his bat. And here, precisely, the batter is most disadvantaged, for hitting has nothing much to do with size or strength but is almost wholly a matter of reflexes. A number of thoughtful students of athletics, including Ted Williams, consider hitting a baseball to be the most difficult reflex—the hardest single act —in all sports.

Almost any strong and passably coordinated young man can learn to pitch, but batting is not generally teachable; even after a lifetime in the game, most pitchers still swing like their old aunties. The solid-gold reflex of the natural hitter is capable of some polishing, but only through many years of practice. There was a time when American boys so endowed spent most of their afternoons playing nothing but baseball, yearned only after a career in baseball, and, once signed, spent at least three years in the minors learning their trade—that is, learning to hit. All this is changed. Boys have more afternoon diversions, many of which do not require seventeen companions and an empty sandlot, and baseball must now compete with pro football, basketball, and golf in signing up the best teen-age athletes. Even if the young phenom does choose baseball, he no longer enjoys the same lengthy apprenticeship. Expansion and television have dried up most of the minor leagues, and the baseball draft now makes it impossible for the parent club to train and protect a promising young slugger down in Rochester or El Paso for more than two years. Hurried through the minors, brushed up in the winter instructional leagues, the would-be Gehringer or Musial suddenly finds himself in the batter's box in a big-league park, where he is expected to begin repaying at once the investment of his owners and the hopes of the fans. Unsurprisingly, he pops up.

Baseball executives might disagree with some of these observations, or place a different emphasis or interpretation on others, but it is difficult to believe that they are totally unaware of the problem itself. Yet their decisions in this decade not only have ignored the imbalance and the decline in quality of baseball but have directly and profoundly worsened it. The expansion of big-league baseball was inevitable and perhaps defensible, but the addition of two new teams to each eight-team league in 1962 permanently watered the quality of the game; the new teams were not permitted anything like a fair share of the available talent, and none of them have yet risen to full contention in their leagues. Since that time, of course, all twenty teams have had to scout and bid in a player market tightened by 25 per cent more buyers. At this moment, four new teams are being created—Montreal and San Diego in the National League and Kansas City and Seattle in the American—and both leagues next year will be divided into six-team Eastern and Western divisions. Every team will play an unbalanced schedule—eighteen games against each team in its own division and twelve against each team in the other division; the divisional champions in each league will meet in three-out-of-five-game autumn playoffs to determine the pennant winners and World Series participants.

However neatly or awkwardly this complex plan works in practice, and however rich a revenue the existing clubs will derive at
once from the price of the new franchises and the attendance of
fans in the new cities, there should be no illusions about the stat-
ure of the new teams or the true quality of the leagues. Each existing club lost six players to the new teams in the draft just concluded, but sympathy should be reserved for the fans of the
Expos, the Padres, the Royals, and the Pilots, who will have to
watch these stitched-together, rivet-necked monsters in action
next year. The rosters of the new clubs have been assembled out
of culls and spare parts—the sixteenth, twentieth, twenty-
fourth, twenty-eighth, thirty-second, and thirty-sixth best ballplayers on each present club. One-third of all the players in the
majors next April would have been minor-leaguers in unex-
panded baseball.

A few owners have opposed expansion for precisely these reasons, but the majority are executives caught up in the old business fiction that says bigger is better. Their usual defense against
charges of greed and shortsightedness is a dictum first pro-
pounded by Branch Rickey in the nineteen-fifties, which postu-
lated that the increase in national population guaranteed an increase in the number of first-class ballplayers, thus justifying
expansion. This year's batting averages do not support the
theory, for reasons I have suggested, and neither do the sharply
declining attendance figures in the parks of some famous old
teams that have not been in recent pennant contention. The new
expansion, in the owners' dreams, will remedy the attendance
anemia, particularly in September, by doubling the number of
pennant races and adding two new playoff extravaganzas before
the Series itself. The scheduling of these playoffs means that baseball will now be extended into mid-October, and that there will
be three full weekends of national television coverage right in the
heart of the professional-football season. Clearly, the conservative
owners—the non-expansionists—never had a chance. It is expected that baseball fans will somehow not notice that the new

playoffs will make most of the long baseball season meaningless, and that the fans will accept at once a system that, had it been in effect this year, would have required the Detroit Tigers to qualify for the Series by winning a playoff against the sixth-place Oakland Athletics, who finished twenty-one games behind them in the standings.

The World Series just past carried an extraordinary burden of hopes. It was counted on to make up for everything—not only the deadly zeros of the Year of the Pitcher but the bad luck of two one-sided pennant races, whose winners were virtually decided by mid-July. This last pre-inflationary, pre-playoff Series meant the end of something, and there was pleasure in the knowledge that both champions represented ancient baseball capitals that had flown a total of eighteen previous pennants. Many of us could remember the last Tiger-Cardinal Series, in 1934, which went seven memorable games and concluded in a riot of acrimony and garbage. Each of the current rivals presented deep, experienced, and exciting teams, whose individual attributes were admirably designed for the dimensions of their home parks— the Cardinals, the defending world champions, quick on the bases, brilliant in defense, knowing in the subtleties of cutoff, sacrifice, and hit-and-run; the Tigers a band of free-swingers who had bashed a hundred and eighty-one homers and could eschew the delicate touch in the knowledge that their runs would come, probably late and in clusters. At almost every position, there were dead-even matchups of ability and reputation. Curt Flood and Mickey Stanley were the best center fielders in their leagues, and Tim McCarver and Bill Freehan the best catchers; Roger Maris, retiring this winter, would play opposite Al Kaline, now in his sixteenth year with the Tigers, who had finally been rewarded for his refusal ever to attend a Series except as a participant; at first base, Orlando Cepeda and Norm Cash presented faded but still formidable reputations as game-busting clean-up hitters. Best of all, the opening game (and probably the key fourth and seventh games) would offer what few sportswriters could resist calling a "meaningful confrontation" between Bob Gibson, the best pitcher in baseball, and Denny McLain, who had won more games in a season than anyone since Lefty Grove. With squads like these, neither Manager Red Schoendienst nor Manager Mayo Smith had been called on through the season to attempt more than minimal prestidigitation. Then, on the eve of the Series, Smith announced that he was moving Mickey Stanley to shortstop, a position he had played in only eight games in the majors. Some sort of shuffle like this was inescapable, because room had to be found in the outfield for Kaline, who had been injured too often of late to hold down a regular spot, but Mayo's switch offered the heady possibility of disaster every time a ball was hit to the left side of the Tiger infield.

A sellout crowd of 54,692 turned out at St. Louis's Busch Stadium for the meaningful confrontation. The meanings were there, if hard to decipher immediately. Gibson fanned two batters in the first, but he threw a lot of pitches and looked less imperious than he had against the Red Sox last fall. In the second, though, he settled into his astonishing, flailing delivery, which he finishes with a running lunge toward the first-base line, and struck out the side on eleven pitches. After four innings, he had eight strikeouts—halfway toward a new Series record. McLain, who stands hunchily on the mound, like an Irish middleweight in his ring corner, was mostly high and wild. He gave up an enormous triple to Tim McCarver in the second, but Mike Shannon and Julian Javier were too eager to nail his chin-level fast balls and went down swinging. McLain escaped again in the next inning, when Lou Brock was stranded at third after stealing second and sailing along to third when catcher Bill Freehan's abysmal throw bounced behind the pitcher and on into center field. Freehan was known to have an ailing arm, but this frail peg promised something like a free visa to all bases for the Cards' winged messengers. In the fourth, Maris and McCarver both walked on four pitches, and this time Shannon and Javier waited for pitches in the strike zone and then hit singles, good enough for three runs, because Willy Horton misplayed Shannon's hit in left, moving up the runners. They were also good enough for the ball game. McLain vanished after the fifth, Brock hit a loud but superfluous homer in the seventh, and then there was nothing to watch but Gibson setting the new Series record of seventeen strikeouts.

It made memorable watching—not just the three last batters whiffed in the ninth but a whole lineup of fine hitters utterly dominated and destroyed by the man on the mound. Gibson worked so fast that I was constantly falling behind the actual ball-and-strike count. His concentration was total. Not once, it seemed, did he look at his outfielders, tug at his cap, twitch his sleeve; he didn't even rub up the new ball after a foul. The instant he got his sign, he rocked, flailed, threw, staggered, put up his glove for the catcher's throw back, and was ready again. He threw more curves than expected—good, sharp-breaking, down stuff—and though he always seemed to be working at a peak of energy, he had reserves when needed. In the sixth, after Dick McAuliffe singled with one out, he fanned Stanley on three pitches, and when Kaline then doubled down the left-field line he fanned Cash on five. He was tired by the ninth, and he had to throw twenty-eight pitches to four batters (Stanley singled, leading off), yet the count never went above two balls on any of them. Kaline went down swinging at a fast ball, which tied Sandy Koufax's old Series record of fifteen strikeouts, and then, after many fouls, Gibson got Cash on a beautiful half-speed curve that may have been the best pitch of the game, and Horton on a called third strike that just nicked the back inside corner. Afterward, in the clubhouse, the Tigers sounded like survivors of the Mount Pelée disaster. "I was awed," said McLain. "I was *awed*." McAuliffe, asked to compare Gibson with some pitcher in his league, said, "There is no comparison. He doesn't remind me of anybody. He's all by himself." Gibson proved just as difficult for the reporters as he had for the batters. He is a proud, edgy, intelligent, and sensitive man, very aware of his blackness and all its contemporary meanings. He could stand in front of a circle of fifty reporters and say something impossible, like "I'm never surprised at anything I do," without making it seem anything less or more than truth. He smiled briefly when someone asked him if he had always been deeply competitive. "I guess you could say so," he said. "I've played a couple of hundred games of ticktacktoe with my little daughter, and she hasn't beaten me yet. I've always had to win. I've got to win."

The next day's baseball was of more human proportions. Detroit's starter, Mickey Lolich, is a swaybacked, thick-waisted left-hander whose sinker ball becomes more difficult to hit as he grows tired in late innings. This curious propensity may account for his near invulnerability in late-season ball; by midsummer this year he was reduced to bullpen work, but his record after August 6 was ten wins and two losses. Here, he fell into difficulties in the first, and was saved from immediate extinction only by Al Kaline's long gallop to right, where he grabbed Cepeda's foul drive just before crashing into and disappearing through an unlocked field gate. The Tiger batters, perhaps relieved at being able to see what they were swinging at, were doing a lot of first-ball hitting, and, in the second, Willy Horton sailed Nelson Briles's first delivery deep into the left-field seats, to the accompaniment of a long, low moan of pain from the local partisans. The only sounds that greeted Lolich's modest round-tripper in the third were hilarious cries from the Detroit bench, for it was his first home run in ten years of professional ball. In the sixth, Norm Cash made it three homers, three runs, and then the Tigers added a pair more modestly, on two singles, a walk, and Dick McAuliffe's low drive to center that skidded off Curt Flood's glove. Lou Brock twice stole second, but Lolich's only anxieties were suddenly eased when, with one run in and two men on base in the sixth, Mickey Stanley flew to his right to seize Shannon's grounder and begin a nifty double play. Mayo Smith's alchemy had produced gold. The Tigers won, 8–1, and the teams moved on to Detroit even up.

After twenty-three years without a pennant, and perhaps a decade without any good news of any description, Detroit could almost be forgiven for its susceptibility to the worst kind of baseball fever—the fence ripped down at the airport by the mob
welcoming the team home; the billboards crying "Tigertown,
U.S.A."; the tiger-striping on dresses, hats, suits, menus, and
street crossings; the prefixative "our" before every mention of the
team in the papers; and the "Sock It to 'Em, Tigers!" motto,
with excruciating variations ("Soc et Tuum, Tigres!" "Duro con
Ellos, Tigres!"), in every bar and department-store window. The
fever reached a critical point in the third inning of the home
opener, when Kaline lined a two-run homer into the top left-field
deck of the boxy old canoe-green stadium, and then it plummeted rapidly as the weather and the ball game turned icy cold.
Curiously, though the Tigers led for almost half of the going,
only the Cardinals looked dangerous, and no one was much surprised when they went ahead at last and won it, 7–3. Brock
had stolen second in the top of the first, but was nailed at third as
Maris fanned. He came up again in the third, singled, stole again,
and was stranded. A Cardinal double steal went awry in the
fourth, when McCarver was thrown out at third on a close call,
but the angry shouting from the Cardinal bench suggested that
this kind of teetery, edge-of-the-cliff shutout could not be sustained for long. Brock singled to lead off the fifth and again
helped himself to second; it was his fifth straight time on base in
two games, and his fifth straight steal of second. Earl Wilson, the
Detroit starter, was by now in an understandably poor state of
nerves, and after he gave up a run-scoring double to Flood and a
walk to Maris he was excused for the afternoon. A moment or
two later, McCarver hit a three-run homer off Pat Dobson, to
put the Cards ahead for good. Ray Washburn, the Cardinal
pitcher, also departed, after a homer to McAuliffe in the fifth and
two walks in the sixth, but the reliever, Joe Hoerner, stopped the
Tigers, and then Cepeda, emerging from an autumn hibernation

that had stretched back through three World Series, hit a low liner in the seventh that just reached the left-field seats, to score the last three runs and conclude the arctic maneuvers.

Sunday's game, played in a light-to-heavy Grand Banks rainstorm and won by the Cardinals, 10–1, offered several lessons, all of them unappreciated by the Tigertowners. (1) Lou Brock does not always steal second. He led off the game with a homer, tripled and scored in the fourth, grounded out in the sixth, and then doubled and stole *third* in the eighth. It was his seventh stolen base of the Series, tying the record he set last year against Boston. He was at this point batting .500 in the Series and .387 for eighteen Series games, going back to 1964. (2) Some meaningful confrontations are meaningless. McLain met Gibson again, and was gone after two and two-thirds innings, having surrendered four runs and six hits. He turned out to have a sore shoulder, and might not be seen again in the Series. Gibson stayed for his customary nine (he was not knocked out of the box once this season), gave up a home run to Jim Northrup, hit a home run himself, and struck out ten batters without the benefit this day of a reliable curve ball. (3) There are several ways to try to delay a ball game, and just as many to try to speed it up. When rain interrupted matters for an hour and a quarter in the third, with the Cardinals ahead, 4–0, the bleacherites set up a chant of "Rain! Rain! Rain!" hoping for a postponement. This didn't work, so in the fourth and fifth, with the score now 6–1, the Tigers tried their own methods—long pauses for spike-digging and hand-blowing by the batters, managerial conferences, and inexplicable trips to the dugout, all conducted while they glanced upward for signs of the final and reprieving deluge. Willy Horton even feigned an error, dropping a fly by Shannon that he had already caught, but the umpire would have none of it. Meanwhile, the Cardinals, fully as anxious to reach the legal limit of five innings as the Tigers were to avoid it, gave their special and highly secret steal-but-steal-*slow* sign to Cepeda and Javier in successive innings; both runners, looking like Marcel Marceau's mime of a

man running while standing still, were thrown out, and the game
eventually went into the books. (4) Some baseball games that
should not be played because of terrible weather are played anyway, especially if they happen to be Series games televised by
NBC on prime Sunday-afternoon time.

At this point, with four one-sided games gone and the Tigers
facing imminent deletion, the strongest memories this Series had
brought forth were of last year's long rouser between the Cards
and the Red Sox. The Sock It to 'Ems filing into their seats for
the fifth game looked distraught, for the papers that morning had
informed them that only two clubs had ever recovered from a
one-three Series deficit. Surprisingly, the Tigers themselves, gathered around the cage during batting practice, seemed in remarkable fettle for a group apparently awaiting only the executioner's
blindfold. Norm Cash was telling George Kell, a retired Tiger
demigod, that he had just figured out how to hit Gibson. "It's
like duck-shooting," he said. "You gotta *lead* the goddam bird.
When he's up here [he imitated Gibson at the top of his
windup], you gotta start swinging. Pow!" Northrup, in the cage,
laced a long fly to right, and several Tigers, watching the ball,
cried, "*Get* out of here!" Northrup then broke two bats on two
swings and was urged to open a lumberyard. There was some
giggling over Vice-President Humphrey's visit to the Tiger clubhouse after the previous game. "He kept *congratulating* everybody," Dick Tracewski said. " 'Congratulations! We're proud of
you.' I mean, didn't he see the game? Didn't he see us get
pasted?" "Maybe he thought he was in the other clubhouse,"
someone suggested.

I concluded that these high spirits among the losers were induced only by anticipation of their coming winter holiday, a
hunch that appeared swiftly verified when the Cards teed off on
Lolich in the top of the first—a double by Brock, a single by
Flood, and a homer by Cepeda. The stands fell into a marmoreal
hush, and the cheering in the third when Freehan, on a pitchout,
finally threw out Brock stealing had a bitter edge to it. But then,

in the Tiger fourth, Mickey Stanley's lead-off drive to right
landed a quarter-inch fair, and he wound up on third. Kaline was
decked by Nelson Briles's inside pitch, but the ball trickled off
his bat and he was out at first. Cash scored Stanley on a fly, and
then Willy Horton bashed a triple to deepest right center field.
Northrup's hard grounder right at Javier struck a pebble on the
last hop and sailed over the second baseman's head, and suddenly
the breaks of the inning were even and the Tigers only one run
down. From then on, it was a game to treasure—the kind of
baseball in which each pitch, each catch, each call becomes an
omen.

Brock doubled again in the fifth, going with an outside pitch
and flicking the ball to left, exactly as he had in the first. Javier
singled to left, and when Brock, in full stride, was within six feet
of the plate it looked as if he had Willy Horton's throw beaten
by yards. He must have thought so, too, for he failed to slide.
The ball came in on the fly, chest-high to Freehan, he and Brock
collided, and umpire Doug Harvey's fist came around in a right
hook: Out! Brock, storming, thought Harvey had missed the call,
and so, I must confess, did I. Later, photographs proved us wrong
(though nothing would have been altered, of course, if they'd
proved us right). The pictures show Brock's left heel planted and
his toes descending on the plate; an instant later he has hit Freehan's right arm and left leg, and his foot, banged away, twists and
descends on dirt instead of rubber.

The game rushed along, still 3–2 Cardinals, and when the
Tigers loaded the bases in the sixth and Freehan, now zero for
fourteen in the Series, came up to the plate, I thought Mayo
Smith would call on a pinch-hitter. He let Freehan bat, and Freehan bounced into an inning-ending force. With one away in the
seventh, and the Tigers only seven outs away from extinction,
Smith also permitted Lolich to bat for himself, and, extraordinarily, his short fly fell safe in right. Hoerner came in to pitch, and
McAuliffe singled just past Cepeda. Stanley walked, loading the
bases, and Kaline came up to the plate. Now I understood.

Clearly, Mayo had planned it all: the famous old hitter up to save the day and the game and the Series in a typical Tiger seventh, and the stands going mad. Kaline swung and missed, took a ball, and then lined the next one to right center for the tying and go-ahead runs. Cash singled another in. Moments later, it seemed, we were in the ninth, and the Cards had the tying runs aboard. Lolich, however, took a deep breath and fanned Maris, pinch-hitting. He then pounced on Brock's weak tap, ran a few steps toward first, and lobbed the ball to Cash, and the great game was over.

In baseball, a saying goes, things have a way of evening up, but the cliché is not usually as quickly or remorselessly proved as it was in the sixth game, back in St. Louis. The Tigers, having racked up two second-inning runs off Washburn, sent fifteen men to the plate in the third and tied a famous Series record by scoring ten runs in one inning. Jim Northrup hit a grand-slammer into the right-field bullpen, Kaline and Cash had two hits apiece, the top three Tiger hitters scored six runs, and eight men reached base before the first out was made, and my totals indicated six singles, one homer, four walks, one hit batsman, one sacrifice bunt, four disheartened pitchers, and one bollixed scorecard. This kind of rockslide is not quite the rarity it might seem, and whenever it happens I am left with the impression that all the players involved are mere bystanders at a statistical cataclysm. The batters become progressively more certain that each hit will drop in for them, the fielders less surprised by each unreachable fly or untouchable grounder, the pitchers more and more convinced that their best stuff will be bombed. In the end, there seems nothing to do but wait until the riot exhausts itself and probability can again be placed under the rule of law. Eventually, the Tigers won the game, 13–1. The beneficiary of all this ferocity and good fortune was Denny McLain, suddenly restored to action by a mixed shot of cortisone and Novocaine, and I was glad for him. McLain, who is also a professional organist, has an immense appetite for celebrity, a hunger for big money, and hopes of a profitable winter career in the night clubs. But he is also an engaging and combative young man who had sustained his prior Series humiliations in good humor. Now he was off the hook and ready for Vegas.

So the Series came down to its last game, and the confrontation, it turned out, was between Gibson and Lolich. Both had won two games, and both had tired arms, though Lolich was starting with one less day of rest. He pitched the first two innings like a man defusing a live bomb, working slowly and unhappily, and studying the problem at length before each new move. He threw mostly sidearm, aiming at corners and often missing. After he had defused Brock for the second time, in the third, he seemed to gain poise and began getting ahead of the hitters. Gibson struck out five of the first nine men to face him, and the game was still scoreless, and now infinitely more dangerous, when Brock led off again in the sixth and singled. After one pitch to the next batter, he took an extraordinary lead off first—a good twenty feet. It was a challenge. Lolich remembered that Brock had succeeded with this identical maneuver in the second game, drawing the throw to first and then beating Cash's hurried peg down to second. Now, given no other choice, Lolich flipped to Cash. Brock burst away and was in full stride, at least halfway down the line, when Cash was able to wheel and throw. This time, the ball whistled right past Brock's left ear to Stanley, covering, and Brock was out, by a hair. One out later, Flood got to first on a single and was erased on almost exactly the same pick-off, ending this time in a rundown. Two singles and no double plays, but Lolich had somehow set down the side in order.

Still no score. Summer and the Series were running out. Gibson had permitted only one base-runner in the game, and here were the Tigers down to their last seventh inning of the year. Gibson fanned Stanley, for his thirty-fourth strikeout of the Series, and Kaline grounded out. At three and two, Cash singled to right. Horton hit to the left side, and the ball went through for a single. Northrup lined the first pitch high and deep, but straight to center, where Curt Flood started in, reversed abruptly, and then stumbled, kicking up a divot of grass. He recovered in an instant and raced toward the fence, but the ball bounced beyond him, a good four hundred feet out; Northrup had a triple, and two runs were in. Freehan doubled past Brock in left, for the third.

Gibson stayed in, of course. It was inconceivable that Schoendienst would take him out. He batted for himself in the eighth and fanned, and gave up another run in the ninth, on three singles. His stillness, his concentration, his burning will kept him out there, where he belonged, to the end. Lolich, too, lasted the distance, surviving an error in the seventh, a walk in the eighth, and a final, anticlimactic homer by Shannon in the ninth, which closed matters at 4–1. It was still the Year of the Pitcher, right to the last, but the Tiger hitters had restored the life and noise that seemed to go out of baseball this year.

The Leaping Corpse, the Shallow Cellar, the French Pastime, the Walking Radio, and Other Summer Mysteries

I first heard about the death of baseball one night last December. A friend of mine, a syndicated sports columnist, called me after eleven o'clock and broke the news. "Hey," he said, "have you *seen* the crowds at the Jets' games lately? Unbelievable! It's exactly like the old days at Ebbets Field. Pro football is the thing, from now on. Baseball is finished in this country. Dead." He sounded so sure of himself that I almost looked for the obituary in the *Times* the next morning. ("Pastime, National, 99; after a lingering illness. Remains on view at Cooperstown, N.Y.") Though somewhat exaggerated, my friend's prediction proved to be a highly popular one. In the next three or four months, the negative prognosis was confirmed by resident diagnosticians representing most of the daily press, the magazines, and the networks, and even by some foreign specialists from clinics like the *New Republic* and the *Wall Street Journal*. All visited the bedside and came away shaking their heads. Baseball was sinking.

Even if the old gent made it through until April and the warmer weather, his expectations were minimal—lonely wheelchair afternoons on the back porch, gruel and antibiotics, and the sad little overexcitement of his one-hundredth birthday in July. I haven't run into my dour friend at any ball games this summer, but I doubt whether the heavy crowds and noisy excitement of the current season, which is now well into its second half, would change his mind. The *idea* of the imminent demise of baseball has caught on, and those who cling to it (and they are numerous) seem to have their eyes on the runes instead of that leaping corpse. This new folk belief centers on the new folk word "image." Baseball, the argument goes, has a bad image. The game is too slow and too private, and offers too little action for a society increasingly attached to violence, suddenness, and mass movement. Baseball is cerebral and unemotional; the other, fast-growing professional sports, most notably pro football, are dense, quick, complex, dangerous, and perpetually stimulating. Statistics are then cited, pointing out the two-year decline in baseball attendance, as against the permanent hot-ticket status now enjoyed by football. (Last year, the National Football League played to 87 per cent of capacity in its regular season.) A recent Harris poll is quoted, which showed football supplanting baseball for the first time as the favorite American sport. The poll, which was taken last winter, indicated that football appeals most to high-income groups and to those between thirty-five and forty-nine years old, while baseball still comes first with old people, low-income groups, and Negroes. Bad, *bad* image.

Most of the statisticians and poll-watchers I have talked to have declined my invitation to come along to Shea Stadium to see what's been happening to the old game this summer, so I must pause here to make my own reading of those same bones and entrails. The decline of baseball at the box office (down from 25,-132,209 in 1966 to 23,103,345 last year) has taken place over two seasons that produced only one real pennant race (in the American League in 1967) and that included last summer's dispiriting

Year of the Pitcher—a complicated phenomenon that, for various reasons, seems to have subsided. Baseball has had previous recessions, including a four-year sag from 1950 through 1953, from which it recovered brilliantly. The larger statistics are more to the point. In the nineteen-sixties, the game has been going through the wrenching, loyalty-testing business of expansion—generally with a minimum of tact and common sense—and yet it is clearly holding its own. Average seasonal attendance between 1960 and 1968, during which time the number of games played per season increased 32 per cent, is up exactly 32 per cent over the ten-year average of the nineteen-fifties, and up 55 per cent over the nineteen-forties. As for the poll, it scarcely came as news to me that pro football has a corner on the young, well-heeled, with-it crowd; this is the same audience, to judge by my own eyeball survey, that snaps up all the available tickets to another status event of short duration, the World Series. The old, the poor, and the black might even prefer football, too, if they could afford a pair of season tickets, which is now the only sure way of getting in. It's hard to see how any of this constitutes a menace to the sunshine game. It's even more difficult to understand why Mr. Harris asked his questions in the first place. Football's regular season encompasses fourteen weekends—from mid-September to Christmas—whereas baseball starts in April and winds up, a hundred and sixty-two games later, with the new playoffs and the World Series in October. Being forced to pick between them seems exactly like being forced into a choice between a martini and a steak dinner. Most fans, I suspect, enjoy different sports precisely because they *are* different, and if it's all right with Mr. Harris I'll take both—pro football (preferably via television, because of the instant replay) for its violence and marvelously convoluted machinery, and baseball (preferably from a seat behind first base) for its clarity, variety, slowly tightening tension, and acute pressure on the individual athlete.

Those who gave up on baseball last winter may have only been watching the carryings-on of the next of kin outside the sickroom door, who went through a screeching, months-long family wrangle sufficient to do in a less hardy patient. In December, the owners suddenly fired the Baseball Commissioner, General William D. Eckert, in what for them has become typical fashion—forcing him to commit executive hara-kiri at a press conference. General Eckert was hired in 1965, apparently because he knew absolutely nothing about baseball and thus would be certain to keep his hand off the tiller; he was fired for the same reason, when it was noticed that the unskippered vessel had drifted toward a bank of nasty-looking reefs. The closest of these, just off the bow, was a threatened players' strike over the renewal of their pension fund, centering on the allocation of funds from a new fifty-million-dollar television package. The owners' first offer was rejected by the Players Association by a vote of 491 to 7, and the subsequent delay of any real negotiations made it clear that some owners and executives were preparing for a test of strength when spring training opened and would risk a full strike, and even a season of baseball played by bush-league replacements, on the chance that they could break the Association and discredit its director, Marvin Miller, a professional labor leader, whose name causes some veteran front-office men to sway and clutch their desks. (This fondness for the Carnegie-Gompers era of labor relations is not unusual in the halls of baseball. Last September, American League President Joe Cronin abruptly fired two veteran umpires—Al Salerno and Bill Valentine—who had been trying to form an umpires' association; Cronin's move instantly fused the new union and very nearly precipitated an umpires' strike at the World Series. Disclaiming union-busting, Cronin explained that Salerno and Valentine were "just bad umpires, that's all." This case is now in the courts.) Meanwhile, the owners went through an unedifying two-month squabble over the selection of a new Commissioner, finally settling, out of sheer exhaustion, on a compromise temporary choice, Bowie Kuhn, who had been the National League's attorney.

Mr. Kuhn, a tall, Princeton-educated Wall Street lawyer who

has been a devout fan and student of the game, set to work instantly, advising all parties to cool it and forcing a sensible compromise that was signed just as the spring-training camps were opening. His subsequent operations have shown more sure-handedness, intelligence, and courage than have been customarily visible in the Commissioner's office in recent decades, and it is expected that he will soon be signed to a full four-year contract. As the season began, he stood up to Judge Roy Hofheinz, the Astros' panjandrum, over a Houston-Montreal player trade that had gone sour when one of the players, Donn Clendenon, refused to play for Houston. Kuhn not only persuaded Hofheinz to accept an alternative, and inferior, player swap but extracted from him a public apology for a bad-tempered attack he had made on the Commissioner's office. Some weeks later, Kuhn called in Ken Harrelson, the Red Sox' outfielder and bead-wearer, who had refused to be traded to the Indians, and taught him to love Cleveland. In both of these curious and difficult negotiations, Kuhn was steering away from a major test of the reserve clause—the system that requires a player to deal for his services only with the club that owns his contract. Owners, players, Congress, and the Supreme Court all know that the reserve clause is probably a violation of the antitrust laws, yet its abolition would so surely destroy team identities and year-to-year play (one can imagine two leagues of pickup teams signed up by entrepreneurs, and a David Merrick–Sol Hurok World Series) that all parties maintain an unspoken pact not to push the matter over the brink. Mr. Kuhn will have to work out an acceptable new plan to ease this persistent anomaly—probably some form of fixed recompense to all traded players. His other large problems include the financial losses suffered by the owners of losing teams and exhausted franchises—losses now far too large to be cured, as in the old days, with one swoop of a millionaire's check-signing arm. This may even require (oxygen to the directors' room!) a partial profit-sharing among all clubs. Ahead, too, may be an enforced shortening of the present hundred-and-sixty-two-game season—

plus payoffs, plus World Series—which is clearly too much for the pitchers' arms and the fans' patience. On his record to date, Mr. Kuhn looks to be the kind of Commissioner who will support baseball's younger executives and thus at last force the game's Cro-Magnons into common-sense planning and a grudging contemporaneity.

This is baseball's hundredth anniversary, a centennial marking the Cincinnati Red Stockings' first professional season, and no innovation in that century has so severely tested its fans as the majors' latest expansion to twenty-four teams and four six-team divisions. Many veteran followers of the game have told me that they still have difficulty remembering the names of the new clubs or the composition of the madly named "East" and "West" divisions. (For a start, I recommend throwing away one's Rand McNally and noting that Chicago is in the West in the American League but is officially East in the National.) What these traditionalists mourn will never come again—the time, a decade ago, when we all knew all sixteen big-league teams as well as we knew the faces and tones of voice of those sitting around the family dinner table at Thanksgiving. That began to go when four new chairs had to be squeezed in, and when several sudden divorces and remarriages added a lot of unfamiliar names to the party. Like everyone else, I was at first unhappy about the new divisional setup, but I must confess now that I have entirely changed my mind. The six-team sub-leagues, whose members play against each other eighteen times and against the teams of the other division twelve times, seem to me a perfect substitute for the departed smaller leagues, and I think that in time most fans will become specialists in the players and the standings within their own chosen division. Already the four families have taken on separate identities and interests. The best of them this year, surely, is the National League West, where four famous old teams—the Braves, the Dodgers, the Giants, and the Reds— are locked in a dusty nonstop scrimmage that will probably go right down to the playoffs. The American League East, which includes the World Champion Tigers, the Red Sox, and the Orioles, promised equally well, but the Orioles, whose pitching and hitting have both come around simultaneously, have played the best ball in either league and now own an apparently insurmountable fourteen-game edge. The National League East, which looked to be a private hunting preserve for the Cardinals, has been saved by the Cards' early bumbling and by the electrifying apotheosis of the Cubs and the Mets. Only in the American League West, where Oakland and the Minnesota Twins are conducting their rather stately maneuvers, does the luck of the draw run thin, bunching two expansion teams, the Seattle Pilots and the Kansas City Royals, with the White Sox and the Angels in a miserable heap of losers, and reminding us that this year's shallower cellars can be just as dank and gloomy as the old abolished dungeons of eighth place.

The highest anxiety about this season centered on the hitters, whose combined efforts last year added up to a batting average of .236 (the worst in history), three hundred and forty shutout games, and a winter of rich reminiscences for most pitchers. Early this spring, Jim Maloney, of the Reds, and Don Wilson, of the Astros, pitched back-to-back no-hitters at Crosley Field, thus repeating a similarly comatose miracle of last summer, but this fearful omen vanished in the cannonade of base hits that has lately been audible on all fronts. At this writing, the averages show nineteen National League and ten American League fulltime players batting over .300, led by Rod Carew's .370. Six of the Cincinnati Reds' regulars have a combined average of .326. The leagues' combined batting averages are up to .249, runs per game stand at 8.29 (the highest since 1962), and so many home runs (1.59 per game, or the best since 1960) are flying out of so many parks that any of a dozen sluggers may wind up with at least forty homers this year. First among the bombardiers is Reggie Jackson, a twenty-three-year-old outfielder with the Oakland Athletics. Jackson is the genuine article—a superior natural left-handed hitter with enormously powerful wrists and shoulders. His startling production of downtowners (forty to date) may bring him within range of Roger Maris's record by mid-September. It is not quite a coincidence that Maris hit his sixty-one homers in another expansion year, 1961; all pitching staffs have been diluted by the draft that manned the four new clubs, and the batters are happily profiting. The sudden jump in averages is equally attributable to an off-season decision to diminish the size of the strike zone and to pare down the pitcher's mound from fifteen to ten inches. One must also ask, in a whisper, whether the ball has not been discreetly juiced. The hitting boom this season is somewhat synthetic, then, but baseball has often made such adjustments in the past; the new rulings that handicap the pitchers are an answer to previous changes in the game that helped to tip the balance their way—larger ballparks, larger pitchers, larger infielders' gloves, night ball, and the slider. No one knows yet whether the balance between hitting and pitching has been truly restored, but the joyful sound of bat on ball is once again loud in the land, and only the most obdurate purist will complain.

The flowering of Reggie Jackson is an especially happy sign, for baseball is in acute need of new superstars. A decade or two ago, the majors' lineup included such all-timers as Musial, Di-Maggio, Williams, Mantle, Mays, Feller, and Koufax, but now, with the retirement of the Mick, the list of one-man gate attractions is reduced to Willie Mays (now thirty-eight), Bob Gibson, and perhaps Carl Yastrzemski. Just behind them, to be sure, is a long list of remarkable ballplayers—Aaron, McCovey, McLain, Banks, Frank Robinson, Marichal, Richie Allen, Killebrew, Frank Howard, etc.—but none of them quite has the flamboyance that makes national household names. For some years now, baseball has not been signing many of the country's finest young athletes, who have chosen instead to accept the enormous bonuses available in pro football and basketball. But this problem will end shortly, when these rival sports reach the saturation point in salaries and when a new All-American halfback or center will be unable to draw one more ticket-buyer into a sold-out stadium. From then on, there is no reason to suppose baseball will not attract its full share of future Alcindors and O. J. Simpsons. Their presence may offer some solution to the game's most nagging current affliction—the half-dozen or so tired franchises where shabby, badly situated ballparks or vapid teams mean perpetually low attendance. Baseball's upward path is not yet assured, and total attendance this season, though currently up by two and a half million, will still require the customary tonic of some September pennant scrambles to show us that the game is truly healthy and still keeping pace with its own expansion. I am optimistic about this, for the reasons stated and also because of the rewarding and frequently riveting nature of the baseball games I have seen around the leagues this summer.

Obeying a pre-season resolution to devote more attention to the young Yankees, whose late push had brought them to a surprising fifth-place finish last September, I paid dutiful calls to the Stadium on several chilly spring evenings. The Yankee attack this year consists largely of quickness on the bases and some opportunistic hitting by a youngster named Bobby Murcer. The team is managed by the estimable Ralph Houk, and Mike Burke, the president, is one of the most intelligent young executives now in baseball, but the players on the field often look less palpable than the stalking, pin-striped specters of a hundred departed Bombers. Lately, the management has tried to keep Stadium fans awake by offering to play any patron's request on the organ. I did see Murcer, then the league's runs-batted-in leader, win one early game, when manager Bill Rigney of the Angels mysteriously ordered his hurler, Rudy May, to pitch to him in the ninth with two on, two out, and first base open. Murcer obliged with a game-winning double, thus providing one of the few bright spots in a disastrous spring for the Bronx Bunnies. Murcer, though eager and talented, is not a true fence-buster, and the pressure on him to de-

liver in countless games in which the Yankees have been trailing
has steadily pushed his average down—a sight too painful for
me to keep watching.

My first visits to Shea Stadium were of the same dispiriting
nature—an early, low-hit squeaker against the Reds, when the
same old Mets came apart in the ninth (two hits, an error, and a
wild pitch) and lost by 3–0, and a mid-May game against Atlanta, when three fast balls aimed by the Mets' skinny, hard-
throwing rookie, Gary Gentry, were redirected by Hank Aaron,
Orlando Cepeda, and Bob Tillman into the distant bullpens, thus
providing all the runs necessary for a 4–3 Braves victory. I was
not present the following night, when the Mets astonished themselves. Hitless through the sixth against Phil Niekro, they erupted
for eight runs in the eighth inning, climaxed by Cleon Jones's
grand-slammer, to win over Atlanta 9–3. I hurried right back
the next afternoon, and my subsequent delightful hours with the
Mets this year are perhaps best summarized in a game diary I
began keeping at that time:

THURSDAY, MAY 15: Beautiful afternoon, beautiful game. Senior Citizens' Day at Shea, but place jam-packed with kids. Attendance: 32,130. National Pastime looks rosy, but what about
schools? Hank Aaron, quickest wrists in West, wafts two (Nos.
516, 517 lifetime), and Metsies dead, down 6–2 in 7th. Metsies *not* dead. Four singles, wild pitch makes it 6–5 in 8th.
Optimist fans screeching. Bud Harrelson singles, bottom 9th,
Grote plunked by pitch, Agee sacrifices them along. Intentional pass loads hassocks. *Everybody* screeching. Harrelson
forced at plate. Cleon Jones up, currently batting .390. (.390?
Yep, .390.) Rips one—*pow!*—to right, but triumph denied
as Millan, Braves' 2B, climbs invisible ladder, turns midair, &
gloves pill backhand. Sudden silence. Damn!

MAY 30–JUNE 1: Mets sweep Giants 3 games while I waste
Memorial Day weekend in country. Bad planning.

JUNE 3, NIGHT: Mets' 6th straight. Pass .500, take 2nd place,
as Seaver 3-hits Dodgers, 5–2. First hit for good guys is
Kranepool's homer in 5th; frequent recent habit with Mets.

Kranepool *another* HR in 6th. Must revise Kranepool estimate; good old Eddie! Curious impression: Mets resemble vets, while young Dodgers (Sudakis, Sizemore, Grabarkewitz, etc.) are kiddie corps. What's going on here?

JUNE 4, NIGHT: Exhausted. Mets win, 1–0, in dawn's early light. 15 innings. Sweep of Giants *and* Dodgers, History made. DiLauro, elderly Met rookie hurler, lucky in early going, then implacable. Mets always look lucky these days; sign of good team. L.A. puts 12 runners on base in extra inns., scores none. Mets unflappable. Save game with incredible play in top of 15th—Al Weis, Mets' 2B, reverses gears, grabs deflected drive off pitcher's glove, throws same instant, and nails L.A. base-runner at plate. Still don't believe it. Mets win on anticlimax: Dodgers' W. Davis lopes in for Garrett's easy single, gives it the old hotdog one-hand scoop—and misses. Ball rolls to CF fence & Agee scores easily all way from first. Hoo-haw. Davis looks for place to hide. Kind of game Mets used to lose.

JUNE 15: Mets away, knocking 'em dead in West. Have just learned why Cleon Jones, Our Boy, throws left but bats right. As lad, played in Mobile sandlot with tiny right field; poke over RF wall counted as out, so Cleon switched to starboard side. Sensible. Cleon played baseball, football with T. Agee, also Our Boy, on same Mobile high-school team. Mobile High first Met farm.

JUNE 22: Sunday doubleheader, Cards. Sunshine. Mets break own record for largest '69 crowd: 55,862. (Leagues break own record for largest Sunday crowds ever: 394,008 paid.) Mets look cool, loose, rich—like old Yanks. Manager Hodges a genius. In opener, Gary Gentry shackles Cards as Mets romp, 5–1. (Gentry third straight excellent rookie hurler—Koosman last yr., Seaver yr. before. Wait till NL sees new phenom hurlers. J. Matlack, J. Bibby, now ripening on Met farms! They say Bibby looks exactly like Don Newcombe.) * Mets rooters show nouveau-riche side: wildly cheer poor Swoboda, hapless Met flychaser, as he fans 5 times. Second game very tight—Koosman vs. Cards' Torrez in scoreless duel—

* Quite a wait. Matlack and Bibby have yet to attain the majors.

but I am distracted by small boy, aged 10 maybe, in next box, who is intent on setting new two-game Eastern Flyweight stuffing record. Order of consumption: 1 pizza, 1 hot dog, 1 container popcorn, 1 Coke, ½ bg. peanuts, 1 Coke, 1 ice cream. No more hot dogs, so settles for 2nd pizza. Asks Pop for French fries. Mets' Boswell doubles in 5th, after 17 straight Met singles today (new record?), but still no score. Boy's dad, worn out by entreaties, leaves seat in search of French fries, thus misses Harrelson triple, Agee double that win game in 7th. Dad returns with Fr. frs., loses temper. Cries, "I knew it! The only G.-d. Fr. frs. were way the h. over behind third base!" Is placated when Rod Gaspar makes great peg in 8th to nail Brock at plate & save 1–0 nightcap. Brilliant baseball. Day to remember.

That same week, I flew north to visit the Expos, a newborn team that has found a happy home in Montreal and in the cellar of the National League East. (Proper baseball-watching now requires field trips, for the inflated schedule means that almost half the season has gone by before all the teams have paraded into one's home park.) I arrived at Jarry Park, a handsome little field that much resembles a country fairground, just in time to watch the Cardinals bat around in the fifth, in the first game of a twi-nighter. Bob Gibson was pitching, so I was disheartened for the home crowd, until I noticed that it didn't seem to mind much. The unroofed stands were packed, and the locals cheered politely for every Expo pop fly and booed every strike called against their team. Though slightly bush, these are real fans, for they have turned out through thick and (mostly) thin, and the whole town is talking baseball. Attendance actually went *up* during a recent twenty-game losing streak, because everybody wanted to be there the day it ended. Montreal is relentlessly bilingual, and as the Cards went on piling up runs that evening I began my first lesson, assisted by the announcer and the scoreboard, in baseball French. A long parade of *lanceurs* trudged to *le monticule* for the Expos before the first game of the doubleheader (*le premier programme double disputé au crepuscule par les Expos*) ended, with the Cards winning 8–1.

The second *partie* started just as dishearteningly, with the visitors scoring three *points* on three *coups sûrs* in the first, but matters improved electrifyingly in the second, when the Expos pulled off a triple play (line drive to Bob Bailey, *au premier but*, who stepped on the bag to double up an occupant Cardinal and then flipped to *l'arrêt-court*, Bobby Wine, who beat the other base-runner to second). It was the first triple play I had ever seen, in any language. The Expos tied it up in the third, on back-to-back (*dos-à-dos?*) homers (*circuits*) by Ron Fairly and Rusty Staub, as the scoreboard put up "VAS-Y!" and "IL NOUS FAUT UNE VICTOIRE!" Staub (a former Astro) and Mack Jones (a former Brave) are the resident gods in Montreal, the latter because he hit a homer and a triple during the Expos' victory in their opening home game in April, still a burning date in these fans' uncrowded memories. The nightcap was still tied in the seventh, and when the Expos put two men on base a tomblike silence descended on the crowd. Puzzled, I asked my neighbor what was going on, and he said, "They know that if we don't score now, we'll lose it." I understood, suddenly remembering what it had been like to be a Mets fan in the lighthearted, hopeless old days at the Polo Grounds. He was right, too; the Expos didn't score, and the Cards racked up five runs in the last two innings. When the *gérant*, Gene Mauch, came out to relieve his willing but exhausted young starter, Mike Wegener, he got the *framboise* from the fans. Mauch didn't mind; he used to manage the Phillies, which is the perfect prep school for his current post.

There were fewer fans at Jarry Park the next afternoon, which was too bad, because the absentees missed an Expos win. The Cards scored five early runs, but then fell into the baffling torpor that has gripped them so often this year, and lost it on bad relief pitching. Staub and Ron Fairly, the old Dodger *voltigeur*, had three hits apiece, and reliever Dan McGinn, a *gaucher*, got the 8–6 win with seven innings of peerless sinker-ball (I give up)

pitching, and I came away happy. *La victoire*, in Montreal, is
rare but sweet.

That home-and-home series waged by the Cubs and Mets last
month, and won by the Mets, four games to two, is too recent
and vivid in memory to require much recapitulation here, except
perhaps to recall the opener at Shea, which was in all respects the
first truly crucial game of the Mets' eight-year history. Five
games back of the Cubs (three in the more significant "lost" column), they had to gain some ground while simultaneously an-
swering for themselves the question that their old friends were
asking: "Are the Mets for *real?*" If this means "Are the Mets real
pennant threats?" the answer is probably still no. With Seaver on
tap, there probably will be no long losing streaks, but Koosman,
Gentry, and the bullpen were frightfully battered by the Astros
in a doubleheader last week. Any further relapse to the Polo
Grounds days, in view of the Mets' continuing lack of true muscle at the plate, may still make the last weeks of their schedule
painful. In other respects, this has been a season in which every
good hope was realized. Bud Harrelson's restored knee, Al Weis's
useful glove, and rookie Wayne Garrett's surprising bat have
contributed to a respectable infield. The young pitching arms
have matured, and Cleon Jones has been up among the league's
batting leaders all year. Best of all, perhaps, has been the dashing
performance of Tommie Agee in center and as lead-off man—a
renaissance that has finally justified the much criticized trade that
brought him here last year. (I'll bet that a lot of local Little
Leaguers have begun imitating Agee's odd batting mannerism
—a tiny kick of the left leg that makes him look like a house guest
secretly discouraging the family terrier.) The Mets even have a
bench this year, at last permitting Manager Hodges to do some
useful platooning. Hodges' instruction has been subtle and superior; the Mets play fine baseball and are no longer surprised at
anything they do.

What they did in that first Cubs game will be remembered for months, and maybe years, by all 55,096 of us who were there that afternoon. Jerry Koosman and Ferguson Jenkins, the towering Cubbie right-hander (and the only pitcher I have ever seen who runs to the mound to start his warmups each inning), had at each other in a flurry of early strikeouts, with the Cubs persistently threatening and just failing to score in the first five innings. The Mets' first hit was a homer in the fifth—a high fly by Kranepool that barely slipped over the wall in right center. Ernie Banks hit an identical miniblast to the opposite side in the sixth, and the Cubs added one more run in each of the next two innings—the last on a real homer by Jim Hickman, an unsentimental ex-Met. (My own sentiments, hopelessly home-towny, did not entirely keep me from enjoying the Cubs—a vastly more experienced and dangerous-looking team than the Mets. They are worth watching for Ernie Banks alone, the nearly legendary, skinny-necked, and exuberant thirty-eight-year-old first baseman, who is so well loved in Chicago that an alderman there once proposed the erection of a gigantic statue of him to replace the city's celebrated fifty-foot Picasso creature. If Manager Durocher can growl and connive these Cubs to a pennant, he will reward a mighty army of North Side bleacherites who are at least as vehement and deserving as the Mets' "Go!" shouters.) So we came down to the bottom of the ninth, with the Mets behind 3–1 and still owning but one hit. No one, absolutely no one, made a move toward the exits. Here, at once, came the necessary piece of luck—a shallow pop by pinch-hitter Ken Boswell that Cub center fielder Don Young lost in the sun for an instant. It dropped in for a double. Agee fouled out, but Donn Clendenon, pinch-hitting, sent Young way back with a long, high drive; Young caught it but slammed into the center-field wall at the same instant, and the ball was banged loose. Cleon up; runners at second and third, and an enormous, pleading din from the stands. He cracked the second pitch to left field, for the third double of the inning, tying up the game. Durocher, thinking hard, ordered the next man walked, and both runners then moved up on an in-

field out. Reconferring with Jenkins on the mound, Leo ordered
outside curves for Kranepool, the next hitter. Eddie took one for
a ball, another for a strike, and swung and missed on the next.
The last pitch was away, too, but Kranepool, going with it,
flicked the ball in a little curving loop that landed it just beyond
the shortstop—not much of a hit, but good enough.

The rest of those games—Tom Seaver's beautiful near-no-
hitter suddenly snipped off by that Qualls single in the ninth, the
Cubs' two successive wins, those raucous and admirable banner-
wavers in the Wrigley Field bleachers, Tommie Agee crashing so
many first pitches, and Al Weis's unexpected homers in the last
two Mets victories—were equally notable for the sight of so
many men on the streets here making their afternoon rounds with
transistor radios against their ears. No one had seen that kind of
midsummer fever in the city since the old Giants-Dodgers blood-
lettings, fifteen or twenty years back. One of those afternoons,
hurrying back to my office TV set, I suddenly wondered what
Mr. Harris's poll-takers were doing just then.

I got away for two more grandmothers' funerals—the first at
Fenway Park, the Taj Mahal of New England, to watch the Red
Sox and the Tigers. The Sox this year have been bashing a lot of
homers, but they have also had injury trouble, pitching trouble,
catching trouble, fielding trouble, and Baltimore trouble. They
stayed close to the Orioles until the weekend of June 13, when
the Athletics destroyed them, racking up thirty-eight runs and
forty-eight hits in three games, during which Reggie Jackson hit
four homers and batted in fifteen runs. Despite all, the Beantown
fans are flocking into the little green ballyard at a rate that may
equal last year's record Boston attendance of 1,940,788. My visit
was on a weekday afternoon, but even standing room was sold
out half an hour before game time. On this day, the park most resembled a huge pet shop—a place of endless squeakings, flutter-
ings, yelpings, hoppings, feedings, and scatterings as hundreds
upon hundreds of kids shrieked and piped during their long after-

noon sociable. The average age of the fans looked to be about twelve, and the Red Sox and the Tigers, successive pennant-winners the past two years, responded by playing a hilariously bad game that looked like a matchup between two day-camp nines. There were five throwing errors, two of them by Boston center fielder Reggie Smith, whose arm is as powerful and just about as random as a MIRV missile. Eventually, the Tigers took it, 6–5, and both teams trooped embarrassedly into the clubhouses for late classes with their managers.

Baltimore, my last stop, has the opposite kind of trouble—a ball team that can do no wrong this year, and a shortage of ticket-buyers. Attendance at Memorial Stadium is running at about the same pace as last year, when the club wound up with a $186,460 deficit; the park has a capacity of fifty-two thousand, but it has never once been filled in a regular-season game. Baltimoreans do care about the Orioles, but their curious affair is mostly conducted at long distance, by radio and television; whenever Manager Earl Weaver yanks a pitcher or decides to rest Frank Robinson for a day, the stadium switchboard is flooded with inquiries, complaints, and counter-advice. I heard a lot of baseball talk downtown, but most of it was centered on the autumn playoffs, which everyone thinks the Orioles will lose. Two other local champs, the football Colts and the basketball Bullets, fell on their faces in postseason tournaments this year, and the Orioles' success fills their townsmen's hearts with despair.

The Orioles have it all—the two Robinsons, Paul Blair, Boog Powell, a solid infield, and a pitching staff good enough to hold the fort until the artillery is unlimbered; Dave McNally's pitching record is now 15–0, but he has been taken off the hook seven times by late rallies. Powell, Blair, and Frank Robinson have seventy-three homers to date. I turned up to watch this formidable equipage in a twi-night doubleheader against the Red Sox, then trailing by thirteen and a half games. The promised mismatch turned out just the other way around, as so often happens in this most unpredictable of all sports; the Bosox swept the bill, 7–4

THE SUMMER GAME   [214

and 12–3, banging out a record (against Baltimore pitching)
twenty-two hits in the nightcap. Yastrzemski, who is swinging
only for the fences this year, had a pair of homers; Mike
Andrews, the dandy Boston second baseman, had five hits and a
walk in the second game; and Reggie Smith, enjoying the longest
hot streak of any American League batter this year, managed
two walks, four singles, two doubles, and one home run in eleven
trips to the plate. Sitting there in the stands, a happy neutralist
surrounded by unhappy locals, I tried to decide which kind of
baseball I like best—the anxious involvement of those taut miracles at Shea Stadium; the gentle, comical back-country begin-
nings in Montreal; or this long banging of bats and the satisfying humiliation of a better team. Then I remembered that I didn't
have to choose, for all these are parts of the feast that the old
game can still bring us. I felt what I almost always feel when I
am watching a ball game: Just for those two or three hours, there
is really no place I would rather be.

Days and Nights with the Unbored

The Series and the season are over—four days done at this writing—and the Mets are still Champions of the World. Below midtown office windows, scraps and streamers of torn paper still litter the surrounding rooftops, sometimes rising and rearranging themselves in an autumn breeze. I just looked out, and they're still there. It's still true. The Mets won the National League's Eastern divisional title, and won it easily; they won the playoffs, beating the Atlanta Braves in three straight; they took the World Series—one of the finest short Series of all— beating the Orioles in five games. The Mets. The New York *Mets?* . . . This kind of disbelief, this surrendering to the idea of a plain miracle, is tempting but derogatory. If in the end we re- member only a marvelous, game-saving outfield catch, a key hit dropped in, an enemy batter fanned in the clutch, and then the ridiculous, exalting joy of it all—the smoke bombs going off in the infield, the paper storm coming down and the turf coming up, and the clubhouse baptisms—we will have belittled the makers of this astonishment. To understand the achievement of these Mets, it is necessary to mount an expedition that will push beyond the games themselves, beyond the skill and the luck. The journey will end in failure, for no victorious team is entirely un- derstandable, even to itself, but the attempt must always be made, for winning is the ultimate mystery that gives all sport its mean-

ing. On the night of September 24, when the Mets clinched their
divisional title, Manager Gil Hodges sat in his clubhouse office
after the game and tried to explain the season. He mentioned
good pitching, fine defense, self-reliance, momentum, and a sense
of team confidence. The reporters around his desk nodded and
made notes, but they all waited for something more. From the
locker room next door came a sharp, heady whiff of sloshed
champagne and the cries of exultant young athletes. Then someone said, "Gil, how did it all happen? Tell us what it all *proves*."

Hodges leaned back in his chair, looked at the ceiling, and then
spread his large hands wide. "Can't be done," he said, and he
laughed.

Disbelief persists, then, and one can see now that disbelief itself
was one of the Mets' most powerful assets all through the season.
Again and again this summer, fans or friends, sitting next to me
in the stands at Shea Stadium would fill out their scorecards just
before game time, and then turn and shake their heads and say,
"There is no way—just *no* way—the Mets can take this team
tonight." I would compare the two lineups and agree. And then,
later in the evening or at breakfast the next morning, I would
think back on the game—another game won by the Mets, and
perhaps another series swept—and find it hard to recall just
how they *had* won it, for there was still no way, *no* way, it could
have happened. Finally, it began to occur to me that if my
friends and I, partisans all, felt like this, then how much more
profoundly those other National League teams, deeper in talent
and power and reputation than the Mets, must have felt it. For
these were still the Mets—the famous and comical losers,
ninth-place finishers last year, a team that had built a fortune and
a following out of defeat and perversity, a team that had lost
seven hundred and thirty-seven games in seven years and had finished a total of two hundred and eighty-eight and a half games
away from first place. No way, and yet it happened and went on
happening, and the only team, interestingly, that did not disbe-
lieve in the Mets this summer was the Houston Astros, a club

born in the same year as the Mets and the owners of a record almost as dismal; the Astros, who also came to competence and pride this summer, won ten out of twelve games from the Mets and were the only rivals to take a season series from them.

The Amazin's amazed us so often that almost every one of the 2,175,373 fans who saw them at home this year (an attendance record that topped all clubs in both leagues) must be convinced that he was there on that one special afternoon or crucial evening when the Mets won *the* big game that fused them as contenders and future champions. Many claim it was that afternoon of July 8, when the Mets, five games behind the Cubs in the standings and two runs behind the Cubs in the game, came up with ninth-inning pinch doubles by Ken Boswell and Donn Clendenon that were both misplayed by a rookie Chicago center fielder; a tying double by Cleon Jones; and a bloop two-out single by Ed Kranepool that won it. Some think it was the next day, when the Mets' shining leader, Tom Seaver, came within two outs of a perfect game, shutting out the Cubs, 4–0, and cutting their lead to three. Some hold out for the televised game at Wrigley Field the following week when Al Weis, the weak-hitting spare infielder, bashed his first homer of the year to drive in three runs in a 5–4 victory. Or the next game there, when Weis hit *another* homer and Tommie Agee delivered a lead-off double and a lead-off homer in the first two innings, as the Mets won again. Others remember the doubleheader against San Diego at Shea on August 16 (four-hit shutout by Seaver in the first; winning pinch single by Grote in the nightcap) that started the Mets back from their midsummer nadir, nine and a half games behind. After that day, the team won twelve of its next fourteen games, all against Western teams, and Seaver and Koosman embarked on a joint record of sixteen wins in their last seventeen decisions. My own choice of *the* game is a much earlier wonder—a fifteen-inning, 1–0 bleeder against the Dodgers on the night of June 4. In the top of the fifteenth, with a Dodger on third, Al Weis, playing second base, darted to his left for a hard grounder that was deflected in

midflight by pitcher Ron Taylor's glove; Weis had to leap the
other way, to his right, for the carom, but came up with the ball
and an instant off-balance throw that nailed the runner at the
plate and saved the tie. Moments later, Tommie Agee scored the
winning run all the way from first on an error. The victory sustained what came to be an eleven-game winning streak and completed successive series sweeps against the Dodgers and the
Giants. Manager Hodges said later that Weis's double reverse and
peg was one of the greatest single infield plays he had ever seen.

    What matters here is not the selection of one winning game
(there were many others as close and perhaps as important) but
the perception of a pattern in them all. Ten separate players,
many of them part-timers or pinch-hitters, figure significantly in
these brief accounts of seven key games. This happened all year,
and in time the Mets began to recognize the pattern as their main
source of strength. This is a phenomenon unique in baseball. The
Mets were the first team in the history of the game to enter a
World Series with only two players (Cleon Jones and Tommie
Agee) who had over four hundred official at-bats in the course of
the regular season. From the beginning, successful big-league
clubs have won with set lineups, which has usually meant send-
ing at least five or six hitters to the plate four or five hundred
times a year. The 1967 Cardinals had eight players with more
than four hundred ABs; the 1964 Yankees had six with more than
five hundred. Even Casey Stengel's famous Yankee platoons of
the nineteen-fifties, even those constantly reshuffled castoffs who
played for the Mets in their first season presented more stable
lineups than the new champions. Hodges' Irregulars, to be sure,
were a creation of pure necessity. Cold bats, injuries, and call-ups
to Army Reserve duty required improvisation all through the
season, but every substitution seemed to work. Young Wayne
Garrett niftily spelled old Ed Charles at third; rookie Bobby Pfeil
and backup glove Al Weis filled in for Bud Harrelson and Ken
Boswell; Ed Kranepool and Donn Clendenon (who was acquired
from Montreal just before the trading deadline in June) together

added up to a switch-hitting first baseman who delivered
twenty-three home runs; Art Shamsky and Ron Swoboda became
a switch-hitting right fielder who hit twenty-three more homers;
Rod Gaspar, mostly played as a pair of fast wheels in late innings,
led the outfielders in assists, which means enemy runners cut
down in key situations. No professional ballplayer likes to sit out
even one game, but in time all the Mets, sensing that no one on
the bench had actually lost his job, were infected with a guerrilla
spirit. Ed Charles, who has played pro ball for eighteen years,
talked about it one day near the end of the season. "I've never
seen it or heard of it before," Charles said. "Every one of us knew
when it was time to pick the other guy up. The bottom of the
order, a pinch-hitter, a man who'd just fanned three times—
everybody figured, 'What the hell, what am I waiting for? Do it
now, baby, because there's no big man going to do it for you.'
Give No. 14 a lot of credit." No. 14 is Gil Hodges.

Other components of the new-Metsian physiology are more
traditional. They include:

PITCHING—Tom Seaver and Jerry Koosman, who appeared
and flowered in succession in the past two seasons, are now the
best one-two starting pair on any team in the majors. This year's
freshman was Gary Gentry, up from Arizona State (the Notre
Dame of college baseball) and only two years in the minors, who
won thirteen games and invariably proved obdurate in the tough,
close ones. A veteran, Don Cardwell, and two more youngsters,
Nolan Ryan and Jim McAndrew, together provided the fourth
and fifth starters, and Ron Taylor and Tug McGraw were the
stoppers from the bullpen. Ryan throws pure smoke (in the minors he once fanned eighteen batters in seven innings), but there
are those who think that McAndrew may be an even better
pitcher in the end. Young hurlers' arms are as delicate as African
violets, and Hodges and the Mets' pitching coach, Rube Walker,
stuck to a five-day rotation through the most crowded weekends
of the schedule, arriving at September with a pitching staff that
was in splendid fettle. Rube has been known to glare at a pitcher

whom he finds playing catch on the sidelines without his permission.

DEFENSE—Gil Hodges, trying to put to rest the notion that his winners were somehow spawned out of sunshine, recently pointed out that last year's team, which finished twenty-four games back, was almost never beaten badly. I looked it up: the 1968 club lost only ten times by six runs or more. Give No. 14 a lot of credit. Even while losing, the young Mets were taught the essentials of winning baseball—hitting the cutoff man, throwing to the right base, holding the runner close. The new Mets do not beat themselves, which is a failing far more common in baseball than one would suspect.

HITTING—Batting is very nearly unteachable, but it thrives on confidence. The Mets' two most talented swingers, Cleon Jones and Tommie Agee, are lifelong friends from Mobile, Alabama; both, curiously, are subject to self-doubt and depression. Hodges has stuck with them for two seasons, patiently playing them in the top of the order and ignoring slumps and glooms. Agee, always a fine center fielder, came back from a terrible .217 season to a solid .271 this year, with twenty-six homers, while Jones, down to .223 at one point last year, was in the thick of the fight for the National League batting title this summer, finishing in third place, with .340. Shamsky, Boswell, Harrelson, and Grote all had surprising years at the plate (Shamsky's .300 was sixty-nine points above his lifetime average), which may be due to example, or to the exuberance of winning, or to just plain

GOOD LUCK—Always, this is the identifying mark of a pennant winner. You can see it beginning to happen: Key hits start to drop in, fair by inches, while the enemy's line shots seem to be hit straight into a waiting glove or to carom off the wall to produce an overstretched hit-and-out. These Mets, however, have been the recipients of several extra kisses of providence. This spring, Commissioner Bowie Kuhn persuaded Donn Clendenon to come out of a month's retirement after he had been traded from Atlanta to Montreal, thus keeping him available for a trade to the

Mets in June. Tom Seaver was illegally signed to a bonus by the Braves in 1966, thus making him available for a lucky draw from a hat by the Mets. The son of a Shea Stadium usher happened to write his father that there was a pretty fair sort of pitcher at his Army camp, thus bringing the name of Jerry Koosman to the attention of Met scouts.

YOUTH AND CHARACTER—The Mets' locker room was a pleasant place to visit this summer—for once, a true clubhouse. These ballplayers are younger than most, the great majority in their mid-twenties, and their lack of superstars and supersalaries accounted for an absence of the cliques, feuds, and barracks irritability to be found on many ball teams. The Mets are articulate and educated (twenty-two of the twenty-six have attended college), and they seem to take pride in their varying life styles and interests, which include love beads and business suits, rock music and reading, the stock market, stewardesses, practical jokes, alligator shoes, and sometimes even world affairs. Donn Clendenon owns a night club in Atlanta and is a vice-president for industrial relations of Scripto, the pen company; Ron Taylor is an electrical engineer, who has been known to say, "Doubleheader tomorrow, barring nuclear holocaust"; Jim McAndrew is a psychologist; Ed Charles sends his inspirational poems to kids who write for autographs; Ron Swoboda talks of entering politics someday, because he wants to do something about racial tensions. Ed Kranepool is the only original Met still with the team, but Swoboda, to my mind, most typifies the change from the old Mets to the new. He arrived in 1965, at the age of twenty—an enormous young man with an enormous, eager smile. He hit prodigious homers and had appalling difficulties with outside curves and high flies. He fell down in the outfield, threw to the wrong base, lost his temper, and was involved in Metsian misadventures. Once, in Candlestick Park, he popped up with men on base, returned to the bench, and stamped so hard on his batting helmet that it could not be pulled off his spikes in time for him to return to the field for the next inning. The Shea fans have stuck with him through sulks and slumps and strikeouts ("RON SWOBODA IS STRONGER THAN DIRT," one banner read), because he is *never* unsurprising—as the Baltimore Orioles will forever remember.

Tom Seaver, still only twenty-four, was the biggest winner in baseball this year (he finished at 25–7) and the undisputed leader of the Mets' upsurge. Arriving two years ago to join a hopeless collection of habitual cellar mice, he made it clear at once that losing was unacceptable to him. His positive qualities —good looks, enthusiasm, seriousness, lack of affectation, good humor, intelligence—are so evident that any ball team would try to keep him on the roster even if he could only pitch batting practice. This is unlikely to happen. In his first three years, he has won fifty-seven games and has been voted onto three All Star teams, and he is now a prime favorite to win both the Cy Young and the Most Valuable Player awards for 1969. Such a combination of Galahad-like virtues has caused some baseball old-timers to compare him with Christy Mathewson. Others, a minority, see an unpleasantly planned aspect to this golden image—planned, that is, by Tom Seaver, who is a student of public relations. However, his impact on his teammates can be suggested by something that happened to Bud Harrelson back in July. Harrelson was away on Army Reserve duty during that big home series with the Cubs, and he watched Seaver's near-no-hitter (which Seaver calls "my imperfect game") on a television set in a restaurant in Watertown, New York. "I was there with a couple of Army buddies who also play in the majors," Harrelson said later, "and we all got steamed up watching Tom work. Then—it was the strangest thing—I began feeling more and more like a little kid watching that game and that great performance, and I wanted to turn to the others and say, 'I *know* Tom Seaver. Tom Seaver is a friend of mine.'"

Most of the other Mets, it seems to me, are equally susceptible to enthusiasm. Young and alert and open, they are above all suggestible, and this quality—the lead-off hit just after a brilliant inning-ending catch; the valiant but exhausted starting pitcher taken off the hook by a sudden cluster of singles—is what made the Mets' late innings so much worth waiting for this year. It is also possible that these intuitive, self-aware athletes sensed, however vaguely, that they might be among the few to achieve splendor in a profession that is so often disappointing, tedious, and degrading. Their immense good fortune was to find themselves together at the same moment of sudden maturity, combined skills, and high spirits. Perhaps they won only because they didn't want this ended. Perhaps they won because they were unbored.

Something else—a sense of unreality, some persistent note of recognition of difference—stayed with me after all my visits to the Mets' clubhouse this year. Only in the end did I realize what it was. Instead of resembling a real ball team, the new Mets reminded me most of a Hollywood cast assembled to play in still another unlikely baseball movie. They seemed smaller and younger and more theatrical than a real team, and their drama was hopelessly overwritten. Certainly the cast was right— Harrelson and Boswell (Bud and Ken), the eager, sharp-faced infielders; Wayne Garrett, the freckle-faced rookie with the sweet smile; Jerry Grote, the broken-nosed, scrappy catcher; Agee and Jones, the silent, brooding big busters; Jerry Koosman, the cheerful hayseed; Ed Charles, the philosophical black elder; Art Shamsky, the Jewish character actor with persistent back pains; Hodges and Berra, the seamy-faced, famous old-timers (neither, unfortunately, called Pop); and Tom Seaver, of course, the hero. And who can say that the Mets didn't sense this, too—that they didn't know all along that this year at Shea life was imitating not just art but a United Artists production?

The only bad luck suffered by the Mets this year was the collapse of their opposition. A few cynics will insist (I have heard them already) that the Mets did not win their divisional title but had it handed to them. They somehow overlook the fact that the Mets won thirty-eight of their last forty-nine regular-season games (twenty-nine of thirty-six when it really mattered), and point instead to the Cubs' loss of ten out of eleven games in early September, to the Cubs' blowing a nine-and-a-half-game lead in less than a month, and to the failure of the powerful Pirates and the pennant-holding Cardinals ever to mount a consistent assault on the leaders. We all wanted that culminating explosion of open warfare similar to the famous Trafalgar staged by the American League in 1967, but the major fleets seemed only to glide past each other in the night. One brief skirmish—a pair of evening games at Shea on September 8 and 9—sufficed to convince me, however, that the Mets would have won just as surely if the issue had come down to the last afternoon of the season. The Cubs by then were a badly rattled club, exhausted by the silences and rages of their manager, Leo Durocher, and apprehensive about the impending loss of their lead, which they had held too long (a hundred and forty-two days) and too easily. Cub pitcher Bill Hands opened the first game by decking Tommie Agee with an inside fast ball—a mistake against the Suggestibles. Jerry Koosman responded classically by hitting the next Cub batter, Ron Santo, on the wrist, and an inning later Agee banged a two-run homer. The Cubs tied it in the sixth, but Agee scored the winning run in the bottom half, sliding in ahead of a sweeping tag by catcher Randy Hundley, who then suggested that the umpire had blown the call. (I was watching at home, and Hundley's enraged leap took him right off the top of my TV screen, leaving only his shoes in view, like Santa's boots disappearing up the chimney.) The next night, Seaver threw a five-hitter, the Mets racked up ten hits and seven runs, and Durocher was treated to several dozen touching renditions of the new anthem, "Good-by, Leo!" The Mets took over first place the next day.

They went on winning—sometimes implacably, sometimes improbably. They won a doubleheader from Pittsburgh in which the only run in each game was driven in by the Met pitcher. They won again from the Pirates the next day, when Ron Swoboda hit the first grand-slam home run of his career. Against the

Cardinals, they set an all-time mark by striking out nineteen times in one game, but beat the brand-new record-holder, Steve Carlton, on two two-run homers by Swoboda. Against the Pirates, a Pittsburgh pop single was converted into a sudden out when Swoboda scooped up the ball and fired it to catcher Jerry Grote, who had raced up the line to take the throw at first base just as the base-runner turned the corner. Had we but seen them, these games contained all the market indications of a brilliant investment coup in the coming playoff and Series.

Fittingly, the game that clinched the Mets' half-pennant was against the old league champs, the Cardinals. Thoughtfully, the Cubs had won that afternoon, thus keeping the Mets from backing in. Appropriately, it was the last home game at Shea, and 54,928 of us had turned out. Undramatically, the Mets won it in the very first inning, bombing out Steve Carlton with two homers—a three-run shot by a new favorite, Donn Clendenon, and a two-run poke by an old favorite, Ed Charles, who clapped his hands delightedly as he circled the bases. It was a slow, humid, comical evening, presided over by a festive orange moon. Plenty of time to read the fans' banners ("QUEENS LITHO LOVES THE METS," "YOU GUYS ARE TOO MUCH!"), to read the scoreboard ("METS WELCOME THE GOODTIME CHARLIE PHYSICAL FITNESS GROUP"; "METS WELCOME THE PASSIONIST RETREATISTS"), to fly paper airplanes, to grin idiotically at each other, to tear programs into confetti, and to join in a last, loud "Good-by, Leo!" rendered *a cappella*, with the right-field tenors in especially good voice. Then, in a rush, came the game-ending double play, the hero-hugging (Gary Gentry had pitched a 6–0 shutout), the sprint for life (Met fans are not the most excited pennant locusts I have ever seen, but they are the quickest off the mark and the most thorough), and the clubhouse water sports (Great Western, Yoo-Hoo, Rise lather, beer, cameras, interviews, music, platitudes, disbelief). Ed Charles sat in front of his locker, away from the television lights and the screeching, and said, "Beautiful, baby. Nine years in the minors for me, then nine more with the Athletics and Mets.

Never, *never* thought I'd make it. These kids will be back next year, but I'm thirty-six and time is running out. It's better for me than for them."

A few minutes later, I saw George Weiss, the Mets' first general manager, trying to push his way through the mob outside Gil Hodges' office. He got to the door at last and then peered in and waved to Hodges, who had played for the Mets in their terrible first season.

"Nineteen sixty-two!" Weiss called.

"Nineteen sixty-two!" Hodges replied.

Rod Kanehl and Craig Anderson, two other Original Mets, met in the middle of the clubhouse, cried "Hey!" in unison, and fell into each other's arms. Soon they became silent, however, and stood there watching the party—two heavy men in business suits, smoking cigars.

The playoffs—the television-enriching new autumn adjunct known officially as the Championship Series—matched up the Orioles and the Minnesota Twins, and the Mets and the Atlanta Braves, who had barely escaped the horrid possibility of three-way or four-way pre-playoff playoffs with the Dodgers, Giants, and Cincinnati Reds in the National League West. Atlanta filled its handsome white stadium to capacity for its two weekend games against New York, but to judge from the local headlines, the transistor-holders in the stands, the television interviews with Georgia coaches, and the high-school band and majorettes that performed each morning in the lobby of the Regency Hyatt House hotel, autumn baseball was merely a side attraction to another good old Deep South football weekend. Georgia beat South Carolina, 41–16; Clemson beat Georgia Tech, 21–10; the Colts beat the Falcons, 21–14; and the Mets beat the Braves, 9–5 and 11–6. The cover of the official program for the baseball games displayed a photograph of the uniformed leg of an Atlanta Brave descending from a LEM onto a home plate resting on the moon, with the legend "One Step for the Braves, One Giant

Leap for the Southeast," but Manager Hodges saw to it that the astronaut never got his other foot off the ladder. Not wanting to lose his ace in the significant first game, he kept Tom Seaver on the mound for seven innings, while Seaver absorbed an uncharacteristic eight-hit, five-run pounding. Tom plugged away, giving up homers and doubles, and resolutely insisting in the dugout that the Mets were going to win it. The lead changed hands three times before this finally happened, in the eighth, when the Mets scored five times off Phil Niekro on three successive hits, a gift stolen base, a fearful throwing error by Orlando Cepeda, and a three-run pinch single by J. C. Martin. The next day's match was just as sloppy. The Braves scored five runs with two out in the fifth, all off Koosman and all too late, since the Mets had already run up a 9–1 lead. Hank Aaron hit his second homer in two days, Agee and Jones and Boswell hit homers for the Mets, and the Braves left for Shea Stadium with the almost occult accomplishment of having scored eleven runs off Seaver and Koosman without winning either game.

Hodges, having demonstrated slow managing in the first game, showed how to manage fast in the last one. His starter, Gary Gentry, who had given up a two-run homer to the unquenchable Aaron in the first inning, surrendered a single and a double (this also by Aaron) in the third, and then threw a pitch to Rico Carty that the Atlanta outfielder bombed off the left-field wall on a line but about two feet foul. Hodges, instantly taking the new ball away from Gentry, gave it to Nolan Ryan, in from the bullpen, who thereupon struck out Carty with one pitch, walked Cepeda intentionally, fanned Clete Boyer, and retired Bob Didier on a fly. Agee responded in obligatory fashion, smashing the first pitch to him in the same inning for a homer, and Ken Boswell came through with a two-run job in the fourth, to give the Mets the lead. Cepeda, who so far had spent the series lunging slowly and unhappily at Met singles and doubles buzzing past him at first, then hit a home run well beyond the temporary stands behind the left-center-field fence, making it 4–3, Braves. Even he must have sensed by then what would happen next: Ryan, a .103 hitter, singled to lead off the home half; Garrett, who had hit but one home run all year, hit another into the right-field loges, for two runs; Jones and Boswell and Grote and Harrelson and Agee combined to fashion two insurance runs; Ryan fanned seven Braves in all, and won by 7–4. Just about everybody got into the act in the end—the turf-moles onto the field again, Nolan Ryan and Garrett under the kliegs, and Mayor Lindsay under the champagne. Forehandedly, he had worn a drip-dry.

After a season of such length and so many surprises, reason suggested that we would now be given a flat and perhaps one-sided World Series, won by the Orioles, who had swept their three playoff games with the Minnesota Twins, and whom reporters were calling the finest club of the decade. There would be honor enough for the Mets if they managed only to keep it close. None of this happened, of course, and the best news—the one *true* miracle—was not the Mets' victory but the quality of those five games—an assemblage of brilliant parables illustrating every varied aspect of the beautiful game.

The Baltimore fans expected neither of these possibilities, for there were still plenty of tickets on sale before the opener at Memorial Stadium, and the first two Series games were played to less than capacity crowds. This is explicable only when one recalls that two other league champions from Baltimore—the football Colts and the basketball Bullets—had been humiliated by New York teams in postseason championships this year. Baltimore, in fact, is a city that no longer expects *any* good news. In the press box, however, the announcement of the opening lineups was received in predictable fashion ("Just *no* way . . ."), and I could only agree. The Orioles, who had won a hundred and nine games in the regular season, finishing nineteen games ahead of the next team and clinching their divisional title on September 13, were a poised and powerful veteran team that topped the Mets in every statistic and, man for man, at almost every position. Their three sluggers—Frank Robinson, Boog Powell, and Paul Blair —had hit a total of ninety-five homers, as against the Mets' *team* total of a hundred and nine. Their pitching staff owned a lower earned-run average than the Mets' sterling corps. Their ace, screwballer Mike Cuellar, had won twenty-three games and led the staff in strikeouts; their second starter, Dave McNally, had won fifteen games in a row this year; the third man, Jim Palmer, had a record of 16–4, including a no-hitter. Since Cuellar and McNally are left-handers, Hodges was forced to start his righty specialists (Clendenon, Charles, Swoboda, and Weis) and bench the hot left-handed hitters (Kranepool, Garrett, Shamsky, and Boswell) who had so badly damaged the Braves. Just *no* way.

Confirmation seemed instantaneous when Don Buford, the miniature Baltimore left fielder, hit Seaver's second pitch of the game over the right-field fence, just above Swoboda's leap. (Swoboda said later that his glove just ticked the ball "at my apogee.") For a while after that, Seaver did better—pitched much more strongly than he had in Atlanta, in fact—but with two out in the Baltimore fourth the steam suddenly went out of his fast ball, and the Orioles racked up three more runs. The game, however, belonged not to Buford, or to the other Oriole hitters, or to Cuellar, but to Brooks Robinson, the perennial All Star Baltimore third baseman, who was giving us all a continuous lesson in how the position can be played. Almost from the beginning, I became aware of the pressure he puts on a right-handed batter with his aggressive stance (the hands are cocked up almost under his chin), his closeness to the plate, his eager appetite for the ball. His almost supernaturally quick reactions are helped by the fact that he is ambidextrous; he bats and throws right-handed, but eats, writes, plays ping-pong, and fields blue darters with his left. In the fifth, he retired Al Weis on a tough, deep chance that leaped up and into his ribs. In the seventh, after the Mets had scored once on a pair of singles and a fly, he crushed the rally when he sprinted in toward Rod Gaspar's topped roller, snatched it up barehanded, and got off the throw, overhand, that retired Gaspar by yards. The Orioles won, 4–1, and Brooks had made it look easy for them.

The Mets were grim the next day (Frank Robinson had baited them after their loss, commenting on the silence in their dugout), and they played a grim, taut, riveting game. Brooks Robinson went on making fine plays, but he had plenty of company—an extraordinary catch and falling throw to second by Baltimore shortstop Mark Belanger, a base-robbing grab by gaunt little Bud Harrelson. (The tensions of the season had burned Harrelson down from a hundred and sixty-eight to a hundred and forty-five pounds.) The Mets led, 1–0, on Donn Clendenon's wrong-field homer off McNally in the fourth, and Baltimore had no hits at all off Koosman until the bottom of the seventh, when Paul Blair led off with a single. Two outs later, Blair stole second on a change-up curve, and Brooks Robinson scored him with a single up the middle. The tie seemed only to make the crowd more apprehensive, and the Baltimore partisans seemed unamused when a large "LET'S GO, METS!" banner appeared in the aisle behind home plate; it was carried by four Met wives—Mesdames Pfeil, Dyer, Ryan, and Seaver, smashers all, who had made it the night before out of a Sheraton bedsheet. There were two out in the top of the ninth before the Mets could act on this RSVP, winning the game on successive singles by Charles and Grote and a first-pitch hit to left by the .215 terror, Al Weis. Koosman, throwing mostly curves in the late going, walked two Orioles in the bottom half, but Ron Taylor came in to get the last out and save Jerry's two-hit, 2–1, essential victory. It was a game that would have delighted John McGraw.

Back at Shea Stadium, before an uncharacteristically elegant but absolutely jam-packed audience, Tommie Agee rocked Jim Palmer with a lead-off first-inning homer—Agee's fifth such discouragement this year. Gary Gentry, who had taken such a pounding from the Braves, was in fine form this time, challenging the big Baltimore sluggers with his hummer and comforted by a 3–0 lead after the second inning. He was further comforted in the fourth, when Tommie Agee, with two Orioles aboard, ran for several minutes toward deep left and finally, cross-handed, pulled down Elrod Hendricks' drive just before colliding with the fence. Agee held on to the ball, though, and carried it all the way back to the infield like a trophy, still stuck in the topmost webbing of his glove. It was 4–0 for the home side by the seventh, when Gentry walked the bases full with two out and was succeeded by Nolan Ryan. Paul Blair hit his 0-2 pitch on a line to distant right. Three Orioles took wing for the plate, but Agee, running to his left this time, made a skidding dive just at the warning track and again came up with the ball. The entire crowd—all 56,335 of us—jumped to its feet in astonished, shouting tribute as he trotted off the field. The final score was 5–0, or, more accurately, 5–5—five runs for the Mets, five runs saved by Tommie Agee. Almost incidentally, it seemed, the Orioles were suddenly in deep trouble in the Series.

It was Cuellar and Seaver again the next day, and this time the early homer was provided by Donn Clendenon—a lead-off shot to the visitors' bullpen in the second. Seaver, who had not pitched well in two weeks, was at last back in form, and Baltimore manager Earl Weaver, trying to rattle him and to arouse his own dormant warriors, who had scored only one run in the past twenty-four innings, got himself ejected from the game in the third for coming onto the field to protest a called strike. Weaver had a longish wait in his office before his sacrifice took effect, but in the top of the ninth, with the score still 1–0 and the tension at Shea nearly insupportable, Frank Robinson and Boog Powell singled in succession. Brooks Robinson then lined into an out that tied the game but simultaneously won the World Series for the Mets. It was a low, sinking drive, apparently hit cleanly through between Agee and right fielder Ron Swoboda. Ron, who was playing in close, hoping for a play at the plate, took three or four lunging steps to his right, dived onto his chest, stuck out his glove, caught the ball, and then skidded on his face and rolled completely over; Robinson scored, but that was all. This marvel settled a lengthy discussion held in Gil Hodges' office the day before, when Gil and several writers had tried to decide whether Agee's first or second feat was the finest Series catch of all time. Swoboda's was. Oh, yes—the Mets won the game in the tenth, 2–1, when Grote doubled and his runner, Rod Gaspar, scored all the way from second on J. C. Martin's perfect pinch bunt, which relief pitcher Pete Richert picked up and threw on a collision course with Martin's left wrist. My wife, sitting in the upper left-field stands, could not see the ball roll free in the glazy late-afternoon dimness and thought that Martin's leaping dance of joy on the base path meant that he had suddenly lost his mind.

So, at last, we came to the final game, and I don't suppose many of us who had watched the Mets through this long and memorable season much doubted that they would win it, even when they fell behind, 0–3, on home runs hit by Dave McNally and Frank Robinson off Koosman in the third inning. Jerry steadied instantly, allowing one single the rest of the way, and the Orioles' badly frayed nerves began to show when they protested long and ineffectually about a pitch in the top of the sixth that they claimed had hit Frank Robinson on the leg, and just as long and as ineffectually about a pitch in the bottom of the sixth that they claimed had *not* hit Cleon Jones on the foot. Hodges produced this second ball from his dugout and invited plate umpire Lou DiMuro to inspect a black scuff on it. DiMuro examined the mark with the air of a Maigret and proclaimed it the true Shinola, and a minute later Donn Clendenon damaged another ball by hitting it against the left-field façade for a two-run homer. Al Weis, again displaying his gift for modest but perfect contingency, hit his very first Shea Stadium homer to lead off the seventh and tie up the game, and the Mets won it in the eighth on doubles by Jones and Swoboda and a despairing but perfectly understandable Oriole double error at first base, all good for two runs and the famous 5–3 final victory.

I had no answer for the question posed by that youngster in the infield who held up—amid the crazily leaping crowds, the showers of noise and paper, the vermilion smoke-bomb clouds, and the vanishing lawns—a sign that said "WHAT NEXT?" What was past was good enough, and on my way down to the clubhouses it occurred to me that the Mets had won this great Series with just the same weapons they had employed all summer— with the Irregulars (Weis, Clendenon, and Swoboda had combined for four homers, eight runs batted in, and an average of .400); with fine pitching (Frank Robinson, Powell, and Paul Blair had been held to one homer, one RBI, and an average of .163); with defensive plays that some of us would remember for the rest of our lives; and with the very evident conviction that the year should not be permitted to end in boredom. Nothing was lost on this team, not even an awareness of the accompanying sadness of the victory—the knowledge that adulation and money and the winter disbanding of this true club would mean that the young Mets were now gone forever. In the clubhouse (Moët et Chandon this time), Ron Swoboda said it precisely for the TV cameras: "This is the first time. Nothing can ever be as sweet again."

Later, in his quiet office, Earl Weaver was asked by a reporter if he hadn't thought that the Orioles would hold on to their late lead in the last game and thus bring the Series back to Baltimore and maybe win it there. Weaver took a sip of beer and smiled and said, "No, that's what you can never do in baseball. You can't sit on a lead and run a few plays into the line and just kill the clock. You've got to throw the ball over the goddam plate and give the other man his chance. That's why baseball is the greatest game of them all."

The Baltimore Vermeers

It was not a year to treasure, nor yet one to forget too quickly. It was a baseball season of satisfactions rather than miracles, of reasonable rather than sudden successes, and a season of much loud foolishness. Attendance and litigation were up, the pennant races and the World Series fell a bit below the wonders of recent autumns, but still there was another long summer of immense noise and involving tension to remember, and hard disappointments, too, and some splendor in the AstroTurf. Most of all, perhaps, it was a year of baseball surprises, in which the bad news, as usual, was often more interesting than the good. The New York Yankees, for example, improved themselves admirably, finishing a solid second to the all-conquering Orioles in their division and compiling a 93–69 won-and-lost record that was bettered, in both leagues, only by the Orioles, the Reds, and the Twins. Their reward for this fine effort was to attract one and a half million fewer fans at home than the Mets drew at Shea Stadium in the course of winning ten fewer games and finishing an abject third in the National League East: the Mets' gate of 2,697,479, in fact, was the second largest total in the history of baseball. Sharing a similarly curious fortune was a field general named Larry Shepard, who was fired a year ago as manager of the Pittsburgh Pirates after his team had won eighty-eight games; his successor, Danny Murtaugh, brought the Pirates home this year with eighty-*nine* victories and was instantly named Manager of the

Year. For Denny McLain, the now erstwhile Detroit ace pitcher
who won a total of fifty-five games in the '68 and '69 seasons,
there was scarcely any good fortune at all. Suspended three
times (twice by Commissioner Bowie Kuhn and once by the
Tigers) for a variety of sins that ranged from a losing venture into
illegal bookmaking to throwing ice water at two sportswriters, he
appeared in fourteen games and won only three. At the end of
the season, he was declared "not mentally ill" by the Commissioner and was then traded to the Washington Senators, against
the wishes of that team's manager, Ted Williams; McLain's sole
immediate consolation may be the thought that he is now the only
right-hander in the American League who is officially sane. Commissioner Kuhn also found it necessary to reprimand another
pitcher-flake, Jim Bouton, whose offense was the co-authorship of
an absorbing and comical baseball book called *Ball Four*. The
volume, which recounts Bouton's somewhat descendant career as
a pitcher with the Yankees, Pilots, and Astros, also includes frank
passages about the pregame amphetamine-popping by his teammates, about their relaxed evening habits on the road, about race
prejudice and minor cheating on the field, and about the habitual
patronizing and financial bullying that most players come to expect from the front office. Commissioner Kuhn did not attack the
veracity of anything in the book, but he indicated his extreme
displeasure with this form of memoir—thus unerringly, if unconsciously, confirming much that Bouton had said about baseball's closed mind and nervous clubbishness. Despite, or perhaps
because of, this warning and the shrill accompanying cries of a
good many Establishmentarian sports columnists (one of them described Bouton and his collaborator, Leonard Shecter, as "social
lepers"), *Ball Four* remained at the upper levels of the best-seller
lists all summer, and is likely to become the most successful sports
book in publishing history. Thus variously rewarded, Bouton
gave up his losing struggle to master the knuckleball, and is now
a sportscaster with a local television station. The lepers are also at
work on a new volume.

Commissioner Kuhn, it can be seen, had a difficult second year in office, and should probably be listed as another victim of the legendary sophomore jinx. Some achievements and standoffs must be granted him. A players' strike was averted through the negotiation of a wide-ranging new three-year contract with the Players Association; the agreement raises minimum salaries and playoff and World Series bonuses, protects players cut during spring training, and establishes new grievance procedures that considerably limit the powers of the Commissioner's office. Still in abeyance, however, is the biggest issue of all—the reserve clause, which was challenged head-on this year by Curt Flood's refusal to report to the Phillies after being traded away by the Cardinals, and his subsequent suit against organized baseball. The case was heard in Federal District Court by Judge Irving Ben Cooper, who listened to fifteen sessions of testimony from owners, executives, and players, and eventually found in favor of the defendants; it was agreed by both sides, however, that the real test of baseball's right to its ancient and unique exemption from the antitrust laws will come during the pending appeal to the Supreme Court. Flood, who is thirty-two, missed a full year at his trade because of his belief that he and his fellow professionals should not be sold and shipped from city to city like crates of oranges, but his sacrifice is still not understood by many of the same megatheriums who were so scandalized by *Ball Four*. When asked about Flood, they shake their heads incredulously and mutter, "How do you *like* that for ingratitude? He was earning ninety thousand a year!"

Outdoors, the news was brighter. Rico Carty, the Braves' ebullient left fielder, won the National League batting title with a mark of .366—the highest average since Ted Williams' .388 thirteen years ago. In all, thirty-one hitters finished the year at .300 or better, which suggests that the recent advantage that pitchers have enjoyed over batters has been almost rebalanced. The Yankees came up with an excellent young catcher named Thurman Munson, who hit .302 in his first year, and a new twenty-game-winning pitcher in Fritz Peterson. Willie Mays, who will be forty next spring (Willie Mays *forty?*), had a splendid season, batting .291 and hitting twenty-eight homers for the Giants, thus running his lifetime total to 628. Hank Aaron, who will be thirty-seven this winter, batted .298 and hit thirty-eight homers for the Braves, running *his* lifetime total to 592. And Hank Morgenweck, who is thirty-eight, worked behind second base during the National League playoff game in Pittsburgh on October 3, thus running his lifetime total of major-league games umpired to one; this record, of course, is shared by George Grygiel, Fred Blandford, and John Grimsley.

Before we move on to those playoffs and the pleasures of the quick, loud World Series just concluded by the Reds and the Orioles, attention must be paid to the painful collapse of the World Champion Mets. It *was* a collapse, although it didn't look that way, because the defenders remained in contention with the Pirates and the Cubs until the very last weekend of the season. From June to October, these three clubs gasped and spluttered and thrashed together at or just below the surface of first place in the National League East; whenever one of them managed two or three strokes in succession and seemed on the point of drawing clear, a clutching hand would reach out and pull it down again. Mostly, it was the Pirates who stayed on top, but the ineptitude of all three teams permitted the Cubs to survive one submersion of twelve straight losses without undue damage, and sustained late pennant hopes that were, in every case, richly undeserved. The Pirates' final 89–73 record was the lowest winning average in the history of the big leagues.

Why the Mets failed to survive even this flabby test, falling seventeen games below their record of last year, is easy to explain but hard to understand. The 1970 Mets encountered many of the accidents and disappointments that befall almost every team in the course of the long season, and their failure to survive them must remind us that last year's Amazin's were largely free of in-

juries and sore arms. They were also a team of extremely limited
power and reserves, which kept winning because every man on
the squad seemed to come through with a key hit or clutch
pitching performance at the precise instant it was needed. This
year, one kept seeing the opposite. Cleon Jones, who led the team
with a .340 average last year, fell into an epochal early slump that
kept him close to the .200 mark until past midseason; no one appeared, from the bench or the farms, to take up this slack. The
bullpen, so obdurate last year, was unreliable until mid-September, when it was too late. Jerry Koosman hurt his arm and broke
his jaw, and still wound up with a 12–7 record—an admirable performance but less good than last year's 17–9, when he
also missed a month of the action. Gary Gentry and Nolan Ryan
were consistently inconsistent. Explanations, excuses . . . What
remains invisible is the weight of success that these young, all-
conquering Mets brought with them into this season. So little was
expected of these players last year that they could plunge head-
long into every key game and series, knowing that they would
not be blamed if they fell on their faces. This year, the opposite
was true. I doubt whether the Mets were surprised or troubled to
find every other club taking dead aim at them in every game, but
what must have been much more difficult was the discovery that
a second success requires different private resources and reserves.
from the first. (This is a hard lesson that New York people understand well; it was what made the Mets' exuberant, astonishing
victory last autumn seem somehow heartbreaking, too.) This
summer, the Mets suffered so many difficult, late defeats in close
games that no one on the team, surely, could have escaped the
chilling interior doubt—the doubt that kills—whispering that
their courage and brilliance last summer had been an illusion all
the time, had been nothing but luck.

Of all the defeats this summer, none was quite so shocking as
the loss the team suffered to the Braves in Atlanta on the night of
August 15. With Tom Seaver in excellent form on the mound,
the Mets led, 2–1, when the Braves, thanks largely to a lucky

infield hit by Carty, loaded the bases with one out in the bottom of the ninth. With the count one and two on Bob Tillman, Seaver wound and threw a called strike three, but the pitch was a fast ball instead of the curve that Jerry Grote had signaled for, and it sailed right by the catcher and back to the screen. The runner scored from third, and when Grote pegged wildly past Seaver, covering at the plate, the runner from second also came in, and the game was suddenly and horribly gone. That one seemed to go on hurting. It dropped the Mets four games behind the Pirates and made Seaver's record 17–7; he was to win only one more game the rest of the year, finishing up at 18–12. Of all the Mets' mysteries, this is the most mysterious. Seaver was not injured or suffering from arm exhaustion, although he did pitch with insufficient rest in the late stages of the race. Throughout September, he made no excuses, except to say that the problem was technical—his left leg was getting too far ahead of his body in his delivery, subtly altering his timing. Yet he looked worse and worse as the season ran out, being hit by humpty-dumpty batters who had never touched him before, and even fielding his position poorly. Tom Seaver is a complicated young man who has enjoyed extraordinary success at his profession, and any tentative explanation of his sudden downfall must also be complicated, beginning with the instant reminder that it was a "downfall" only in comparison with his own past record; his 18–12 mark was below last year's 25–7, but he still led the league this year with an earned-run average of 2.81 and two hundred and eighty-three strikeouts. And here, perhaps, is a clue. Last year, Seaver came within two outs of pitching a perfect game, that finest of all baseball feats, and during the early part of this season it sometimes looked as if his personal goal, in a career that had quickly brought him almost every other achievement, was to win that game back—to attain, if only once, perfection on the mound. Several times this spring, he came unscathed to the middle innings, only to see a scratchy infield hit trickle through or a bloop fly drop in against him and ruin things. He was visibly angry at such times, kicking the mound and glaring at the base-runner; later, he was curt and haughty with reporters. At about the same time, Seaver began striking out more hitters than ever before. He tied a record by fanning nineteen batters in a game against the Padres, during which he set another all-time mark by striking out ten batters in a row. This is impressive but just possibly fatal. As real fans know, a pitcher who strikes out a great many men in a game is often working at less than his best level; a blend of whiffs, grounders, and flies is more effective, and much easier on the arm. What suggests itself, then, is that, subtly and perhaps unconsciously, Seaver began relying too often on his hummer, his strikeout pitch, to get him out of difficulties in a hard season. This is what happened in Atlanta that night, and it may have gone on happening, even to the point where he imperceptibly altered the natural and beautiful rhythm that had made him almost indomitable. In trying for perfection, he may have suffered the first true defeat of his life.

And yet, and yet . . . Even down to late September, a reprieve, a tarnished but acceptable second miracle, seemed quite possible for the Mets. The last fourteen days of the schedule offered seven games with Pittsburgh and four with Chicago. The Mets lost the first two games to the Pirates at Shea on September 18 and 19, each by an excruciating one-run margin, and slid into third place, two games behind the Cubs and three and a half back of the leaders. Then, on the twentieth, the largest home crowd of the year—54,806—turned out for the Sunday doubleheader. Long before game time, there were turned-away fans standing three-deep on the roofs of some parked buses behind the visiting-team bullpen in left field; they stood there, craning and hoping, all through the warm late-summer afternoon. They were rewarded with a superb performance by Jerry Koosman in the opener. Tendonitis has robbed Koosman of his old, sweeping fast ball, but he is perhaps more of a pitcher now than ever before. Working resolutely, always around the corners, he served up an assortment of down-breaking curves and changes that set down the first fifteen Pirate batters in order. José Pagan hit a home run to lead off the sixth, but by that time the home side had compiled a modest three runs, and Jerry gave the Pirates only one other hit, winning 4–1. Now! A sweep would put us back in the thick of things. Seaver was opposed by a young pitcher named Fred Cambria, who was in only his second year of organized ball, yet it was Seaver who was instantly in difficulties, giving up singles and loud outs in profusion. Some good luck and a costly Pirate error kept it tied at 2–2 until the sixth, when Tom departed amid a shower of hits and boos—a sound I never expected to hear directed at him—and the score went to 5–2 against the Mets. Stubbornly, almost sullenly, they rallied—a Boswell homer in the sixth, three hits in the seventh—to tie it once more at 5–5, to an enormous storm of shouting, but the effort clearly exhausted them. The visitors' Willie Stargell hit a homer off McGraw to open the tenth, and a moment or two later Tommy Agee and Rod Gaspar collided in right field, not far from the site of Agee's second famous catch in the World Series last year, and Gene Alley's liner rolled all the way to the wall. The Pirates won, 9–5, and the two-year age of wonders came to its end. Official extinction descended a week later, when the Mets dropped three more games in Pittsburgh, all of them by one-run margins. In the seven key games against the Pirates, they had batted into sixteen double plays and stranded no fewer than sixty-six base-runners, which is the mark of an old, old ball team.

The most riveting figures visible on the first day of the National League playoffs between the Pirates and the Cincinnati Reds at Pittsburgh's new Three Rivers Stadium were neither the home team's conglomeration of old and young hitters— Roberto Clemente and Manny Sanguillen, Willie Stargell and Rich Hebner, Bill Mazeroski and Bob Robertson—nor even such celebrated Red cannoneers as Johnny Bench, Tony Perez, Lee May, and Pete Rose; they were the umpires, the aforementioned Messrs. Morgenweck, Grygiel, Blandford, and Grimsley, who had been hastily summoned up from the minors (and into the Trivia Hall of Fame) to replace the regular six-man National League crew, which had that day (*O tempora!* O Bill Klem!) gone on strike for higher playoff and World Series wages. The American League umps working the Orioles-Twins playoffs in Minnesota were also out. Negotiations between the Umpires Association and the Commissioner's office had dragged on in a desultory fashion for some weeks, with no more than a couple of thousand dollars separating the two, and it seemed clear that no one had truly expected the issue to be drawn. Thus, it was not until just before game time that the strikers slipped their painted-cardboard sandwich signs ("Major League Umpires on Strike for Wages") over their uniforms and formed a ragged, self-conscious picket line outside the stadium. One of them, Harry Wendelstedt, kept explaining to entering fans that he felt embarrassed about the whole thing. "I'm a professional man," he said. "I belong out on that ballfield, not here looking like a clown." Whatever irresolution might have been indicated by this remark was probably dispersed when Warren Giles, the former president of the National League, shook hands with Wendelstedt on entering the park and then turned to a nearby special cop and said, "Move 'em away from here—about a mile and a half away." The umps stood fast, and during the afternoon their number increased as more of their colleagues arrived from around the country and joined the line.

Inside, and almost incidentally, the ball game went on—fortunately, without any especially difficult calls to challenge the bush-league bluecoats. The matchup brought together teams both known for their good hitters and their aching pitchers. Both had compiled a team average of .270; the Reds had led the league in homers, the Pirates in hits; throughout the season, both had been forced to rely heavily on bullpen veterans and newly called-up young fireballers to help out a corps of starting pitchers who sometimes seemed to be made of blown glass. Expecting a bombardment, we were given, of course, a pitching duel—a languid

Indian-summer afternoon of pop fouls and infield outs, only occasionally vivified when the starters, Gary Nolan for the Reds and Dock Ellis for the Pirates, worked out of mild jams. I had plenty of time to study the new ballpark, which is situated just across the Allegheny River from Pittsburgh's downtown Golden Triangle, and to wonder how ballplayers nowadays can remember which town they are playing in as they look up at the same tiered, brightly painted circles of seats that, rising above fields of fake grass, identically and anonymously surround them in so many big-league cities. More and more, these stadia remind one of motels or airports in their perfect and dreary usefulness; they are no longer parks but machines for sports. In time, though, I found the difference here—an immense glassed-in dining room and bar called the Allegheny Club, which occupies much of the third and fourth tiers beyond first base at Three Rivers Stadium, permitting affluent locals (who may also lease private boxes, at a price of $38,000 for five years) to take their baseball à la carte. Pittsburgh has six chandeliers in right field. It also, on this particular day, had some twenty thousand bright orange empty seats in upper center field—an embarrassing reminder that these Championship Series, as the postseason playoffs are officially known, have not yet won the fealty of the fans. I was aroused from these reveries by the first loud, sharp noise of the day as Ty Cline, a Cincinnati pinch-hitter, led off the tenth inning with a triple past Clemente in right field; a moment or two later, he trotted in with the first run of the game, and then Lee May drove in two more with a double to left, and the Reds won it, 3–0.

I got to the stadium early the next day, but not as early as the striking umpires, who had set up their picket line at five in the morning and now had the place buttoned up like Fort Knox. Pittsburgh, of course, is a union town, and the various locals representing the stadium's ushers, ticket-takers, groundskeepers, electricians, and such enforced a total embargo in honor of the umps' grievance. It was a chill, blowy day, and we all milled around together cheerfully under the fortress walls—strikers, unioneers, fans, reporters, Baseball Annies, cops, photographers, and excited small boys. Negotiations, we were told, were in progress within. Umpires Doug Harvey and Paul Pryor gave out autographs and TV interviews like a couple of Musials, and once a cigar-smoking shop steward pushed forward through the crowd to rumble loud reminders of solidarity at the driver of an approaching cab, who, it turned out, was merely lost. Then, just an hour before game time, the word came: "It's over!" National League President Chub Feeney and Jack Reynolds, the lawyer for the Umpires Association, announced together that negotiations would be resumed in good faith; later that week, the two sides settled on umpires' fees of $4000 per man for the playoffs and $7500 ($8000 after 1972) for the World Series—a fair sum, it might seem, for a handful of games, but one that each umpire will draw, in rotation with his fellows, only every five years or so. The whole impasse, in retrospect, seemed faintly bush, but it had been a very near thing. That morning, one Pirates executive had approached another inside the empty park and said, "Look, if this strike isn't cleared up, do you think you could ask Clemente and some of the other players if they'd mind helping take up the tarpaulin?"

"Who," said his associate, paling, "*me?*"

The victorious umpires received a fat round of boos from the fans as they came onto the field, but then lapsed into invisibility when the baseball began. Better baseball, too. Bobby Tolan, the quick young Cincinnati center fielder, gave us an edifying lesson in one o'cat, scoring the Reds' first run on a single, a stolen base, an error, and a wild pitch; their second run on a prodigious homer to right center; and their third and final run on another single and a dash around the bases on Tony Perez' double. The home team, having put up fourteen straight goose eggs on the board, scraped together a run in the sixth, but Sparky Anderson, the Reds' manager, called in a nineteen-year-old left-hander named Don Gullett, who retired Willie Stargell with two men on and blew down the Pirates the rest of the way. Gullett, who was pitching for his high school in Kentucky a year and a half ago, throws *hard;* afterward, his catcher, Johnny Bench, said, "He can throw the ball through a car wash and not get it wet."

The playoffs now moved along to Cincinnati's Riverfront Stadium, which is another 1970-model four-decker, but with different accessories: no chandeliers, AstroTurf instead of Tartan Turf underfoot, and no dirt on the base paths, which have utterly vanished except for a miniature sandbox around each base. (Ballplayers, it must be said, are almost unanimous in their praise of these new surfaces, which improve their fielding averages by eliminating the bad bounce. A thrown or batted ball jumps off the ungrass with such alacrity that anything hit up the left- or right-field power alley almost invariably streaks through for extra bases, but outfielders who remember to keep their pegs down low—for the bounce—suddenly discover that they all have developed shotgun arms. All this, of course, has changed the game in ways that have yet to be measured—if anyone should ever care to conduct such useless, *ex post facto* researches.) Now facing deletion in the three-out-of-five series, the Pirates painstakingly worked the Reds' starter, Tony Cloninger, for a run in the first inning. In the bottom half, however, Tony Perez and Johnny Bench hit two balls over the left-field fence in such quick proximity and succession that the second resembled an instant-replay shot of the first. The Pirates retied in at 2–2 in the fifth, but Anderson brought in another postpubescent from the bullpen, a twenty-year-old right-hander named Milt Wilcox, who quickly restored order. The crowd, larger and much noisier than the Pittsburgh turnouts, now sensed whatever it is that can so often be sensed about the outcome of a tight, important game; they kept up a happy, expectant screeching, even though Bob Moose, the Pittsburgh starter, was now pitching almost indomitably, setting down nineteen of twenty Redleg batters in a row. Sure enough—with two out in the eighth, Moose walked Ty Cline, and then had to face Pete Rose, who is perhaps the world's most dangerous hitter in such a situation. Rose singled. Thinking hard, Murtaugh now brought in a lefty, Joe Gibbon, to throw to left-handed Bob Tolan, but Tolan took two quick strikes and then poked a wrong-field single to left on the next pitch, bringing in Cline with what turned out to be the deciding run. The Orioles, the scoreboard announced, were champions again, having wiped out the Twins in three straight for the second year in a row. And here, minutes later, Don Gullett was in again to retire the last Pirate batter, and the Reds were champions too. Time for the champagne: champagne over everybody and everything, champagne all over the nice red rug on the clubhouse floor, and also—hoo, hoo! ho, ho!—all over the Reds' other rug, which is Lee May's hairpiece.

All of us, I think, had been waiting through the summer for this Series and for the collision of these two enormous teams. Both had utterly flattened the opposition in their divisions, holding first place unchallenged after April. The Reds' three sluggers, Perez, Bench, and May, had combined for a hundred and nineteen home runs—a total six entire *teams* failed to reach this year—and three hundred and seventy-one runs batted in. Bench, the Reds' leader and, at twenty-two, already one of the finest catchers in baseball history, had led both leagues with forty-five homers and a hundred and forty-eight RBIs. Against this, the Orioles could offer Boog Powell (thirty-five homers), the two famous Robinsons, three twenty-game-winning pitchers—Cuellar (24–8), McNally (24–9), and Palmer (20–10)—and a hovering, almost visible smolder of resentment over the team's unexpected beating by the Mets last fall.

The opener, back at Riverfront Stadium, brought the expected early clang of armor—a Lee May homer and three quick Cincinnati runs, which were instantly won back on homers by Powell and Elrod Hendricks, the Baltimore catcher. It was still 3–3 in the bottom of the sixth, when Lee May, leading off, rifled a hard grounder to left; Brooks Robinson, the Orioles' thirty-three-year-old perennial third baseman, leaped to his right, speared the ball cross-handed just above the base, and, whirling and throwing in the same instant, let go a fallaway peg from foul ground that got to first on the bounce and still nipped the runner. This wonder (not an unexpected wonder for those of us who remembered Robinson's play in last year's Series) saved a double, and made possible the famous and disorderly scene that now began after Bernie Carbo walked and was singled to third. Ty Cline, pinch-hitting, chopped at a Jim Palmer pitch and bounced it high in the air, directly in front of the plate. Hendricks stepped forward, waiting for the ball to descend, and Carbo suddenly and foolishly set sail for the plate. Home-plate umpire Ken Burkhart, apparently forgetting all about the base-runner, stepped forward to see if the ball would come down fair or foul, and Jim Palmer, approaching from the mound, had an incomparable view of the ensuing carnage.

"I knew Carbo was coming," he said later. "I could hear him —*clomp, clomp, clomp*—on the AstroTurf, so I yelled to Hendricks, 'Tag him! Tag him!' " Carbo slid, Hendricks whirled and lunged for him, and Burkhart, now horribly resembling a dog on a highway, was struck simultaneously from two directions. He landed on the seat of his pants, facing the outfield, but bravely raised his fist in the air for the "out" sign. That settled the matter, of course, though dissenting views were delivered by Carbo, Sparky Anderson, and 51,531 other expert witnesses. The Reds lost the game in the next inning, 4–3, when Brooks Robinson lofted a high sailer into the alley behind the left-field fence. Detailed-sequence photographs in the papers the next day reminded one of the fatal business at Sarajevo. They clearly showed that all three participants had failed in their missions: Carbo never touched the plate, Hendricks tagged the runner with his glove but not the ball, and Burkhart, trying to look down the small of his back, did not see the play.

The Reds briskly disposed of Cuellar in the second game, racking him for three runs in the first inning and a Tolan homer in the third; more damage impended, but Brooks Robinson jumped for a hard shot by Lee May and turned it into a double play, and Boog Powell, for the second day in a row, began the Orioles' catch-up with a fourth-inning homer. They did more than just catch up this time; in the fifth, five singles drove out the Reds' starter, Jim McGlothlin, and then Elrod Hendricks, who bats left-handed, barely clipped a pitch with the very tip of his flailing bat, banking it the wrong way, over third, and driving in the fifth and sixth Baltimore runs—a piece of pure bad baseball luck that cost the Reds the game. Bench hit a subsequent homer that brought it up to 6–5, but the home-towners could do nothing against the Orioles' relief pitcher, Dick Hall, who set down the last seven batters in order. Dick Hall is a Baltimore institution, like crab cakes. He is six feet six and one-half inches tall and forty years old, and he pitches with an awkward, sidewise motion that suggests a man feeling under his bed for a lost collar stud. He throws a sneaky fast ball and never, or *almost* never, walks batters; he has given up exactly twenty unintentional bases on balls in the past four hundred and eighteen innings, dating back to 1965. Hall is almost bald; he has ulcers, a degree in economics from Swarthmore, a Mexican wife, four children, and an off-season job as a certified public accountant; and he once startled his bullpen mates by trying to estimate mathematically how many drops of rain were falling on the playing field during a shower. After the game, I saw Dick Hall laughing and talking with teammates and reporters in the clubhouse, with a crust of dried Gelusil on his lower lip; his pitching opponent for the last two innings had been Don Gullett, the nineteen-year-old, and I suddenly wondered which of the two would remember this day longer.

On to Baltimore, then, to real (if rather scruffy) grass, and, for the next two games, to the awed further inspection of that other local monument, Brooks Robinson. Long ago, his teammates adopted a cool, unsurprised tone, which is part put-on, in discussing Robinson's feats. "Oh, that's nothing," they say to a sportswriter or rival player about some dusty new miracle behind third. "Brooks does that sort of thing all the time." In the third game —a 9–3 laugher that was settled in the sixth, when Oriole pitcher Dave McNally hit a grand-slam homer—Brooks Robinson hit two doubles and batted in two runs, snuffed out a Cincinnati threat in the first with a nifty double play, robbed Tommy Helms in the second by dashing in for a grab and flip of his slow bouncer, and broke Johnny Bench's heart in the sixth with a full-length portside dive to snare Bench's liner in the top of his glove webbing, some four inches above the ground. The Series had given us so many of these Brooksian masterpieces, in fact, that I found myself beginning to collect and compare them in memory, like Vermeers. After the game, Oriole manager Earl Weaver merely smiled and said, "Yes, I've enjoyed watching him," but the unhappy Reds' pilot, Sparky Anderson, kept shaking his head and muttering, "He's the whole Series so far." Pete Rose, glumly pointing a thumb upward, said, "Brooks Robinson belongs in a Higher League."

During the fourth game, the following afternoon, Brooks Robinson did nothing much in the field, but he put in a useful day at the plate, rapping a homer and three singles in four trips. It looked to be a quick and nearly monotheistic Series as Baltimore moved smoothly out to a 5–3 lead. Then, in the eighth, with the season running down and the Reds' power coming to the plate for perhaps the last time this year, Tony Perez worked Jim Palmer for a walk, and Johnny Bench singled solidly to left. Eddie Watt, a right-handed reliever, came in for the Orioles. He warmed, then got his sign, stretched and threw, and Lee May hammered the pitch into the deeper part of the deep-left-field bleachers; none of the Baltimore infielders even turned to watch the flight of the ball. The Reds' best reliever, Clay Carroll, set down the home side in the eighth and ninth, and the Reds won it, 6–5. It was the Orioles' first defeat in the past eighteen games, and even a few of the Baltimore rooters must have sensed that the Reds, who had reached the Orioles' pitchers for twenty-nine hits so far, had deserved at least this one evening of renewed hope and raised voices. Lee May, laughing, said, "I got *hold* of it! Had to keep it away from that Hoover Robinson, you know. He's been suckin' up everything I sent down his way." Johnny Bench, deadly serious, said, "We've really got a shot now. We win it tomorrow and it's back to our home park, and *then* let's see who takes it all."

Bench didn't quite convince me then, but he almost did in the first inning the next afternoon, when he singled and Pete Rose and Lee May and Hal McRae all doubled, to score three light-ning-fast runs off Mike Cuellar. Earl Weaver convened a mound conference with his ace and, having seen something that was en-tirely invisible to everyone else in the park, left Cuellar in the game. This, of course, is what managers are paid for; Cuellar did not give up another hit until the seventh inning, by which time the game and the Series and the season were, in effect, over. The Other Robinson—Frank—had started things off with a two-run homer in the bottom of the first, and then there were two more Oriole runs in the second and still two more in the third, and it became clear that the Reds' pitching, which had never been in true health, was at last finished. With the Orioles leading by 7–3, Brooks Robinson came up to bat in the eighth, fanned, and returned to the dugout to the accompaniment of what may stand for some time as the longest and loudest standing ovation given to a ballplayer who has just struck out. And then, in the ninth, Brooks returned the compliment prettily—another air-borne flight across third base, to grab Bench's lead-off liner. Af-terward, after Baltimore had won the game by 9–3 and the Se-ries by 4–1, Pete Rose sat in the quiet Reds' clubhouse and said, "That last shot? Oh, that was nothing for Brooks. That's nothing for him." Quite right, and so let us conclude by saying only that there were several of us who, along with Earl Weaver, enjoyed watching the Orioles' third baseman play baseball this autumn, when he and his teammates entirely destroyed what has sometimes (but never so late) been called the Big Red Machine.

Part of a Season: Bay and Back Bay

Baseball, it seems, has declared an advance special dividend for 1971. The old mutual concern, barely a third of the way into its new business year, has rarely found itself in such splendid early fettle, and its supporters have already been enriched beyond their customary late-summer expectations. These are the latest market quotations on some of the firm's gilt-edge securities: Oliva, .371; W. Davis, .357; Brock, .352; Torre, .351; Mays, .323; Frank Robinson, .308; Kaline, .321; Brooks Robinson, .304, after a recent sell-off; and the junior Alou Frères, Ltd.—Jesus, .333, and Mateo, .316. Good performances have also been recorded by such comparatively recent issues as Kranepool (.309), Staub (.325), Murcer (a resounding .359), and a new high-flier called Garr of Atlanta (.349). Having thus bankrupted my supply of financial metaphors (even without mention of Bobby Bonds or a Blue Chip named Vida), I will go on to observe, more plainly, that the sluggers have been busily at work, too. The Pirates' Willie Stargell has twenty-one homers currently in hand, which represents something of a slump from his record opening burst of eleven in April; Hank Aaron has wafted nineteen, Johnny Bench sixteen, Bonds fifteen, and Billy Williams and Orlando Cepeda fourteen each. The American League long-ball hitters are a bit laggard, but it is unsafe to assume that Yastrzemski, Frank Howard, Harmon Killebrew, and the rest will not suddenly catch up in the

course of some loud, hot summer week. And the pitching—
well, the pitching, in both leagues, has been of such a quality
that one cannot entirely understand who it is all these hitters
have been swinging against. Vida Blue, the phenomenal young
Oakland fireballer, has struck out a hundred and twenty-five batters in a hundred and thirty innings, and has a record of 13 wins
and 2 losses. Mike Cuellar, of the Orioles, stands at 10 and 1;
Larry Dierker, of the Astros, at 10 and 2; and the Cardinals'
Steve Carlton at 10 and 3. At this rate, all of them have a crack at
winning thirty games or more this year. Four pitchers with six or
more decisions to their credit have earned-run averages of less
than two runs per game—Cooperstown stuff.

Attendance, unsurprisingly is up—a jump of about 220,000
in the American League and better than 358,000 in the National
League. The more modest AL mark is probably the more significant, since the NL totals include an artificial boost attributable to
the opening of the Phillies' new ballpark, Veterans Stadium. But
even the White Sox, still resident in ancient Comiskey Park and
holding what has been recently considered an exhausted franchise, have almost doubled their attendance so far this year. Statistics bore everybody but the superfan (who already knows them
anyway), but these are offered with a purpose: to me they suggest that in 1971 most of the baseball news is being made out on
the playing field, instead of in the courts or in the front office, its
habitat in recent years. And even the kind of baseball happening
that is not easily encapsulated in a box score seems to have an unusual savor in this unusual season. There has been the brief retirement of Clete Boyer, the Atlanta third baseman, who almost
talked himself out of baseball because he could not bear the character of his general manager, Paul Richards, and said so, repeatedly. Also the bemusement of Alex Johnson, the Angels' defending American League batting champion, who has walked himself
into semi-permanent suspension because he cannot bear to run on
the base paths. Also the self-exile of Carl Taylor, a Kansas City
outfielder who, dissatisfied with his own professional perfor-

mance, pushed at an umpire, punched a teammate, and set fire to
his uniform in the clubhouse before departing the pastime for a
period of reflection.

Baseball thrives on personality, but the cult of the team is even
more essential to its well-being than the cult of the star. Two decades ago, the sixteen major-league clubs were entirely distin-
guishable; one knew them by heart and could recognize them as
quickly and surely as one recognized the different flavors in a jar
of sourballs. Now there are twenty-four teams, split into four
subdivisions, and, because of expansion and the shifting and scattering of franchises, there sometimes seem to be no more than half
a dozen teams that are *known* to us—not just the names of
their stars or managers but the way they play ball, the way they
look on the field, the way they are remembered. Only sharper
competition, marked by the arrival of new challengers at the
upper levels of contention, can alter this, and it is precisely that
phenomenon which has brought such a sense of quickening and
excitement to the young season. Who does not know the news?
The Baltimore Orioles, who so admirably and drearily discour-
aged all opposition in their division for the past two years, took
wing in rather leaden fashion this year, thus permitting hope in
such unexpected places as Boston and Detroit; the world champions have only recently retaken their accustomed topmost perch,
and there may be a good deal of teetering and flapping there before all is secure. Meanwhile, the American League West has
been entirely dominated by the startling Oakland A's, a team
heretofore notable only for its white baseball shoes and the Ca-
ligulan whims of its owner, Charles O. Finley, who has fired ten
managers in ten years. The National League East is once again
the scene of a two- or three-team fight that may not be resolved
until the final days or hours of the season. The contenders—the
Cardinals, Mets, and Pirates—have offered a sustained lesson in
different styles of winning baseball; the best of the three may be
the Cardinals, back from two years of utter despond, whose new
style is hitting. The Cincinnati Reds, last year's pennant winners,

are in disarray, their pitching almost nonexistent and the other parts of the Big Red Machine sputtering badly or in the repair shop. Their demise was predicted even before the season started; their successors at the top of the National League West, everyone agreed, were to be the Dodgers—an excellent prediction entirely ignored by the San Francisco Giants, who almost ran away from the field in the first six weeks. Many of these clubs, it will be noticed, have honored, familiar names, but as 1971 contenders they are not at all the same good old clubs we thought we knew —as we may discover when we call on the good old (or, in most ways, much better and not so old) Giants in their airy seaside home.

Before that journey, though, a brief further look should be directed at the Mets, whose baseball personality has subtly altered. Last year, the memory of their brilliant, unforgettable success of the previous autumn seemed to hang on them like a sea anchor. They played somberly, warily, and, in the end, exhaustedly, as if they had forgotten how many games they had once captured on sheer exuberance. This season is much more like '69; the players are mature, but one sometimes catches glimpses on the field of that same mad young expectation—the conviction that the team just might win every single game from now to October. This is a hope still unreinforced by such baseball realities as the long ball. The team has won on hitting by gentle belters like Jerry Grote, Dave Marshall, and Bud Harrelson, and by the surprise of the year, if not the century, Eddie Kranepool, now in his tenth summer in a Mets uniform. The pitching has been excellent, of course—most especially the bullpen of McGraw, Taylor, and Frisella—and Nolan Ryan has succeeded Jerry Koosman as the stopper next to God, Tom Seaver. Watching Ryan work can be wearing; a typical Ryan inning (as confirmed by my scorecard of a recent game against Houston) consists of a walk, another walk, a swinging strikeout, another swinging strikeout, *another* walk, and a line drive straight into the glove of the right fielder. One way or another, he gets the job done—he has won six games so far, and has an earned-run average of 1.72. For that matter, watching the Mets in almost any game can be exhausting; things are often settled, along about the ninth or tenth or eleventh inning, by a piece of wild baseball luck—an enemy drive that *just* falls foul, or a Metsian screamer that suddenly becomes the game-closing DP. This kind of baseball requires a superior infield, enormous team courage, and strong-hearted, insatiable fans—exactly what the Mets have the most of.

Giant fans are famous front-runners. Made wary over the years by the Giants' obligatory June swoon and patented furious, insufficient September rush, which have kept the team habitually in second place, the fans have stayed away from Candlestick Park in notable numbers. It is in many ways an excellent place to avoid —a dour, wind-whipped gray concrete tureen that is currently being enlarged, of all things, so that it may similarly test the loyalties of pro football fans this autumn. When I arrived there on a Friday night in mid-May, I thought for a moment that I would be just in time for the Forty-Niners' opening kickoff, because the fans around me were accoutered in mackinaws, scarves, gloves, and watch caps, and carrying steamer rugs and Thermosed fortifiers. But they were baseball fans, in sensible Bay-side evening attire, who had finally appeared in real numbers to see the beginning of a three-game set against the Dodgers and warily to encourage their Giants, off to the greatest start in their history, with a lead of eight full games in their division. The Dodgers added to the wind-chill factor with two instantaneous runs on a long double by Willie Davis, but reassurance was quickly supplied. The second home-sider to come to the plate was Chris Speier, a thin twenty-year-old shortstop, still only in his second year of organized baseball, who has nailed together the Giant infield for the first time in a decade and driven San Franciscans into an uncharacteristic tizzy of admiration; he lofted one of Al Downing's pitches up into the westerly gale, which carried it over the right-field fence. The next pitch was hit somewhat more

firmly by Willie Howard Mays and disappeared in the direction
of San Leandro. It was Speier's first major-league homer (he
waved his clenched fist in the air as he rounded the bases), and,
with its successor, it raised the record for most combined home
runs by a still active shortstop and center fielder on the same
team to six hundred and thirty-seven.

The game was a brisk, noisy affair that kept us continuously, if
not warmly, entertained. The Giants went ahead on the second
of Willie McCovey's three hits, were passed in the fourth on a
two-run Dodger homer by Duke Sims, and then put the game
away, 8–4, in the seventh on a long succession of singles, walks,
sacrifices, and Dodger mistakes. Dodger manager Walter Alston
made two defensive infield shifts in this inning, and each of his
specialists committed an error—the kind of gift that streaking
teams like the Giants accept without surprise.

The next afternoon, another big crowd, now reassured by the
Giants' *nine*-game lead, saw an even better game—a vivid
pitchers' battle between the Dodgers' Bill Singer and the perennial Juan Marichal, who has won more games for the Giants
than anyone except Carl Hubbell and Christy Mathewson. The
innings zipped along, and, washed in sunshine and a river of
clean ocean air, I had plenty of time to admire the new Giants
and sympathize with the new Dodgers. The Los Angelenos' Willie Davis, now resplendent in the largest Afro in baseball, is hitting the ball and playing the outfield as never before in his life;
his celebrated new teammate Richie Allen is also hitting the ball
as never before—which is to say that he is hardly hitting it at
all. The Giants, so far, have been entirely free of such mysteries
and bad luck. Willie McCovey has sore knees, but they do not
prevent him from batting with his old exciting, scythe-swinger's
style. The pitching, recently no deeper than Marichal and Gaylord Perry, has been firmed up by admirable younger arms belonging to Ron Bryant and Steve Stone and a reliever named
Jerry Johnson, whose ERA at this writing is 0.70. The
outfielders—Mays, Ken Henderson, and Bobby Bonds—are

wonderfully fast afoot, an essential attribute on Candlestick's slick AstroTurf, which now covers the whole infield except for dirt cutouts around the mound and the bases. (The all-chemical lawn is perhaps forgivable at Candlestick, for it has done away with the appalling dust storms that used to swirl among the cowering participants.) Chris Speier, I suspect, is a model of baseball's infielder of the future, the AstroPlayer—wide-ranging, with extremely quick hands and the ability to get off deep, rifle-shot throws with almost no visible arm-cocking or windup. Old-time Giant front-office men think he may turn out to be the finest Giant shortstop since Travis Jackson, back in the early thirties. (Speier, by the way, is a local product, who still lives at home in Alameda, across the Bay. His fourteen-year-old brother, Bill, one may imagine, is grappling with something of a sibling problem this year. When a reporter recently asked Speier if Bill gave him much flak at the family's breakfast table, the new star shrugged and said, "Not much. I mean, what can he *say?*")

Candlestick's classic pastime—and the best entertainment in baseball this year—is watching Willie Mays. Now just turned forty, and beginning his twenty-first year in the majors, he is hitting better than he has hit at any time in the past six or seven seasons, and playing the game with enormous visible pleasure. Veteran curators in the press box like to expound upon various Maysian specialties—the defensive gem, the basket catch, the looped throw, the hitched swing, and so forth. My favorite is his base-running. He may have lost a half-second or so in getting down to first base, but I doubt whether Willie Davis or Ralph Garr or any of the other new flashes can beat Mays from first to third, or can accelerate just as he does, with his whole body suddenly seeming to sink lower when, taking his turn at first and intently following the distant ball and outfielder, he suddenly sees his chance. Watching him this year, seeing him drift across a base and then sink into full speed, I noticed all at once how much he resembles a marvelous skier in midturn down some steep pitch of fast powder. *Nobody* like him.

No one knows how long Mays can sustain all this. He will sit out perhaps thirty or forty games this year, resting, but the only other concession to age is his habit, in a Giants' half when he is unlikely to come to bat, of sitting down with the pitchers out in the right-field bullpen, thus saving himself the trip to the dugout. His real race with his years is measured—in the mind of the public, at least—in that perpetual comparison with Babe Ruth's home-run record of 714. Willie is at 641 as this is written, and he will need three homer-productive years—say, twenty-five more this season, then thirty, then twenty—to make it. I doubt whether he will quite run the course—but I care much less about his breaking the record than I care that the last Mays homer, whenever it comes and whatever its number, be struck with joy.

The Singer-Marichal matchup sailed scorelessly along into the later innings, with the Dodgers seeming to have a little the better of it. Singer was striking out Giants in clusters, while Marichal —who throws like some enormous and dangerous farm implement—was putting men on but still managing to get through innings on no more than eight or ten pitches. Mays led off the seventh and took a huge cut at a Singer fast ball, kicking up a puff of dust in the batter's box as he missed. Singer now craftily essayed a curve (the strategy of pitchers is limited), which Willie leaped at and lined into deepest left field for a double. It was the Giants' first hit of the game, and a few moments later Dick Dietz, the excellent Giant catcher, delivered the second—a single that scored Mays with the only run of the afternoon. Afterward, in his clubhouse office, Giant manager Charlie Fox poured a little Galway Mist for a visiting reporter and said, "It's always *useful* to watch him play this game. You know he moves the players around out in the field? Hell, he's been in this game twenty years—he's picked up a couple of pointers. Yes, it's a nice feeling to come to the ballpark every day and know he's on your side. The leader is still leading."

Charlie Fox, who has been in the Giant organization for thirty

years, ascending to the helm last May, gets along splendidly with
Willie Mays. ("We're like brothers," Fox says, "only I'm the big
brother.") The center fielder, who has a distaste for time-wasting,
occasionally posed difficulties for some of Fox's less accomplished
predecessors. A few seasons ago, when Willie was suffering
through an epochal slump, striking out repeatedly or popping up
in crucial situations, it occurred to the Giant management that
their star might benefit from a checkup by an oculist. Somehow,
neither the manager nor any of his coaches nor anyone in the
front office felt any eagerness to make this suggestion to Mays,
and eventually somebody approached a San Francisco sportswriter named Charles Einstein, who is a biographer and close
friend of Willie's, and asked if he would undertake the mission. A
little startled, Einstein agreed, and a few days later he greeted
Mays near the batting cage. The exchange, Einstein says, went
like this:

> EINSTEIN: Er—say, Buck [some of Mays' friends call him
> Buck], have you noticed how many players are wearing glasses
> this year?
> MAYS: Like who?
> EINSTEIN: Well, let's see. . . . Oh, yes—Howard. Frank
> Howard is wearing glasses now.
> MAYS: He ain't hittin' either.

The subject was never reopened.

On Sunday, a sellout crowd confidently turned out to watch
another Dodger-Giant pitching classic—Claude Osteen vs.
Gaylord Perry—and a further extension of the home team's infinitely extensible lead. It was Cap Day at Candlestick, and the
rows of kids in the top deck, each wearing a dark baseball cap
with white central insignia, looked exactly like a congress of rac-
coons. Noise and delight everywhere—except, it turned out, on
the playing field. The ball kept coming loose in the infield; there
were four errors in the first two innings and eight errors in all,
and at one point Tito Fuentes, the Giants' second baseman,
struck out on a wild pitch and eventually came around to score.

That kind of baseball. Still, all seemed saved when the Giants pulled ahead on a three-run homer by Bobby Bonds in the sixth, but then Don McMahon, the Giants' elderly relief pitcher, found it impossible to get anybody out during his eight-hundred-and-forty-ninth (and perhaps his worst) lifetime mound appearance; Chris Speier, in an admirably eager and youthful but absolutely hopeless and mistaken attempt at a double play, threw a ball away that he should have held on to; the Dodgers scored six runs in the last two innings, beating their old rivals by 9–6; and the San Francisco fans went home with the anxiously renewed knowledge under their new caps that the season still had a few weeks to run after all.

Ten days later, I paid a visit to the American League side of San Francisco Bay, calling upon the other surprise of this baseball season—the Oakland A's, who, like the Giants, had opened a startling lead over their Western Division rivals. The two Bay-area teams have coexisted amicably since the A's migrated from Kansas City in 1968, competing only for the annual regional low-attendance crown, which the Giants carried off by a whisker last year, 740,220 to 778,355. The A's, in spite of their recent and discouraging success at winning ball games, have come back bravely this year, opening up a margin of over a hundred thousand fewer fans than the Giants in their first twenty home games; this time the issue may not be settled until after the World Series. My first view of the handsome new triple-decked Oakland Coliseum, just before game time on a cold Tuesday night, suggested that the tenants of Candlestick Park held an unfair advantage, but then I observed that almost every one of the fifty thousand shiny, brightly painted seats in the place was entirely visible, being empty. The umpires and the teams—the A's and the visiting California Angels—took the field; a serenade played by a strolling jazz combo echoed thinly among the few hundred patrons scattered between the two dugouts; the familiar icy Pacific winds whistled up my pant legs; and I sensed myself, as in a Terence

Rattigan bad dream, exiled to a dying seaside resort in January.

Nobody knows why northern California has taken so gingerly to big-league baseball. The population of the immediate area— perhaps three and a half million, if Sacramento is thrown in— is probably too meager to sustain two baseball teams, but this has not proved to be a difficulty for the two pro football teams, the two major college football teams, and the professional basket-ball team that also sell tickets in the region. The subject is end-lessly speculated upon in local bars and pressrooms, and the only sensible theory I have heard put forward suggests that there are a good many other things to do outdoors in the summer in the en-virons of San Mateo and Marin and Contra Costa Counties. The owner of the A's, Charles O. Finley, has attacked the problem in characteristic style, with a numbing flood of promotions, but it is still possible that his talented and exciting ball team, with its in-comparable new hero, Vida Blue, may eventually succeed in at-tracting more people into the Coliseum than have yet turned out for Hot Pants Day, cow-milking contests, or a gate prize of two free season tickets to the home games of Charles O. Finley's hockey team, the Golden Seals.

The game that first night went to the Finleyites, 7–5, in thir-teen gelid innings; the next evening the Angels reversed matters by the same score in twelve. The two games, in fact, had a creepy, mirrorlike similarity. On Tuesday, the Angels jumped away to a 3–0 and then a 4–1 lead on home runs by Ken McMullen and Roger Repoz, but the bottom of the Oakland bat-ting order kept bashing the ball, too—a homer by catcher Dave Duncan, a three-run job by second baseman Dick Green. Dun-can, a tall young receiver with a pleasingly mobile style behind the plate, hit a double in the seventh, but when he came up to bat with two out in the ninth, the A's were still one run shy. He ran the count to three and two and then lined another homer to left. I was startled. More accustomed to the sight of looped two-hundred-foot bingles in Shea Stadium, I had forgotten about this style of baseball. Bob Locker, a veteran relief man for the A's, now entirely muffled the visitors with his sinker ball, and in the thirteenth Dagoberto Campaneris, the Oakland shortstop, got on via an error and then stole second—quite unnecessarily, it turned out, because his teammate Reggie Jackson hit one out into an uninhabited and perhaps unexplored section of the bleachers, to end matters. It was the fifteenth home run for the A's in seven games—fifteen homers hit by nine different players.

The next evening (before an enormously increased audience of 4354), the Oakland starter, Catfish Hunter, in search of his ninth win in a row, was staked to an early five-run lead, which he slowly but obdurately threw away, surrendering twelve hits to the visitors, including, of course, a tying ninth-inning homer, by Jim Spencer. The winning round-tripper (the tenth of the two-game series) was struck in the twelfth by pinch-hitter Jim Fregosi, the Angels' All Star shortstop, who has been absent most of this season with an ailing foot. The visitors' lineup also included a stranger named Alex Johnson, who had been sprung that afternoon by manager Lefty Phillips from the most recent of his many suspensions for languid play; *almost* languidly, Johnson lined out three singles.

The Athletics (to give them their honored ancient name, which the front office is, for some reason, phasing out) are a poised, eager, and extremely dangerous *équipage*. Their speed and power (an unusual combination that also distinguishes the Giants) are personified in Bert Campaneris, who has won the AL title for stolen bases in five out of the past six years, and Reggie Jackson, who hit forty-seven homers in 1969. Jackson had a miserable season last year, full of sulks and strikeouts, but he seems to have flowered under this year's manager, Dick Williams (who might even be next year's manager, too). Among the other regulars is Sal Bando, an experienced and hard-bitten third baseman. Only the pitching, surprisingly, may be a trifle below championship caliber; the bullpen, for instance, is mostly untested, having rusti-

cated through a span of weeks this spring when two starters,
Vida Blue and Catfish Hunter, ran off a string of eighteen wins
without defeat.

Vida Blue. The name (it is pronounced "Vye-da") could have
been invented by Ring Lardner or Damon Runyon—Lardner
or Runyon on a good day. It can be sung with feeling (I have
heard it) to the tune of "Lida Rose," the quartet from *The Music
Man*. It suggests other baseball monickers—summertime names,
now all but lost to memory: June Green, Jimmy Lavender, Lu
Blue (a switch-hitting first baseman with the Tigers, long ago). It
also suggests, to current American League batters, a quick and
unrewarding day's work. Blue, still only twenty-one years old
and playing his first full season in the majors, has struck out
about three times as many batters as he has walked, which is phenomenal control for a young fireballer; his 13-and-2 record (at
this writing) includes five shutouts. Last year, up from the minors
for six late appearances, he threw a no-hitter and a one-hitter. I
did not see Blue pitch in Oakland (I had a better plan), but I had
no difficulty in picking him out in the clubhouse, or even on the
field during batting practice, for he went everywhere with a
small attendant cloud of out-of-town and local sportswriters.
Their task was unenviable. Every one of them was there to ask
what is, in effect the sportswriter's only question—the question
that remains unanswerable, because it scratches at the mystery
that will always separate the spectator from the athlete: "How
does it *feel* to be you?" Vida, to give him credit, did his best.
One day, pushed for the hundredth time to explain what he, a
young black ballplayer from a small town in Louisiana (Mans-
field, thirty-five miles south of Shreveport), thought when he
heard himself favorably compared to Sandy Koufax and Bob
Gibson and Bob Feller, Blue said, "I find it quite astounding."

Vida Blue, by the way, is not the most publicized member of
the Oakland A's. That honor goes, by a wide margin, to Charles
O. Finley, who must be the only baseball executive whose biog-
raphy takes up more pages in the team's souvenir yearbook than

the space given to any of his stars or to his manager. He is the sole owner of the A's and, in effect, their stage manager. He designed the team's horrendous uniforms ("Kelly Green, Wedding Gown White, and California Gold") and put his ballplayers into white spikes, a combination that makes them look like members of a tavern-league bowling team. At each home game, his signature, spelled out in lighted script on the scoreboard, begins the announcement "Charles O. Finley presents his Million Dollar Baby. . . . I hope you find her very entertaining." He has pushed hard for multicolored bases and for the awarding of first base on three balls instead of four. He is, in short, an embarrassment to baseball and an infuriating goad. Only one thing can be said in his defense: The Oakland A's are *his* ball team. Through player development, through trades, through drafts, through planning and hiring and spending and firing—all with the absolute minimum of outside advice or delegated authority—he alone has fashioned the personnel and character of this excellent club. He is a baseball man.

My better plan about Vida Blue was to see him pitch in the proper surroundings—in front of a crowd. That happened just two nights later, on Friday, at baseball's prettiest diamond, the Bijou of the East, Fenway Park. The game promised wonders. It simultaneously matched up the league's two division-leading teams and two best pitchers. Blue was coming into the game after those ten straight wins, having lost only on the opening day of the season; five of his victories had been shutouts, and he had not permitted an earned run in his previous twenty innings. His opponent, the Red Sox' Sonny Siebert, stood at 8 and 0 for the year, and, going back to the middle of the 1970 season, had won seventeen of his last twenty decisions; he had surrendered a total of four runs in his last four games, and not a single home run this year. Vida, a southpaw, would be pitching for the first time in Fenway Park, whose hovering, over-adjacent green left-field wall is known as a ravenous devourer of lefties. There were other

vibes: Dick Williams, the Oakland manager, was returning to the
park in which, from the opposite dugout, he had led the Red Sox
to their extraordinary pennant in 1967. He was fired two years
later, when the Red Sox slid to third place. That 1969 season
ended for the Red Sox, in effect, during a disastrous June series at
Fenway Park in which the visiting Oakland A's—Kismet!—
scored thirty-eight runs in three games; in one of those games
Reggie Jackson bombed Dick Williams' pitchers for ten runs batted in.

None of this was lost on the Boston fans. An hour before game
time, there were standees stacked three-deep behind the seats
back of home, and a swarm of young human flies had alighted on
the rooftop billboard behind left field. The paying crowd
—35,714—was the biggest at Fenway Park in more than
three years. What we saw fulfilled every wish—a dashing and
memorable party that was over almost before we knew it.
Reggie Jackson, third up for the A's in the first inning, banged a
Sonny Siebert pitch into the right-field bleachers; Reggie Smith
singled off Vida Blue in the bottom half, and Rico Petrocelli, batting clean-up, bombed a Blue darter ten or twelve rows up into
the triangular fold of bleachers above the wall in exact center
field. Enormous noises rose into the spring air.

The two pitchers, thus quickly relieved of several of their statistical burdens, now settled into stride. Vida Blue, I discovered,
is a pitcher in a hurry. Each inning, he ran to the pitcher's
mound to begin his work and ran back to the dugout when it
was done. (He also ran to the batter's box to take his licks—
and ran back, three times, after striking out.) In the field, he
worked with immense dispatch, barely pausing to get his catcher's sign before firing; this habit, which he shares with Bob Gibson and a few others, adds a pleasing momentum to the game.
His motion looked to be without effort or mannerism: a quick,
lithe body-twist toward first base, a high lift and crook of the
right leg, a swift forward stride—almost a leap—and the ball,
delivered about three-quarters over the top, abruptly arrived, a

flick of white at the plate. His pitches, mostly fast balls and always in or very close to the strike zone, did not look especially dangerous, but the quick, late cuts that most of the Red Sox batters were offering suggested what they were up against. Siebert, for his part, was retiring batters just as easily, but with a greater variety of stuff; he fanned Dave Duncan once on three pitches delivered with a sensitive yet thoughtful selection of tempi— *presto, largo*, and *allegro, ma non troppo.*

Now, in the bottom of the sixth, Vida made his first mistakes. (The Petrocelli homer had been struck off an excellent fast ball.) Yastrzemski lashed violently at a high first-pitch delivery and, catching it just a fraction too low, flied out to Rick Monday in deep center. Petrocelli then swung quickly and economically at the very next pitch and stroked the ball into the screen above the left-field wall. 3–1. All at once, the game had altered; it no longer belonged to the pitchers. Moments later, in the Oakland seventh, Dave Duncan sailed a Siebert delivery even higher into the screen, to bring things back to 3–2, and in the bottom of the same inning Siebert himself drove Reggie Jackson all the way to the bullpen to collar his line drive. Jackson was similarly disappointed in the top of the eighth, when Billy Conigliaro, with his back flattened against the fence, pulled down his shot to center. In the home half, Smith singled, and Dick Williams came out to the mound, patted his pitcher on the rump, and excused him for the rest of the evening. The happy cries of the Boston fans turned to prolonged waves of applause as Vida left the field. George Scott then brought Smith home with a little roller, hit off Bob Locker, that just got through between Bando and Campaneris.

Almost over now. Everyone was standing, clapping, laughing. Oops!—there went *another* Oakland home run into the screen, this one by Bando, to make it only 4–3. With two out, the count on Dave Duncan ran to three balls and one strike, the last two pitches floating up to the plate with so little zing that it was suddenly plain that Siebert had used up his arm. He departed, amid plaudits, and Bob Bolin took his place on the mound. Warmed up, he stretched and threw, and Duncan rocketed the pitch to left, up and out and—a long pause—*foul!* The consensus was four inches. Bolin threw, and Duncan whacked another foul into the upper darkness—four feet, maybe five. Bolin threw again, Duncan swung and just ticked the ball, and catcher Duane Josephson held it and jumped straight up into the air, with ball and glove held high.

The season hastens toward its summer discoveries. Vida Blue, drawing enormous audiences on the road, has launched a new winning streak, now three games long. The Red Sox, after beating Vida that Friday, lost five games in a row and eventually surrendered first place to the Orioles, perhaps forever. The Giants' June swoon—at one point, eight losses in nine games—is in full flower. One of their few recent successes was a victory over the Mets that was achieved almost entirely by their first baseman, who tied the game with a home run in the eighth inning, saved it three times in the next two innings with spectacular infield plays, and then scored the winning run in the eleventh. The first baseman, filling in for McCovey, was Willie Mays. Six days later, Mays beat the Phillies with a home run in the bottom of the twelfth inning. The leader is still leading.

Some Pirates and Lesser Men

Baseball has concluded its annual exercises in the obligatory fashion—with another World Series and another franchise shift. A riot followed the wrong event. A long evening of win-dow-breaking, car-burning, and assorted carnage in downtown Pittsburgh was touched off by a marvel of good news—the Pi-rates' stimulating victory over the Orioles in a turnabout seven-game Series—while the atrocious circumstances surrounding the Washington Senators' sudden removal from the capital to a roadside stand west of Dallas were greeted not with the torch but a shrug. The latter happening, to be sure, was followed by some legislative rumblings and an editorial outcry that was nearly unanimous outside Texas, but most fans or ex-fans I have talked to about the matter can summon up only a cynical and helpless grimace over this latest and apparently most arrogant corporate flourish by the owners of the old game. Since 1953, baseball loy-alists in nine other cities, from Boston to Seattle (*ten* cities, ac-tually, since Washington lost its original Senators to Minnesota after 1960 and was given a substitute, Inflato model for the next season), have had to watch such abrupt departures, and the ugly style and detail of this latest decampment are so familiar that the temptation is merely to ignore the whole thing and turn our at-tention at once to the loud surprises of the Series. But this is surely what the baseball moguls would prefer us to do. ("Wow, sonny, how about those Buccos!")

Meeting with his fellow American League owners in Boston in mid-September, Bob Short, a Minneapolis millionaire who purchased the Senators three years ago, cited dropping attendance (a falloff of 169,633 ticket-buyers from last year's unawesome total of 824,789) and rising debts (he claims to have taken a three-million-dollar bath in the Potomac) as compelling reasons for his pulling up stakes instanter. Previously, he had sought redress from Congress and the District of Columbia, offering to stay put in Robert F. Kennedy Stadium in return for impossible rent concessions or, alternatively, to unload the team on the first buyer who came forward with twelve million dollars. He also made ungracious remarks about the loyalty of Washington fans, whom he had stuck with the highest ticket prices and perhaps the dullest team in the majors. (Mr. Short had helped put his own mark on the club by trading away most of his infield last year in return for Denny McLain, a hundred-thousand-dollar-a-year pitcher who lost twenty-two games for the Senators this summer.) There was also the long-range handicap of the World Champion Baltimore Orioles next door, and, very close-range, an imminently payable note of two million dollars. Help for such problems, one might suppose, comes only from Heaven, but Texas sometimes does just as well. Better. At the Boston meeting, Mr. Short introduced the mayor of Arlington, Texas, a hamlet midway between Dallas and Fort Worth, who offered safe harbor to the Senators, along with a low-interest, delayed-amortization seven-and-a-half-million-dollar bank loan; a one-dollar lease on a ballpark called Turnpike Stadium, which could be enlarged to forty-five thousand seats within two years; and a million-dollar television-and-radio contract. Unspoken but also guaranteed was the certainty that, with the eyes of Texas upon them, the same somnolent Senator ball team—now renamed the Rangers or the Horns or the Rustlers or the Spurs, or perhaps the Absconders, and improved if not by the purchase of any new ballplayers then surely by a set of those far-out double-knit Mod uniforms and a winter of heavy down-home public relations (Frank Howard in a ten-gallon Stet-

son! Manager Ted Williams astride a prize Hereford heifer!)—
would surpass the old Washington box-office figures by God
only knew what unimaginable margins for . . . well, at least for a
couple of years. The American League owners voted, ten to two,
to accept the offer.

They did so, it must be added, with pain and distress. Commissioner Bowie Kuhn fought a long, almost frontal campaign
against the switch, and the final meeting dragged along for thirteen and a half hours as the executives considered and finally rejected a counter-offer of nine and a half million dollars (from the
owner of a chain of Washington supermarkets) that turned out to
be incompletely financed. After the vote, American League President Joe Cronin said, "Our conscience is clear," but it is fair to
suppose that no one there was untroubled by the sudden erasure
of such an ancient and affectionately regarded franchise ("First in
war, first in peace, and last in the American League"), or by the
implications of the disappearance of baseball from the baseball na-
tion's capital. One may look on the event with anger, or with
sentimentality (President Nixon said he was heartbroken), or with
sociological dispassion, seeing it as merely another case history in
the economic shift away from the black inner city and toward
the white, autoborne, and nearly cityless suburban middle class
—the Turnpike People. Strangely, the act seems least defensible
when it is regarded from the baseball owners' point of view—
as a straight business deal. Professional baseball *is* a national business, and the abandonment of the capital territory must therefore
be taken as a confession of enormous corporate ineptitude. Fur-
thermore, even the most muttonheaded investor might have
doubts about a concern that proposes to save a losing line simply
by changing its name and then trying to fob off the same shabby
item on unsuspecting consumers in a different territory.

The truth of the matter, it would seem, is that the other baseball owners have absolutely no defense against an impatient and
reckless entrepreneur like Bob Short, because they insist on re-
serving for themselves the same last-ditch privilege they extended

to him in September—the right to run a franchise into the ground and then merely move it along to another address, the right to bail out when the going gets bumpy. The fundamental and now very widespread complaint against the owners and operators of baseball does not really concern any *planned* expansion of their business or any reasonable alteration of it in response to new tastes or population trends; it does concern their actual motives and record in these matters, and their sensitivity to the public's interest. Sustaining baseball in Washington may have become a difficult proposition, to be sure, and perhaps, in the end, an impossible one, but it is clear that in recent years it was never really tried. The idea of building a clientele by building a better ball team apparently did not occur to anybody. Two years ago, the Senators became a competitive club for a time, mostly in response to the presence and tutelage of their new manager, Ted Williams, and improved on their previous year's record by more than twenty games; attendance in Washington that summer rose from 546,661 to 918,106—a gain of sixty-eight per cent. This year, two recently floundering American League teams, the Chicago White Sox and the Kansas City Royals, bettered themselves dramatically on the field and, between them, picked up more than half a million new customers. The best recent example of what can be done in the business of baseball with a modicum of patient hard work and intelligent planning is the Baltimore Orioles, who arrived on the Senators' back doorstep as tattered orphans—the erstwhile St. Louis Browns—in 1954. Encountering many of the same regional problems that have bedeviled the Washington team, and competing for the same cramped regional audience, the Orioles struggled for several years, losing consistently on the field and at the gate, but they have since become the most powerful club in baseball, the winners of four pennants in the past six years, and the operators of a farm system that has captured twenty minor-league pennants in the past decade. Jerold C. Hoffberger, who owns the Orioles, was one of the two men who voted against the Senators' shift to Texas.

The real victim of the owners' nineteenth-century doctrine of total public unaccountability is, of course, the fan, whose financial and emotional expenditures in baseball and other professional sports remain wholly unprotected. He is not only the consumer in the enormous business of sports but also, in areas where municipal funds have helped to build new stadiums and arenas, a co-investor. Yet in the absence of any federal regulation of sports —an athletic Securities and Exchange Commission, a bleacherite Food and Drug Act—he continues to receive Short shrift. It is barely possible that this may not continue forever. To one degree or another, all professional sports are monopolies, controlling exclusive regional franchises and exclusive contractual rights to their athletes' services only because of Congressional and judicial leniency. These often violated privileges are now being challenged by the Curt Flood suit, which the Supreme Court will hear during this session, and by Congressional inquiries into such matters as the proposed merger of the two professional basketball leagues and the football Giants' announced shift from Yankee Stadium to the Jersey Meadows. Senator Sam Ervin, of the Senate Judiciary Committee, has already said that if sports do indeed require their existent monopolies to sustain themselves, they must expect the same federal supervision of profits and practices that now regulates public utilities. If he is right—and it seems impossible not to agree with him—the appropriate laws should be enacted. Then sports reporters will happily stop sounding like Dickens on the workhouse, the baseball owners may be saved from their own mad laissez-faire dreams, and the Washington Senators will not have Gone West entirely in vain.

For the first time since the leagues split in half in 1969, some true expectation centered on the divisional playoffs this year (only TV announcers refer to them by their full, Avenue of the Americas title, "the Championship Series"), because all four pennant races had fallen so flat. By early August, the Orioles, the Pirates, the A's, and the Giants had opened fat, dull leads over their

respective opponents, and only the descent of a near fatal cata-
lepsy upon the San Franciscans provided a late *frisson* of interest.
The Giants and the Dodgers played two wildly exciting games at
Candlestick Park in the middle of September—batters knocked
sprawling, fighting players ejected, late-inning homers flying, old
rages soaring—and the Dodgers, winning both, fought to
within a game of the leaders. Unfortunately, neither team could
do better than split the remaining fourteen games of its schedule,
and what had become a pennant race suggested thereafter nothing so much as two men walking side by side down an up escala-
tor; the final Giant margin, preserved by a Marichal win over
San Diego on the last night, was still that one game.

The National League playoffs, beginning in San Francisco (and
seen by me on the tube), opened with a brisk, noisy entertainment, which the Giants finally won, 5–4, after some appallingly butterfingered work afield in the early innings. The Giant
starter, the perennial Gaylord Perry, pitched resolutely and intelligently, and survived, while his younger opposite number,
Steve Blass, pitched brilliantly and dashingly, and did not. Blass,
posted to an early 2–0 lead, struck out no fewer than nine
Giant batters in the first four innings, and was gone after the
fifth, in which he gave up two two-run homers, the second an in-
tercontinental ballistic missile launched by Willie McCovey. The
Pirates evened matters the next afternoon, when they battered
various Giant second-line pitchers for fifteen hits, including three
home runs by first baseman Bob Robertson, and won 9–4. The
Giants' *first*-line pitching had been reduced by this point in the
season to Perry and Marichal (only one other starter or reliever
won a game for them in their final sixteen decisions), and when
Juan lost the third playoff game, in Pittsburgh, by 2–1, it was
clear that the Giants were *in extremis*. Marichal gave up only
four hits, but two of them were homers—by Robertson again
and by Richie Hebner—and he was beaten by a fast-baller
named Bob Johnson.

It was Perry and Blass once more the next day, and almost instantly the score stood at 5—5, the two teams having rapped out fourteen hits, three homers, and ten runs in the space of two innings. Blass departed, giving way to a skinny sidearmer named Bruce Kison, who set down the Westerners until his teammates ended the Giants' long year with a four-run sixth inning—the last three runs coming home, in a cloud of confetti and yowling, on a three-run homer by Al Oliver. The Pirates had their well-earned pennant.

A missing name in this account, it may be noticed, is that of Willie Mays. He played in all four games and did not exactly or entirely fail: two doubles, one homer, a stolen base, four hits. But these totals do not suggest the true level of his contribution, and by this, for once, I mean that he was less of a player than the statistics suggest—a much older player, who looked every year and month of his forty years; a player gone quite gray-faced with exhaustion and pain and the pressures of leadership. Willie had seen all his splendid early-season triumphs worn away to bare competence; in the late going, he had managed but four hits in forty at-bats, had gone a whole month without a homer, and had been striking out almost half the time. He apologized to his fans at the end of the regular season. During the playoffs, after I had seen Mays taking called third strikes or trying to bunt his way aboard or slicing a weak little pop hit on a fast ball he could no longer get around on, I began—for the first time in my life, and with enormous sadness—not to want him to come up to the plate. I dreaded it, in fact, and I was embarrassed by the feeling, and ashamed of myself. But I still feel the same way, and I think it should be said: Hang them up, Willie, please. Retire.

In Baltimore, meanwhile, the sporting crowd filled the hotel lobbies with cigar smoke and gossip in anticipation of the opening playoff feature of Vida Meets the Birds—a drama that was delayed and deepened by an initial rainout. The Baltimore-Oakland collision was actually between two fine teams—the champs back for a crack at their third straight playoff sweep,

having won over a hundred regular-season games for the third
year in a row through the efforts of *four* twenty-game-winning
pitchers, and the challengers a band of free-swinging youngsters
who had found themselves this year under their new manager,
Dick Williams, and had shattered their opposition to capture
their demi-flag by a sixteen-game margin. All very well, but Vida
Blue was what we had come for. The phenomenal young Oakland fireballer had beaten the Orioles twice in the early season,
by 1–0 and 2–1; all his further meetings with them had been
washed out by repeated bad weather. The new downpour added
to Blue's burdens, for it canceled the playoff's only travel day
and meant that he would not be sufficiently rested to pitch twice
against the Orioles; the first game, in all likelihood, would be crucial. Blue's statistics in this, his first full year in the majors, were
admirable—twenty-four wins and eight losses, an earned-run
average of 1.82, three hundred and one strikeouts, eight shutouts
—but still somehow disappointing, for he trailed off considerably
from the explosive early-season performance that had brought
him to such sudden and total celebrity. He had won only four
games since August 7, and the word was that his fast ball had lost
a bit of its zing and that he could be beaten in late innings.

I hoped not. I had no particular emotional stake in this series, but I had noticed one other figure in Vida Blue's hard-to-
believe statistics for the year—three hundred and twelve innings
pitched. The great majority of the big-league pitchers do not
work as many as three hundred innings in a single season in their
entire careers; the average innings-per-year figure, even if one ig-
nores relief men and part-timers, must be much closer to two
hundred. This season, in both leagues, there were only three
pitchers (Ferguson Jenkins, Mickey Lolich, and Wilbur Wood)
who appeared in more innings than Vida Blue, and all of them
were far older than he. This last is the point, of course. Young
pitchers' arms are so fragile, so easily susceptible to permanent injury, that many clubs have various self-imposed rules to protect
them. One team limits its youngsters to a maximum of a hundred

pitches per game; another does not allow its pitchers to learn the slider until they are at the Class AAA level, and thus presumably into their twenties. Vida Blue turned twenty-two last July, and his left arm just might be the most valuable natural asset to turn up in the majors in a decade. He has powerful legs, and thus throws without effort or strain; he has excellent control, and thus does not waste many pitches. In these and other ways, he reminds me at times of another left-hander, Jerry Koosman, who pitched in two hundred and sixty-three innings in *his* brilliant first full season, at the age of twenty-four, and has never since been able to throw a decent fast ball. Well, young pitchers are eager and forever anxious to get out there and fire; it is the management that decides when to call on them. Vida Blue made winners out of the A's this summer and also, of course, brought out enormous crowds whenever he was slated to pitch. The true balance sheet and final assessment of his first season may not be known for another year or two.

The game arrived at last, and Oakland staked Vida to a quick two-run lead in the second inning, on a triple sandwiched between two doubles. The outfield at Memorial Stadium, which had been patched up and painted various shades of watery green, was still soggy, and anything hit to the corners died there, good for extra bases. With a man at second and none out, the A's now elected to play some uncharacteristically uptight ball. Manager Williams had the runner, catcher Dave Duncan, sacrificed to third, and, with Blue now at bat, ordered a squeeze play; Duncan, however, set sail for the plate a fraction early, and the Oriole pitcher, Dave McNally, threw wide and outside. Blue stabbed helplessly at the ball with his bat, Duncan was chased down and tagged, and a moment later Vida fanned for the third out. It didn't seem to matter much at the time, for Vida looked to be in form. His fast ball was flaring and jumping, and he dismissed the Oriole power—Merv Rettenmund, Frank Robinson, and Boog Powell—on successive swinging strikeouts. He was ahead by 3–1 when the seventh began. Now he gave up a walk and a

single, and, with two out, another, run-scoring single, to Mark
Belanger. The Oakland bullpen was working, but Vida, who had
now thrown something like a hundred and twenty pitches in the
game, was allowed to face pinch-hitter Curt Motton, who thereupon doubled, to tie the score. Still no one emerged from the visitors' dugout to consult or console the young star, and a moment
or two later Paul Blair hit another double, and the big first game
was gone. It was a characteristic kind of victory for the Orioles,
and a mysterious and deadening losing performance by the challengers.

In the clubhouse, Vida Blue sat on a trunk and submitted himself for the last time to the horde of reporters that has dogged
him and surrounded him ever since early summer. His answers
came almost in a whisper; in an agony of disappointment and
anxiety, he kept sighing and staring at the ceiling. He looked terribly young, and then I realized, or remembered at last, that the
rest of us, pushing in around him with out notebooks and our
questions, were much older and supposedly grown up. Once
again we were demanding too much of him; I went away.

The next day, it was Mike Cuellar against Oakland's other
twenty-game winner, Catfish Hunter, who likes to challenge hitters with his fast ball in tight situations, and who this time kept
getting the gauntlet flung right back in his face. Four home runs
—one each by Brooks Robinson and Ellie Hendricks, and two
by Powell—accounted for all the Baltimore runs in a 5–1
win. Boog played with a badly banged-up wrist, and, in the
eighth, tried twice to bunt a runner along; failing, he delivered
him with his second round-tripper. After the game, Catfish
Hunter shook his head and said, "People at home are going to ask
me all damned *winter* how I could throw two home-run balls to
a cripple."

The A's winter began late the next afternoon, in California.
Baltimore's Jim Palmer gave up three solo homers, two of them
to Reggie Jackson, but five Oakland pitchers could not keep matters in order; Brooks Robinson hit a key single in a 5–3 victory

that was never really close. The Orioles' win was their fourteenth in a row, and they had swept the playoffs once again. Piece of cake.

This feeling persisted when the Series began in Baltimore and the home side moved off smartly and inexorably to a two-game lead. We had watched this same fine Oriole team winning so many games on so many October afternoons, going back to 1966, that the occasion had grown easy and familiar—less a contest than the renewal of a permanent autumn holiday. It had become the kind of regular reunion one used to have with the Yankees, the Baltimore fans, like their old counterparts in the Stadium, could pass the time by smugly discovering marvelous but insufficiently appreciated ballplayers hidden in their lineup—regulars like Belanger and Buford and Davey Johnson, who were not quite famous, but only because they played every day next to luminaries like Boog and Frank and Brooksie. Well, there were some other fine players here, too, on the other side—Roberto Clemente, naturally, and the large and dangerous Willie Stargell, who had led all the National League sluggers with forty-eight homers this year, and an exuberant young catcher, Manny Sanguillen. The Pirates, in fact, had led the Orioles in almost every offensive department during the season—runs, hits, and batting averages—but the Orioles' unmistakable pitching advantage was the answer to *that*, and their edge in experience was, well, immeasurable. No one, then, was particularly worried when the visitors notched three runs in the second inning of the opener, all attributable to uncharacteristic Oriole mistakes—a wild pitch and two infield errors. Sure enough, Frank Robinson began the rebound with a lead-off, sky-scraping homer in the third, struck off Pittsburgh's ace, Dock Ellis, and then, an inning later, Belanger and Buford singled and Merv Rettenmund lined a long, low drive that carried all the way to the Baltimore bullpen; Willie Stargell, the Pirate left fielder, ran up the wire fence like a squirrel, but the ball was beyond him, and the Orioles had gone ahead.

They won, 5–3, and Dave McNally, who is sometimes unfairly known in Baltimore as McLucky, set down twenty-one of the last twenty-two Pirates to come to the plate.

Another Maryland monsoon washed out the Sunday game, but there was a rare sellout crowd of 53,239 partisans on hand the next afternoon, presumably to bid farewell to their heroes until springtime. Jim Palmer, working with remarkable haste or impatience, kept walking Pirate batters and then striking out their successors. His opposite number, Bob Johnson, barely survived the second inning, when three Baltimore snipers fired line shots at him—one off his foot, another just over his cap button, and one more that he flagged down in self-defense. He did not survive the fourth inning, and neither did his replacement, Bruce Kison. Then, in the fifth, the Orioles sent eleven batters to the plate, scoring six runs, and the game had become a laugher. The final tally was 11–3; Baltimore had fourteen hits, all singles. Roberto Clemente seemed notably unimpressed. Carrying his bat up to the plate like a surveyor setting up his transit, he precisely measured out a low single, a high line drive that was caught, and a long, beautiful geodetic line straight to the foot of the right-field barrier, good for two bases. In the field, he whirled and threw a burning strike from deep right all the way to third base; this was during the ridiculous goings-on of the fifth inning, but Clemente has no sense of humor about baseball.

As the teams moved along to Pittsburgh, it seemed there was nothing to do but commiserate with the Pirate manager, Danny Murtaugh. His best pitcher, Dock Ellis, was finished for the year with a sore elbow; all his remaining starters had been recently shelled or injured. His big bat, Willie Stargell, was deep in a slump that had gripped him since the onset of the playoffs. His team, badly beaten in two games, had been entirely unable to employ one of its true assets—speed on the bases. Murtaugh—a seamed, tobacco-chewing, contemplative pilot—could only murmur that his outfit was at home now and did not seem to have lost any of its confidence. Baltimore had been terrific, he

said, but still, perhaps . . . These are managerial bromides, but
accurate enough in their way, for in this sport, game plans and
rousing rhetoric are of no use; managers must wait, like the rest
of us, for the disclosures and marvels of each new game. The
marvel of the third game played in the immense plastic cylinder
called Three Rivers Stadium, was Steve Blass. Pitching this time
with an almost surgical finesse, and using his slider and changeup
in textbook fashion to set up the fast ball, he dispatched the Orioles, inning by inning, in minutes. His rival, Mike Cuellar, was
almost as fine, and by the bottom of the seventh inning the Pirates were leading by a minimal 2–1. It was a glazy, beautiful
late-summer day, hot in the sunshine and cool and autumnal in
the shaded stands. Each infielder moved in company with his
etched attendant shadow on the ground, and a hushed, blurred
quiet, broken by an occasional clank of cowbells, had fallen over
the anxious multitude. It was ended by a groan and then a sudden shout: Roberto Clemente, swinging for the seats this time,
half topped a pitch and sent an easy bouncer back to the mound.
Cuellar turned to make the leisurely toss and was astonished to
discover Clemente running out the play at top speed; now hurrying, Cuellar flipped the ball high, pulling Powell off the bag, and
Roberto was on. Disconcerted, Cuellar walked Stargell, and an
instant later Bob Robertson, the dour and muscular Pirate first
baseman, sailed a drive over the fence in deepest right center, to
put the game away at 5–1. Ecstasy along the Monongahela.
Robertson, it turned out, had missed a bunt sign when he hit the
homer, but Danny Murtaugh somehow forgave him.

Game Four, now not quite crucial, brought out a record 51,-
378 Steeltowners; being the first World Series game in history to
be played in prime evening time, it also opened to an estimated
sixty-one million home freeloaders. For a few minutes, it seemed
certain that millions of sets would shortly be tuned to *The Carol
Burnett Show*, because the first three batters in the game hit
dinky little singles and were brought around, dully and undra-

matically, to put the Orioles way ahead. The ratings were saved,
however, by a walk and two doubles in the bottom half that
made it 3–2, and by the Emmy Award performance now
staged by the Pirates' relief pitcher, Bruce Kison. A lanky, long-
legged twenty-one-year-old who seems to have recently out-
grown his uniform, Kison throws a swift, riding fast ball, delivered sidearm, that arrives from the direction of third base and
sometimes ends up in a right-hand batter's ribs. Kison gave up
one bloop double in the second inning, and from then until he retired for a pinch-hitter, after the seventh, the only Baltimore hits
were plunked batters—a record-breaking three. Although the
Orioles were clearly unnerved, the enormous effort involved in
bringing home the tying and winning Pirate runs kept the audience in a lather of excitement. In the Pittsburgh dugout, Dock
Ellis, wearing a warmup jacket and white golf gloves, kept jabbing and weaving like a prizefighter, urging his teammates on-
ward. In the third, with a man on, Clemente leaned over and
struck an outside pitch so severely that the ball streaked away
and, without the smallest discernible fade or droop, banged high
off the right-field wall—foul, by perhaps two inches. Thus
spared, the Oriole pitcher, Pat Dobson, tried a different serving,
which Clemente rapped almost as swiftly into right for a single,
and Al Oliver thereupon singled in the tying run. After that, the
Bucs, who were swinging joyfully and taking liberties on the
base paths, kept putting runners on, moving them along, and not
quite scoring them. In the seventh, with Robertson and Sanguillen aboard, pitch-hitter Vic Davalillo hit a drive to deep left,
which Paul Blair caught after a long chase and then dropped;
Sanguillen came skidding around second and was wiped out by a
fine relay and tag, and appalled groans rose into the night air. But
the next pinch-hitter, for Kison, was another twenty-one-year-
old, named Milt May, and he immediately cracked a single to
right that at last put the rackety, wonderful game away, 4–3.
Dave Giusti retired the next six Orioles in order with his palm
ball, and the Series was all even.

The following afternoon, the Pirates continued to have things all their own way, fashioning runs out of speed, power (another Robertson homer), and various Baltimore mistakes (including, of all things, an error by Brooks Robinson). I kept my eyes on their pitcher, the admirable Nelson Briles, late of the Cardinals, who was pitching even better than his two recent predecessors. In the end he shut out the now almost ex-champions, 4–0, on exactly two hits, and I had plenty of fresh material for the doctoral thesis I have been preparing on the subject of monosyllabically moni- kered Pirate pitchers. As all baseball scholars know, the one un- challengeable all-time Pittsburgh mark in the record books is "Most years leading league in pitchers with one-syllable names." That record, by my computation, now stands at seventeen con- secutive years, going back to the Pirate squad of 1955, which in- cluded the three great perennial Pittsburgh spondees, Bob Friend, Vern Law, and Roy Face, along with two other blurts, Ron Kline and Dick Hall (now of the Orioles). The World Champion Pirates of 1960 counted on pitchers Friend, Law, Face, Green, Gross, and Witt, and the decade rose, in an inexorable staccato, to the great vintage year of 1964, when the Pittsburgh mound staff was Friend, Law, Face, Veale, Blass, Sisk, Schwall, and a couple of foreigners named Gibbon and McBean. This year's Buccos recklessly disposed of Mudcat Grant, but with Blass, Briles, Moose, Lamb, and Veale still on hand (I plan an extensive footnote on this startling incursion of ungulates), and the club's coffers now heavy with championship loot, they can easily swing a deal for Vida Blue that should bring them safely through the seventies.

There was no joking about the sixth game, back in Baltimore; it was late now, and the baseball had grown grim and dangerous. Clemente tripled off the center-field fence in the very first inning. He died on third, but the next time up, in the third, he hit Jim Palmer's first pitch into the right-field bleachers. The Pirates, ahead now by 2–0, continued to get men aboard—they had base-runners in twenty consecutive innings—but Palmer had his pitching rhythm back, and Manager Earl Weaver let him bat for himself in the fifth, though the Birds were still two runs shy. Buford homered in the sixth for the first Oriole run in twenty-three innings, and in the seventh Mark Belanger singled with one out. Palmer was up again, facing reliever Bob Johnson, and the infield came way in. With the crowd shrieking, with the benches whimpering and cursing at each called ball and strike, with the bunt sign on and off and then on again, Palmer ran the count to three and two and fanned. Two out now, and, with Buford up, Belanger flew away for second and made it by a whisker, barely nipping in under Sanguillen's peg. Dave Giusti came in and walked Buford, and then Davey Johnson hit a weak little looper to short left that dropped in and tied it up at last.

It went along like that, through the eighth and ninth and beyond—excruciating baseball, almost painful to watch. Giusti set down the O's in order in the eighth; in the Pirate ninth Sanguillen hit an easy bouncer to Belanger that suddenly leaped over the shortstop's head, but Manny, sensing a championship only three bases away, tried to stretch it and was nailed at second. Two Orioles were stranded in their half, after Clemente unfurled a peg to the plate that sent the runners scurrying like mice back to their bases. Palmer at last departed for a pinch-hitter, and Earl Weaver brought in Pat Dobson to pitch the tenth. Cash singled and stole second, and, with two out, Clemente was walked intentionally. Dave McNally was now summoned to face Stargell (this must have been the first baseball game in which two twenty-game winners were used in relief in the same inning), and walked him, to load the bases, and then retired Al Oliver on a fly, and the home crowd breathed again. The end came very swiftly: a one-out walk by Bob Miller to Frank Robinson, and then a little single by Rettenmund, *just* past second, that barely brought Robby, sliding on his belly, safely into third. Now Brooks hit a short fly to Vic Davalillo in left; Robinson, his long legs churning, raced for the plate, and the peg came in, a little up the line and bouncing high. Robinson slid in under Sanguillen's spikes, and the Series was tied up for the last time.

We forgathered for the last day, a Sunday, and several unanimous conclusions seemed to have been reached. There had been some disappointments, to be sure—too many mistakes in the field by the Orioles, too many men left on the bases by the Pirates—but no matter who won this we had watched a Series that both teams fully deserved to win. Instead of determining a loser, one wished in some way to continue these games indefinitely, to play until winter came, and then throw away the scores. And then, too, there was the shared experience, already permanently fixed in memory, of Roberto Clemente playing a kind of baseball that none of us had ever seen before— throwing and running and hitting at something close to the level of absolute perfection, playing to win but also playing the game almost as if it were a form of punishment for everyone else on the field. He is a frightening batter. He can be retired at times by low curves to the very outside sliver of the plate, but a pitch that comes in a half-inch higher is in his power zone, and thus in imminent danger of departure. *One* of his power zones. During batting practice one day, I saw Clemente step into the cage and take up an unnatural stance, with his legs and feet together. Frozen like that, and swinging only from the waist up, merely getting his eye in, he lined the next three pitches successively to right, to center, and to left—*pop, pop, pop*—all hits in any game. A proud and bitter man, with a haughty, striking profile, Clemente is convinced that he is the finest ballplayer in the world. He believes that for various reasons—his frequent injuries, the fact that he is black, the fact that he is a Puerto Rican and speaks English with an accent—he has been deliberately damaged by the press and kept from the kind of recognition and adulation that we have given to the Aarons and Mayses and Mantles of our time. Before that last game he said to me, "I want everybody in the world to know that this is the way I play all the time. All season, every season. I gave everything I had to this game."

There are other styles of winning in baseball, of course. During batting practice just before this last game of all, I saw Steve Blass, who would start for the Pirates, hit a fly ball that just dropped into the front row of the half-empty bleachers in left. Blass, who hit .120 this year, watched it go and then arched his back, cricked his neck oddly, rolled his head a few times, took up a stance in the back corner of the batter's box, with his bat held high, and glared out at the pitcher imperiously—Clemente, to the life. Blass is a bright, witty, and self-depreciating man, and his dazzling successes on the mound this year may have been of less value to his team than his contribution as the main inventor and sustainer of the Pirates' clubhouse tone, which is warm and profoundly unserious.

An hour or so later, in the third inning, Clemente—standing, as usual, too far back in the box, and swinging, as usual, off the wrong, front foot—hit Mike Cuellar's first pitch to him on a line toward left center; the ball, withdrawing itself rapidly, became smaller, became a speck, then vanished over the fence. It was the first Pittsburgh hit of the game, the first run for either side. After that, it was a pitchers' game, right to the end—Cuellar against Blass again. We knew their styles by heart: Cuellar hunched on the mound, staring at the ground and slowly shaking both his arms, then a quick glance up for the sign, and the pitch—a fast ball in or the screwball away—arriving in a swift port-side swoop; Blass, a right-hander, standing almost primly on the right-hand, first-base corner of the mound, and throwing with a quick pump and a double flurry of legs and elbows ending in an unstylish little stagger. They each gave up two hits through the seventh, and there were some breathtaking infield plays—Cash for the Pirates, Belanger for the Orioles—to keep the proceedings brisk and close.

With nothing to wait for now, the game rushed along into the eighth and its quick resolution. Stargell, dropped for the first time out of his clean-up slot and down to sixth place in the order, led off the inning with a single up the middle, past Belanger, who was over behind second in the standard Stargell shift. José Pagan now drove a long poke that bounced off the left-center-field wall. Rettenmund bobbled the ball for just an instant out there —a fraction of a second, at most—and since the subsequent relay was perfect and Stargell was running at top speed all the way, that amounted to the game and the Series. Powell cut off the peg just as Willie began to slide, but I don't think the play would have caught him. The two runs were just enough, because the dogged old champions scored one in their half and brought the tying run around to third. That was all, though. Blass wrapped up his nifty bundle in the ninth and hurried indoors for deserved refreshments. Champagne, one wanted to cry, for *everybody!*

PART 6

The Interior Stadium

The Interior Stadium

Sports are too much with us. Late and soon, sitting and watching—mostly watching on television—we lay waste our powers of identification and enthusiasm and, in time, attention as more and more closing rallies and crucial putts and late field goals and final playoffs and sudden deaths and world records and world championships unreel themselves ceaselessly before our half-lidded eyes. Professional leagues expand like bubble gum, ever larger and thinner, and the extended sporting seasons, now bunching and overlapping at the ends, conclude in exhaustion and the wrong weather. So, too, goes the secondary business of sports—the news or non-news off the field. Sports announcers (ex-halfbacks in Mod hairdos) bring us another live, exclusive interview in depth with the twitchy coach of some as yet undefeated basketball team, or with a weeping (for joy) fourteen-year-old champion female backstroker, and the sports pages, now almost the largest single part of the newspaper, brim with salary disputes, medical bulletins, franchise maneuverings, all-star ballots, drug scandals, close-up biogs, after-dinner tributes, union tactics, weekend wrapups, wire-service polls, draft-choice trades, clubhouse gossip, and the latest odds. The American obsession with sports is not a new phenomenon, of course, except in its current dimensions, its excessive excessiveness. What *is* new, and what must at times unsettle even the most devout and unselective fan, is a curious sense of loss. In the midst of all these successive spectacles and instant replays and endless reportings and recapitulations, we seem to have forgotten what we came for. More and more, each sport resembles all sports; the flavor, the special joys of place and season, the unique displays of courage and strength and style that once isolated each game and fixed it in our affections have disappeared somewhere in the noise and crush.

Of all sports, none has been so buffeted about by this unselective proliferation, so maligned by contemporary cant, or so indifferently defended as baseball. Yet the game somehow remains the same, obdurately unaltered and comparable only with itself. Baseball has one saving grace that distinguishes it—for me, at any rate—from every other sport. Because of its pace, and thus the perfectly observed balance, both physical and psychological, between opposing forces, its clean lines can be restored in retrospect. This inner game—baseball in the mind—has no season, but it is best played in the winter, without the distraction of other baseball news. At first, it is a game of recollections, recapturings, and visions. Figures and occasions return, enormous sounds rise and swell, and the interior stadium fills with light and yields up the sight of a young ballplayer—some hero perfectly memorized—just completing his own unique swing and now racing toward first. See the way he runs? Yes, that's him! Unmistakable, he leans in, still following the distant flight of the ball with his eyes, and takes his big turn at the base. Yet this is only the beginning, for baseball in the mind is not a mere returning. In time, this easy summoning up of restored players, winning hits, and famous rallies gives way to reconsiderations and reflections about the sport itself. By thinking about baseball like this—by playing it over, keeping it warm in a cold season—we begin to make discoveries. With luck, we may even penetrate some of its mysteries. One of those mysteries is its vividness—the absolutely distinct inner vision we retain of that hitter, that eager base-runner, of however long ago. My father was talking the other day about some of the ballplayers he remembered. He grew

up in Cleveland, and the Indians were his team. Still are. "We
had Nap Lajoie at second," he said. "You've heard of him. A
great big broad-shouldered fellow, but a beautiful fielder. He was
a rough customer. If he didn't like an umpire's call, he'd give him
a faceful of tobacco juice. The shortstop was Terry Turner—a
smaller man, and blond. I can still see Lajoie picking up a
grounder and wheeling and floating the ball over to Turner. Oh, he
was quick on his feet! In right field we had Elmer Flick, now in
the Hall of Fame. I liked the center fielder, too. His name was
Harry Bay, and he wasn't a heavy hitter, but he was very fast
and covered a lot of gound. They said he could circle the bases
in twelve seconds flat. I saw him get a home run inside the park
—the ball hit on the infield and went right past the second baseman and out to the wall, and Bay beat the relay. I remember
Addie Joss, our great right-hander. Tall, and an elegant pitcher. I
once saw him pitch a perfect game. He died young."

My father has been a fan all his life, and he has pretty well seen
them all. He has told me about the famous last game of the 1912
World Series, in Boston, and seeing Fred Snodgrass drop that fly
ball in the tenth inning, when the Red Sox scored twice and beat
the Giants. I looked up Harry Bay and those other Indians in the
Baseball Encyclopedia, and I think my father must have seen that
inside-the-park homer in the summer of 1904. Lajoie batted .376
that year, and Addie Joss led the American League with an
earned-run average of 1.59, but the Indians finished in fourth
place. 1904. . . . Sixty-seven years have gone by, yet Nap Lajoie
is in plain view, and the ball still floats over to Terry Turner.
Well, my father is eighty-one now, and old men are great re-
memberers of the distant past. But I am fifty, and I can also bring
things back: Lefty Gomez, skinny-necked and frighteningly wild,
pitching his first game at Yankee Stadium, against the White Sox
and Red Faber in 1930. Old John McGraw, in a business suit and
a white fedora, sitting lumpily in a dark corner of the dugout at
the Polo Grounds and glowering out at the field. Babe Ruth,
wearing a new, bright yellow glove, trotting out to right field—

a swollen ballet dancer, with those delicate, almost feminine feet
and ankles. Ruth at the plate, uppercutting and missing, staggering with the force of his swing. Ruth and Gehrig hitting
back-to-back homers. Gehrig, in the summer of 1933, running
bases with a bad leg in a key game against the Senators; hobbling,
he rounds third, closely followed by young Dixie Walker, then a
Yankee. The throw comes in to the plate, and the Washington
catcher—it must have been Luke Sewell—tags out the sliding
Gehrig and, in the same motion, the sliding Dixie Walker. A
double play at the plate. The Yankees lose the game; the Senators
go on to a pennant. And, back across the river again, Carl Hubbell. My own great pitcher, a southpaw, tall and elegant. Hub
pitching: the loose motion; two slow, formal bows from the
waist, glove and hands held almost in front of his face as he piv-
ots, the long right leg (in long, peculiar pants) striding; and the
ball, angling oddly, shooting past the batter. Hubbell walks
gravely back to the bench, his pitching arm, as always, turned
the wrong way round, with the palm out. Screwballer.

Any fan, as I say, can play this private game, extending it to
extraordinary varieties and possibilities in his mind. Ruth bats
against Sandy Koufax or Sam McDowell. . . . Hubbell pitches to
Ted Williams, and the Kid, grinding the bat in his fists, twitches
and blocks his hips with the pitch; he holds off but still follows
the ball, leaning over and studying it like some curator as it leaps
in just under his hands. Why this vividness, even from an imaginary confrontation? I have watched many other sports, and I
have followed some—football, hockey, tennis—with eagerness, but none of them yields these permanent interior pictures,
these ancient and precise excitements. Baseball, I must conclude,
is intensely remembered because only baseball is so intensely
watched. The game forces intensity upon us. In the ballpark,
scattered across an immense green, each player is isolated in our
attention, utterly visible. Watch that fielder just below us. Little
seems to be expected of him. He waits in easy composure, his
hands on his knees; when the ball at last soars or bounces out to

him, he seizes it and dispatches it with swift, haughty ease. It all looks easy, slow, and, above all, safe. Yet we know better, for what is certain in baseball is that someone, perhaps several people, will fail. They will be searched out, caught in the open, and defeated, and there will be no confusion about it or sharing of the blame. This is sure to happen, because what baseball requires of its athletes, of course, is nothing less than perfection, and perfection cannot be eased or divided. Every movement of every game, from first pitch to last out, is measured and recorded against an absolute standard, and thus each success is also a failure. Credit that strikeout to the pitcher, but also count it against the batter's average; mark this run unearned, because the left fielder bobbled the ball for an instant and a runner moved up. Yet, faced with this sudden and repeated presence of danger, the big-league player defends himself with such courage and skill that the illusion of safety is sustained. Tension is screwed tighter and tighter as the certain downfall is postponed again and again, so that when disaster does come—a half-topped infield hit, a walk on a close three-and-two call, a low drive up the middle that just eludes the diving shortstop—we rise and cry out. It is a spontaneous, inevitable, irresistible reaction.

Televised baseball, I must add, does not seem capable of transmitting this emotion. Most baseball is seen on the tube now, and it is presented faithfully and with great technical skill. But the medium is irrevocably two-dimensional; even with several cameras, television cannot bring us the essential distances of the game—the simultaneous flight of a batted ball and its pursuit by the racing, straining outfielders, the swift convergence of runner and ball at a base. Foreshortened on our screen, the players on the field appear to be squashed together, almost touching each other, and, watching them, we lose the sense of their separateness and lonesome waiting.

This is a difficult game. It is so demanding that the best teams and the weakest teams can meet on almost even terms, with no assurance about the result of any one game. In March 1962, in St.

Petersburg, the World Champion Yankees played for the first time against the newborn New York Mets—one of the worst teams of all time—in a game that each badly wanted to win; the winner, to nobody's real surprise, was the Mets. In 1970, the World Champion Orioles won a hundred and eight games and lost fifty-four; the lowest cellar team, the White Sox, won fifty-six games and lost a hundred and six. This looks like an enormous disparity, but what it truly means is that the Orioles managed to win two out of every three games they played, while the White Sox won one out of every three. That third game made the difference—and a kind of difference that can be appreciated when one notes that the winning margin given up by the White Sox to all their opponents during the season averaged 1.1 runs per game. Team form is harder to establish in baseball than in any other sport, and the hundred-and-sixty-two-game season not uncommonly comes down to October with two or three teams locked together at the top of the standings on the final weekend. Each inning of baseball's slow, searching time span, each game of its long season is essential to the disclosure of its truths.

Form is the imposition of a regular pattern upon varying and unpredictable circumstances, but the patterns of baseball, for all the game's tautness and neatness, are never regular. Who can predict the winner and shape of today's game? Will it be a brisk, neat two-hour shutout? A languid, error-filled 12–3 laugher? A riveting three-hour, fourteen-inning deadlock? What other sport produces these manic swings? For the players, too, form often undergoes terrible reversals; in no other sport is a champion athlete so often humiliated or a journeyman so easily exalted. The surprise, the upset, the total turnabout of expectations and reputations—these are delightful commonplaces of baseball. Al Gionfriddo, a part-time Dodger outfielder, stole second base in the ninth inning of the fourth game of the 1947 World Series to help set up Lavagetto's game-winning double (and the only Dodger hit of the game) off the Yankees' Bill Bevens. Two days later, Gionfriddo robbed Joe DiMaggio with a famous game-saving catch of a four-hundred-and-fifteen-foot drive in deepest left field at Yankee Stadium. Gionfriddo never made it back to the big leagues after that season. Another irregular, the Mets' Al Weis, homered in the fifth and last game of the 1969 World Series, tying up the game that the Mets won in the next inning; it was Weis's third homer of the year and his first ever at Shea Stadium. And so forth. Who remembers the second game of the 1956 World Series—an appallingly bad afternoon of baseball in which the Yankees' starter, Don Larsen, was yanked after giving up a single and four walks in less than two innings? It was Larsen's *next* start, the fifth game, when he pitched his perfect game.

There is always a heavy splash of luck in these reversals. Luck, indeed, plays an almost predictable part in the game; we have all seen the enormous enemy clout into the bleachers that just hooks foul at the last instant, and the half-checked swing that produces a game-winning blooper over second. Everyone complains about baseball luck, but I think it adds something to the game that is nearly essential. Without it, such a rigorous and unforgiving pastime would be almost too painful to enjoy.

No one, it becomes clear, can conquer this impossible and unpredictable game. Yet every player tries, and now and again—very rarely—we see a man who seems to have met all the demands, challenged all the implacable averages, spurned the mere luck. He has defied baseball, even altered it, and for a time at least the game is truly his. One thinks of Willie Mays, in the best of his youth, batting at the Polo Grounds, his whole body seeming to leap at the ball as he swings in an explosion of exuberance. Or Mays in center field, playing in so close that he appears at times to be watching the game from over the second baseman's shoulder, and then that same joyful leap as he takes off after a long, deep drive and runs it down, running so hard and so far that the ball itself seems to stop in the air and wait for him. One thinks of Jackie Robinson in a close game—any close game—playing the infield and glaring in at the enemy hitter, hating him and daring him, refusing to be beaten. And Sandy Koufax pitching in the last summers before he was disabled, in that time when he pitched a no-hitter every year for four years. Kicking swiftly, hiding the ball until the last instant, Koufax throws in a blur of motion, coming over the top, and the fast ball, appearing suddenly in the strike zone, sometimes jumps up so immoderately that his catcher has to take it with his glove shooting upward, like an infielder stabbing at a bad-hop grounder. I remember some batter taking a strike like that and then stepping out of the box and staring back at the pitcher with a look of utter incredulity—as if Koufax had just thrown an Easter egg past him.

Joe DiMaggio batting sometimes gave the same impression—the suggestion that the old rules and dimensions of baseball no longer applied to him, and that the game had at last grown unfairly easy. I saw DiMaggio once during his famous hitting streak in 1941; I'm not sure of the other team or the pitcher—perhaps it was the Tigers and Bobo Newsom—but I'm sure of DiMaggio pulling a line shot to left that collided preposterously with the bag at third base and ricocheted halfway out to center field. That record of hitting safely in fifty-six straight games seems as secure as any in baseball, but it does not awe me as much as the fact that DiMadge's old teammates claim they *never* saw him commit an error of judgment in a ball game. Thirteen years, and never a wrong throw, a cutoff man missed, an extra base passed up. Well, there was one time when he stretched a single against the Red Sox and was called out at second, but the umpire is said to have admitted later that he blew the call.

And one more for the pantheon: Carl Yastrzemski. To be precise, Yaz in September of the 1967 season, as his team, the Red Sox, fought and clawed against the White Sox and the Twins and the Tigers in the last two weeks of the closest and most vivid pennant race of our time. The presiding memory of that late summer is of Yastrzemski approaching the plate, once again in a situation where all hope rests on him, and settling himself in the batter's box—touching his helmet, tugging at his belt, and just touching the tip of the bat to the ground, in precisely the same set of gestures—and then, in a storm of noise and pleading, swinging violently and perfectly . . . and hitting. In the last two weeks of that season, Yaz batted .522—twenty-three hits for forty-four appearances: four doubles, five home runs, sixteen runs batted in. In the final two games, against the Twins, both of which the Red Sox *had* to win for the pennant, he went seven for eight, won the first game with a homer, and saved the second with a brilliant, rally-killing throw to second base from deep left field. (He cooled off a little in the World Series, batting only .400 for seven games and hitting three homers.) Since then, the game and the averages have caught up with Yastrzemski, and he has never again approached that kind of performance. But then, of course, neither has anyone else.

Only baseball, with its statistics and isolated fragments of time, permits so precise a reconstruction from box score and memory. Take another date—October 7, 1968, at Detroit, the fifth game of the World Series.* The fans are here, and an immense noise —a cheerful, 53,634-man vociferosity—utterly fills the green, steep, high-walled box of Tiger Stadium. This is a good baseball town, and the cries have an anxious edge, for the Tigers are facing almost sure extinction. They trail the Cardinals by three games to one, and never for a moment have they looked the equal of these defending World Champions. Denny McLain, the Tigers' thirty-one-game winner, was humiliated in the opener by the Cardinals' Bob Gibson, who set an all-time Series record by striking out seventeen Detroit batters. The Tigers came back the next day, winning rather easily behind their capable left-hander Mickey Lolich, but the Cardinals demolished them in the next two games, scoring a total of seventeen runs and again brushing McLain aside; Gibson has now struck out twenty-seven Tigers, and he will be ready to pitch again in the Series if needed. Even

* This game and this Series are also discussed on pages 186–196.

more disheartening is Lou Brock, the Cards' left fielder, who has already lashed out eight hits in the first four games and has stolen seven bases in eight tries; Bill Freehan, the Tigers' catcher, has a sore arm. And here, in the very top of the first, Brock leads off against Lolich and doubles to left; a moment later, Curt Flood singles, and Orlando Cepeda homers into the left-field stands. The Tigers are down, 3–0, and the fans are wholly stilled.

In the third inning, Brock leads off with another hit—a single—and there is a bitter overtone to the home-town cheers when Freehan, on a pitchout, at last throws him out, stealing, at second. There is no way for anyone to know, of course, that this is a profound omen; Brock has done his last damage to the Tigers in this Series. Now it is the fourth, and hope and shouting return. Mickey Stanley leads off the Detroit half with a triple that lands, two inches fair, in the right-field corner. He scores on a fly. Willie Horton also triples. With two out, Jim Northrup smashes a hard grounder directly at the Cardinal second baseman, Javier, and at the last instant the ball strikes something on the infield and leaps up and over Javier's head, and Horton scores. Luck! Luck twice over, if you remember how close Stanley's drive came to falling foul. But never mind; it's 3–2 now, and a game again.

But Brock is up, leading off once again, and an instant later he has driven a Lolich pitch off the left-field wall for a double. Now Javier singles to left, and Brock streaks around third base toward home. Bill Freehan braces himself in front of the plate, waiting for the throw; he has had a miserable Series, going hitless in fourteen at-bats so far, and undergoing those repeated humiliations by the man who is now racing at him full speed—the man who must surely be counted, along with Gibson, as the Series hero. The throw comes in chest-high on the fly from Willie Horton in left; ball and base-runner arrive together; Brock does not slide. Brock does not slide, and his left foot, just descending on the plate, is banged away as he collides with Freehan. Umpire Doug Harvey shoots up his fist: Out! It is a great play. Nothing has changed, the score is still 3–2, but everything has changed;

something has shifted irrevocably in this game.

In the seventh inning, with one out and the Tigers still one run shy, Tiger manager Mayo Smith allows Lolich to bat for himself. Mickey Lolich has hit .114 for the season, and Smith has a pinch-hitter on the bench named Gates Brown, who hit .370. But Lolich got two hits in his other Series start, including the first homer of his ten years in baseball. Mayo, sensing something that he will not be able to defend later if he is wrong, lets Lolich bat for himself, and Mickey pops a foolish little fly to right that falls in for a single. Now there is another single. A walk loads the bases, and Al Kaline comes to the plate. The noise in the stadium is insupportable. Kaline singles, and the Tigers go ahead by a run. Norm Cash drives in another. The Tigers win this searching, turned-about, lucky, marvelous game by 5–3.

Two days later, back in St. Louis, form shows its other face as the Tigers rack up ten runs in the third inning and win by 13–1. McLain at last has his Series win. So it is Lolich against Gibson in the finale, of course. Nothing happens. Inning after inning goes by, zeros accumulate on the scoreboard, and anxiety and silence lengthen like shadows. In the sixth, Lou Brock singles. Daring Lolich, daring the Tiger infielders' nerves, openly forcing his luck, hoping perhaps to settle these enormous tensions and difficulties with one more act of bravado, he takes an excessive lead off first, draws the throw from Lolich, breaks for second, and is erased, just barely, by Cash's throw. A bit later, Curt Flood singles, and, weirdly, he too is picked off first and caught in a rundown. Still no score. Gibson and Lolich, both exhausted, pitch on. With two out in the seventh, Cash singles for the Tigers' second hit of the day. Horton is safe on a slow bouncer that *just* gets through the left side of the infield. Jim Northrup hits the next pitch deep and high but straight at Flood, who is the best center fielder in the National League. Flood starts in and then halts, stopping so quickly that his spikes churn up a green flap of turf; he turns and races back madly, but the ball sails over his head for a triple. Disaster. Suddenly, irreversibly, it has hap-

pened. Two runs are in, Freehan doubles in another, and, two innings later, the Tigers are Champions of the World.

I think I will always remember those two games—the fifth
and the seventh—perfectly. And I remember something else
about the 1968 Series when it was over—a feeling that almost
everyone seemed to share: that Bob Gibson had not lost that last
game, and the Cardinals had not lost the Series. Certainly no one
wanted to say that the Tigers had not won it, but there seemed
to be something more that remained to be said. It was something
about the levels and demands of the sport we had seen—as if
the baseball itself had somehow surpassed the players and the results. It was the baseball that won.

Always, it seems, there is something more to be discovered
about this game. Sit quietly in the upper stand and look at the
field. Half close your eyes against the sun, so that the players re-
cede a little, and watch the movements of baseball. The pitcher,
immobile on the mound, holds the inert white ball, his little lump
of physics. Now, with abrupt gestures, he gives it enormous
speed and direction, converting it suddenly into a line, a moving
line. The batter, wielding a plane, attempts to intercept the line
and acutely alter it, but he fails; the ball, a line again, is redrawn
to the pitcher, in the center of this square, the diamond. Again
the pitcher studies his task—the projection of his next line
through the smallest possible segment of an invisible seven-sided
solid (the strike zone has depth as well as height and width) sixty
feet and six inches away; again the batter considers his even more
difficult proposition, which is to reverse this imminent white
speck, to redirect its energy not in a soft parabola or a series of
diminishing squiggles but into a beautiful and dangerous new
force, of perfect straightness and immense distance. In time, these
and other lines are drawn on the field; the batter and the fielders
are also transformed into fluidity, moving and converging, and
we see now that all movement in baseball is a convergence toward fixed points—the pitched ball toward the plate, the

thrown ball toward the right angles of the bases, the batted ball toward the as yet undrawn but already visible point of congruence with either the ground or a glove. Simultaneously, the fielders hasten toward that same point of meeting with the ball, and both the base-runner and the ball, now redirected, toward their encounter at the base. From our perch, we can sometimes see three or four or more such geometries appearing at the same instant on the green board below us, and, mathematicians that we are, can sense their solution even before they are fully drawn. It is neat, it is pretty, it is satisfying. Scientists speak of the profoundly moving aesthetic beauty of mathematics, and perhaps the baseball field is one of the few places where the rest of us can glimpse this mystery.

The last dimension is time. Within the ballpark, time moves differently, marked by no clock except the events of the game. This is the unique, unchangeable feature of baseball, and perhaps explains why this sport, for all the enormous changes it has undergone in the past decade or two, remains somehow rustic, unviolent, and introspective. Baseball's time is seamless and invisible, a bubble within which players move at exactly the same pace and rhythms as all their predecessors. This is the way the game was played in our youth and in our fathers' youth, and even back then—back in the country days—there must have been the same feeling that time could be stopped. Since baseball time is measured only in outs, all you have to do is succeed utterly; keep hitting, keep the rally alive, and you have defeated time. You remain forever young. Sitting in the stands, we sense this, if only dimly. The players below us—Mays, DiMaggio, Ruth, Snodgrass—swim and blur in memory, the ball floats over to Terry Turner, and the end of this game may never come.

FOR THE BEST IN PAPERBACKS, LOOK FOR THE

In every corner of the world, on every subject under the sun, Penguin represents quality and variety—the very best in publishing today.

For complete information about books available from Penguin—including Pelicans, Puffins, Peregrines, and Penguin Classics—and how to order them, write to us at the appropriate address below. Please note that for copyright reasons the selection of books varies from country to country.

In the United Kingdom: For a complete list of books available from Penguin in the U.K., please write to *Dept E.P., Penguin Books Ltd, Harmondsworth, Middlesex, UB7 0DA.*

In the United States: For a complete list of books available from Penguin in the U.S., please write to *Dept BA, Penguin*, Box 120, Bergenfield, New Jersey 07621-0120.

In Canada: For a complete list of books available from Penguin in Canada, please write to *Penguin Books Ltd, 2801 John Street, Markham, Ontario L3R 1B4.*

In Australia: For a complete list of books available from Penguin in Australia, please write to the *Marketing Department, Penguin Books Ltd, P.O. Box 257, Ringwood, Victoria 3134.*

In New Zealand: For a complete list of books available from Penguin in New Zealand, please write to the *Marketing Department, Penguin Books (NZ) Ltd, Private Bag, Takapuna, Auckland 9.*

In India: For a complete list of books available from Penguin, please write to *Penguin Overseas Ltd, 706 Eros Apartments, 56 Nehru Place, New Delhi, 110019.*

In Holland: For a complete list of books available from Penguin in Holland, please write to *Penguin Books Nederland B.V., Postbus 195, NL-1380AD Weesp, Netherlands.*

In Germany: For a complete list of books available from Penguin, please write to *Penguin Books Ltd, Friedrichstrasse 10-12, D-6000 Frankfurt Main I, Federal Republic of Germany.*

In Spain: For a complete list of books available from Penguin in Spain, please write to *Longman, Penguin España, Calle San Nicolas 15, E-28013 Madrid, Spain.*

In Japan: For a complete list of books available from Penguin in Japan, please write to *Longman Penguin Japan Co Ltd, Yamaguchi Building, 2-12-9 Kanda Jimbocho, Chiyoda-Ku, Tokyo 101, Japan.*

FOR THE BEST IN PAPERBACKS, LOOK FOR THE

☐ **CAN'T ANYBODY HERE PLAY THIS GAME?**
Jimmy Breslin

Breslin's celebrated account of the New York Mets' first year of life—a year that produced a record number of losses and an unforgettable collection of oddballs—is a jubilant toast to the tenacity of the human spirit.

"Jimmy Breslin has written a history of the Mets, preserving for all time a remarkable tale of ineptitude, mediocrity, and abject failure."—Bill Veeck

124 pages   ISBN: 0-14-006217-3   **$5.95**

You can find all these books at your local bookstore, or use this handy coupon for ordering:

Penguin Books By Mail
Dept. BA Box 999
Bergenfield, NJ 07621-0999

Please send me the above title(s). I am enclosing _____ (please add sales tax if appropriate and $1.50 to cover postage and handling). Send check or money order—no CODs. Please allow four weeks for shipping. We cannot ship to post office boxes or addresses outside the USA. *Prices subject to change without notice.*

Ms./Mrs./Mr. _____

Address _____

City/State _____ Zip _____

Sales tax: CA: 6.5%   NY: 8.25%   NJ: 6%   PA: 6%   TN: 5.5%